A HUNDRED YEARS' WAR

By the same author:

THE TENDER YEARS

BASS OF GRAYS

OLIVE IN CHINA

THE YORKSHIRE LAD

BLACK RIVER

RELUCTANT HERO

JOHN THE UNLOVED

THE YOUNG WILLIAM BOOTH

A HUNDRED YEARS' WAR

WAR

The Salvation Army

by
BERNARD WATSON

HODDER AND STOUGHTON

Printed in Great Britain for Hodder and Stoughton Ltd., St. Paul's House, Warwick Lane, London, E.C.4, by Lowe & Brydone (Printers) Ltd., London

CONTENTS

PART III

THE SOLDIERS

FOREWORD

by

GENERAL FREDERICK COUTTS

The Salvation Army remains a frontier movement, even though a century ago that frontier was restricted to a Whitechapel sidewalk and, at its widest, extended no farther than the boundaries of that Paradise Lost, the East End of London.

At that time William Booth could hardly have dreamed that a day would come when his soldiers—and these laymen and women account for nine-tenths of the Army's strength—would be drawn from all levels of society and be as much an accepted part of the social scene in the Eastern Highlands of New Guinea as in the suburbs of Toronto.

In those pioneer days the frontier was plainly defined. A flapping sole or a greasy shawl were obvious signs that the foe was around. The unkempt children in the sleazy streets were tokens of his handiwork.

This fact greatly aided the early day Salvationist. He did not need to be told who was responsible for the individual and collective misery which confronted him. None but an enemy could have sown such ferocious tares.

Nowadays the frontier is less clearly defined. For more miles than are conducive to the Christian soldier's peace of mind there seem to be no boundary posts at all. But instead of wasting his time deploring the current situation, the Salvationist today makes his front line where he is. Thus the new frontier may run through a Clydeside shipyard, or by Leichhardt River at Mount Isa, or through Transport House or Times Square, along the Pasir Panjang Road in Singapore or across the University quad in Auckland. In this holy war the twentieth century Salvationist knows that the best means of defence is attack, so he is ever on the Christian offensive without being offensive.

What follows in these pages provides a set of variations on this theme but, lest it be supposed that each individual soldier warreth as seems him good, it should be added that, as part of the universal fellowship known as the Body of Christ, the Salvation Army possesses stated articles of faith, offers the means of grace to all who desire to share its worship, and provides manifold opportunities for Christian work and witness to all who join its ranks upon a profession of faith in Jesus Christ as Lord and Saviour.

International Headquarters,
May 1964.

AUTHOR'S NOTE

On various Salvation Army assignments, and to obtain material for this book, I flew round the world, stopping all too briefly at many points, but finding everywhere the same cause for wonder at the devotion and competence of the modern Salvationist.

One thing is sure: the salvation war that began a hundred years ago still wages—a war of truth, healing, aid and peace that God can smile upon. Some of the heroes of that fight are named in these pages. Many are not: the story is too great to be encompassed in one book or even a hundred.

The real names in the case-histories have been withheld for obvious reasons. Alcoholics, drug-addicts, unwed mothers and other unfortunates aided by the Army rightly expect to be protected from painful publicity. But they are real people. In personal interviews I was constantly impressed by their candour and honesty and the will of many of them to begin again and live a better life. Many are so doing.

Numerous busy and enlightened people gave me their time and patience when I sought information from them. Others were prompt and courteous in checking what I had written. I thank them all. Any errors of fact which may still remain are mine.

BERNARD WATSON

Part I

THE ARMY

1. THE SOLDIER

While women weep as they do now, I'll fight; while little children go hungry as they do now, I'll fight; while men go to prison, in and out, in and out, as they do now, I'll fight; while there is a drunkard left, while there is a poor lost girl upon the streets, while there remains one dark soul without the light of God, I'll fight — I'll fight to the very end!

WILLIAM BOOTH, Founder of the Salvation Army, in his last public address at the Royal Albert Hall, May 9th, 1912, just before the operation which left him blind. Three months later, on August 20th, he 'laid down his sword'.

William Booth was the first salvation soldier and the greatest. For the purposes of reckoning up the Salvation Army he founded takes his action of 1865 as its beginning. In that year the Revd. William Booth, who resigned from the Methodist New Connexion in 1862, accepted an invitation to lead a tent mission down Whitechapel Road, in the East End of London.

People have said that he poked his umbrella into the ground and talked to it, like a man mad, to attract a crowd. Others asserted that he was so striking in appearance, and eloquent in speech, that he would not have needed such a device.

Booth was tall, dark, handsome, with a Hebraic nose, inherited from a mother whose part-Jewish descent is hinted at in a surviving photograph—a biographer suggests that her family name of Moss had been Moses. William, her only surviving son, was schooled in poverty and loneliness. The home was sombre, the boy's early life lacking in affection.

Samuel Booth, the father, was embittered by his inability to make good in the new world of machines and mass production. These had robbed him of his employment as a nail-maker, by hand, at Belper. When he moved to Nottingham to become a builder of the tiny houses for the growing population, ever-recurring trade depressions ruined him.

'Make money,' he said to his son, and died a bankrupt.

William Booth's 'odd man out' status in the home was due partly to the fact that he was the only male in a house with four females and also because he left the Church of England to become a Methodist. Mary Booth, his mother, had pretensions to gentility. Methodism was implicated in much of the radical agitation of the time. She probably felt that her boy would never have become involved with the sick, the dirty, and the hungry, if he had been safely in the fold of the Established Church.

Young Booth was, for a time, poised on the brink of working class rebellion, and probably signed the Charter. Perhaps because of his own gifts as a speaker, the eloquence of Feargus O'Connor, the Chartist leader, appealed to him. Booth's awareness of the suffering of the poor, who came in pale-faced procession down the narrow, dark alley to the pawnshop, made him yearn to do something for them. This gave him something in common with the impassioned Irishman who talked of votes for the suffering workers, and hinted at bullets for their oppressive masters.

But O'Connor's Chartism fizzled out like a damp Gunpowder Plot, and young William was converted in a Wesleyan chapel in Nottingham. After a hard struggle, he became a Methodist New Connexion minister. Not Wesleyan: his educational shortcomings made that unlikely, as well as his suspected sympathies with the reforming elements in Methodism.

Possessed of a gifted wife who urged him to study, and who fanned his cool fires of personal ambition, he became a markedly successful revivalist preacher of the John Wesley, Moody and Sankey, Billy Graham sort. He had sand in his religious shoes. The administration of a circuit, the regular pulpit and pastoral care of souls in one town did not suit him. He was constantly in demand as a visiting campaigner, and when the Methodists refused him permission to do this, he resigned.

So it was that, as a minister without a flock, he was down the Mile End Road among the weak and the wicked of the slums that summer day in June 1865 when he first spoke in the open-air service before The Blind Beggar public-house. The taste of failure was bitter in his mouth and his future was dark before him. Often subject to black moods which sometimes dimmed his faith, he had even thought of withdrawing from the struggle.

When he took charge of the Tent Mission on July 2nd, he was thirty-six years of age, and practically a pauper with a wife and six infant children to support—a seventh child being on the way. Even now, although his ability as a speaker was recognised, and the East-Enders delighted to hear him, long years of trial and error lay in wait for him. His first shots in the salvation war were a distant prelude to his world-wide attack. There were many heart-breaking failures between.

One thing he did know—what it was all about. Three months earlier another Booth, John Wilkes, in Washington, D.C., had shot the President dead. He exclaimed 'Death to tyrants!' as he did so. Yet another Booth, Charles, up in Liverpool, was making a fortune that would enable him to journey to London and become the 'Father of Sociology', to write *Life and Labour of the People in London* and set legions of social scientists about their tasks to this day.

William Booth reckoned the methods of both to be incompetent.

Methodism had fixed his mind, possessed his heart with a 'burning love for souls', a passionate conviction that only God could save men. Bismarck was making modern Germany, Garibaldi was leading his troops to war, Marx urging the proletariat to take arms to strike off its chains. Booth called men to prayer, and began to arm his tiny regiment with the might that is in God:

> *O boundless salvation! deep ocean of love,*
> *O fulness of mercy, Christ brought from above,*
> *The whole world redeeming, so rich and so free,*
> *Now flowing for all men, come, roll over me!*

So he wrote, so he believed, and so his Army sings to this day, all over the world.

It is ironic that the tent in which Booth first campaigned was in a cemetery, let to the mission by the Society of Friends. There peace-loving Quakers had lain quietly for years. Now the man with the deep, rasping voice preached his hour-long sermons interpolated by the loud 'Hallelujahs' of his converts and supporters. The oft-spoken warnings of death, hell and judgment,

the prayers of penitents, the mockery of the vulgar outside the
tent, all created a rowdy scene alien to the polite, dignified
Friends.

Sewage was emptied directly into the Thames; in 1866 there
were more than 8,000 deaths from cholera and other waterborne
diseases.

The Civil War in America had caused great economic hardship in Britain. The dirt, the hovels, the hunger and misery
made men and women ready to sing with great expectations,
'My home is in Heaven!' The workhouses were full of
dehumanized, degraded people and dying children. A *Lancet*
enquirer reported:

'Conditions are abominable, the guardians negligent, incompetent and impudent beyond all palliation. The privations and
sufferings of the inmates are a disgrace to civilization: even the
milk provided for the children being stolen and sold by
nurses . . .'

Though Booth was not by upbringing a rabid total abstainer,
conditions in the East End soon made him share his wife's
loathing of the drink trade. Bestial abuses abounded. Beer-shops
were open from 4 a.m. to 10 p.m. Drunkenness was the general
escape from the intolerable reality of existence. For liquor,
parents neglected their children, girls traded their virtue, men
became criminals, women fell beneath a load of debt.

Unclean, ill-clad, the horde of townspeople, a new breed
brought into being by the factory machines and growing industrial life, were divorced from the churches. Illiterate, they found
it hardly worthwhile to go to worship where they would not
understand the sermon of the educated priest, read the hymns
or know the tunes. Besides, as they thought, the churches were
for 'the gentry'. In their opinion nobody was for them.

Booth's Tent Mission was. The Quakers let their ground to the
mission for 'the purpose of religious services amongst the poorer
classes not in the habit of attending any place of worship'. The
very sight of them, after the socially up-graded Methodist congregations to which he had been accustomed in the provinces,
might have frightened Booth at first, caused him to share the
sentiments of the Duke of Wellington, who remarked with the
forthrightness for which he was famed: 'Our army is composed

of the scum of the earth—the mere scum of the earth.' But Booth, who was not, like Wellington, an aristocrat, would never have said any such thing. He always loved the poor, even before they were washed, in water or in the blood of the Lamb. Arriving about midnight at his Hammersmith home, after wonderful tent services where the 'saints' had been inspired, and 'sinners' had been 'saved', he exclaimed to Catherine: 'Darling, I have found my destiny.'

Soon the Christian Mission was in being. Mr. Samuel Morley, of Nottingham, had promised £100 a year in its support; the advance guard of the Salvation Army was attacking the enemy. Yet Booth, who always had a healthy respect for the devil, found the going hard. After one year he had only sixty faithful followers: casualties and desertions had been numerous. Booth was not yet the autocratic General but he was always the authoritarian, and not always easy to agree with.

'He carried religion too far': holiness, the penitent-form, long prayer meetings. His followers were subject to baptisms of fire from the roughs and mockers of the Mile End Road. He even acquired a bodyguard, Peter Monk, a converted boxer. On occasions this big man went about the floor of the tent where the 'greatest ruffians of Whitechapel' were gathered to listen to Mr. Booth. 'Some were mocking, some were laughing . . . I threw off my coat and walked round the ring . . . and in two minutes all those blackguards were as quiet as lambs.'

From the first, Booth made his attacks out in the open-air where, after all, the Master he served had preached, healed the sick, and died. . . . It was William Booth's battle-school. When his circus tent rallying point became unusable because of rain, he hired Professor Orson's Dancing Academy and Assembly Rooms. Later he moved to the Effingham Theatre, then a wool warehouse and various other rooms, including, aptly, 'a stable up a court off Whitechapel Road'. As early as this, some of his uninhibited converts began to compose rough rhymes for use while they marched, or sang at the services indoors.

A publican complained that it was not pleasant to be shaving on Sunday morning and hear William Booth's people thundering that 'The publican is going to hell'. And not only that, but have to listen to this consecrated ditty:

We'll throw down the bottle
And never drink again.

A lot of them were doing this: it was all very bad for business.
Booth took some of his converts on a jaunt to Epping Forest.
They sang as they went:

In Three Colts Land in an old wool-shed,
Glory Hallelujah!
We frighten the living, and raise the dead,
Sing Glory, Hallelujah!
Shout Glory, Hallelujah!
And while the rats were running round
The boys and girls salvation found.

Pointer to the future, he mixed outings, teas, parties, suppers
and festive occasions of various kinds with Bible-reading, hymns
and prayers. Some of the gatherings he called 'Jam and Glory
Meetings'. They were noisy and, doubtless, vulgar. Many of the
refined Victorians were shocked by them, but the poor liked them
and the mission began to grow.

As yet, William Booth did not know that he was beginning
another Christian denomination. With his hero, John Wesley, he seems to have had the idea that he was a link between
the churches and the un-churched. The East-Enders, having
been sobered, converted, and more or less matured, would be
sent to church. But, with Wesley, he found that this would not
work. The reasons, as Booth gave them, were:

First, they would not go when sent.

Second, they were not wanted.

Third, we wanted at least some of them to help us in the
business of saving others.

The last consideration prevailed. A woman convert wrote,
'They put me to work right away. We had open-air meetings
and I remember having to stand conspicuously in my own street.
They also gave me sick-visiting to do.'

Booth's people learned to be fighting soldiers, and he found
that he had an army whether he wanted one or not. In two years
the Eastern Star public house had become his headquarters, with

reading room, penny bank, seating accommodation for 300 people, and living space for eight missioners. New centres of work were opened in London, and Booth had designs upon the provinces. A summer campaign was waged at Margate in 1867. Mrs. Booth and her husband spoke in the West End and south of the Thames. A number of gifted sympathizers enrolled as speakers and workers, including George Scott Railton, Booth's first Commissioner, whose contribution to the organization was of paramount importance.

Money and strong moral support came, not only from Samuel Morley of Nottingham, but also John and Richard Cory of Cardiff—the ship and colliery owners. Henry Reed, who had made a fortune in Australian sheep-farming, assisted, as did R. C. Morgan of the publishing firm—who also gave valuable publicity. Barnardo, as a medical student, assisted at the Mission, which gave him training for the great work he was later to accomplish. Lord Shaftesbury was at first friendly, but later cooled off. There were many helpers. Without the financial and other assistance given to William Booth in these early years by well-to-do friends and by members of various churches the Salvation Army could not have been created.

Already the pattern of Booth's tactics was becoming evident: evangelical conversion was to be a concomitant of drastic social and economic change—less a religion of stained-glass windows and the music of J. S. Bach, than of soap and a square meal, with noise, cheerful songs, and everyone so busy that they could not be bored.

As early as 1868 women of the streets who knelt at his penitent-form sought refuge and a respectable job within his mission. The alternative would be return to prostitution. He failed in his first attempt to open a rescue home, but resolved that it should be done, and presently it was done.

Booth became editor of *The East London Evangelist*. Mrs. Booth began writing, fluently and powerfully. Bramwell Booth, the couple's eldest son, began his staff work for the movement of which he was to become the second General. From the first, if William Booth was the all-conquering Hindenburg, then Bramwell Booth was the Ludendorff. A sensitive, artistic man, one imagines Bramwell as being more suited to the medical or legal professions, towards which he had leanings. But when William Booth gave his all to God he included his wife and eight children. If they had an option, none of them chose to exercise it. Bramwell's genius for organization of man-power and finance, his skilful navigation of the shoals of international cross-currents, made the present world-wide status of the Salvation Army possible.

A man in the pulpit often stands afar off from people. William Booth's close proximity to the misery of Londoners stimulated him to the compassionate effort which transformed his Christian Mission into the Salvation Army. The open-air meeting rings, like Wellington's squares, are seen to have been a protective measure against the attacks of 'the enemy', which pressed hard against the missioners, and often threw bad eggs, bags of wet flour and over-ripe tomatoes. George Lansbury, whose own religious ardour was to cause him pain in the Trade Union movement, saw the early-day Salvationists maltreated down Whitechapel Road.

The bonnet, large, black and strong, was at first designed to protect the Army lassies from the missiles of the mobs and even, very rarely, the truncheon of a policeman. It was happier for the girls when the smaller bonnet, prettily trimmed, even glamourous, was unnecessary as protection. But the Army always thrived better on opposition.

The decision not to celebrate the Lord's Supper as an outward and visible act, but rather to observe the inner and spiritual meaning of the sacrament, aligned the mission with the Society of Friends. Booth had found that many of his formerly drunken converts could not safely take even one sip of wine from the cup; and some of his women preachers were embarrassed at having to administer the sacraments. Victorian women were not sufficiently emancipated, or more probably Victorian men were not sufficiently enlightened to tolerate it. Booth's renunciation of the communion service was yet another evidence of his empiric method that displeased the ecclesiastical scholars and hierarchy, but which did not bring the dire consequences they predicted.

In 1870 Booth gave his Christian Mission a democratic constitution, one which made the Annual Conference his master. It also came near to being his Shirt of Nessus. Interminable discussion, differences of opinion, delays and timidity well-nigh foundered his movement.

To save the mission the founder staged a personal takeover. In 1878 the Annual Conference became a Council of War, no longer a legislative assembly. There were a few mutineers but no need for shooting. They faded into oblivion when deprived of the inspiration that emanated from William Booth.

The move to autocracy was followed by dramatic advances. Spontaneously, all over the country, military terminology came into existence. Elijah Cadman at Whitby (with Gypsy Smith as his assistant) found that the fishermen termed him 'the Captain'. When Booth visited him to preach, Cadman, who could not read or write, omitted the word 'Superintendent' from the bills, and simply advertised him as 'General of the Hallelujah Army'. It was, of course, a jingoist age. Moody and Sankey had recently been in London singing 'Hold the Fort'. The Revd. Baring Gould's still new 'Onward Christian Soldiers' was immensely popular. The Archbishop of Canterbury, Tait, declared: 'I believe that the only way to maintain the cause of our Lord is to welcome every volunteer who is willing to assist the regular forces; to arm as far as we can the whole population in the cause of Jesus Christ.'

Missioner Cadman, a fiery little man who had been a flue-boy, small enough to go up the chimneys to do the sweeping, displayed banners up at Whitby, worded:

WAR IS DECLARED: RECRUITS ARE WANTED

Booth and Railton were pleased. When Railton and Bramwell Booth prepared an annual report on the mission, carrying the phrase, 'The Volunteer Army', the proof was shown to the General Superintendent. He did not like the association with the Volunteers, a force of amateur soldiers formed during the troubled times of threatened invasion in the reign of George III. Replaced later by the Territorial Army they were allegedly notable for their inability to shoot straight, stay sober, or sit up on a horse.

'No,' said William Booth. 'We are not volunteers . . . We are always on duty.'

He struck out the word 'Volunteer' and wrote in 'Salvation', and that was that.

If it is ever true that any movement is but the lengthened shadow of its founder, it is true of the Salvation Army. Healthy regard for William Booth has tended to become adoration. Thousands of his busts—long beard and Hebraic nose prominent—rest in Salvationist homes. What the Founder said in 1885 means much more to his followers than what Mr. Gladstone said at the same time. Though among the young, a healthy sign, there has been in late years a disposition to put the grand old man of the Salvation Army into history where he belongs.

The Army now has new Generals, new frontiers, new failures and successes. What it prays about, fervently, and strives to preserve, is William Booth's original passion to save souls. It is under no illusion that its admired brass bands, social service, street-corner preaching, youth work or missionary endeavour are achieving this great objective on a grand scale, although there are successes and trophies won in many lands. The battle is much tougher than before; agonizing reappraisals of methods have been necessary.

The perimeter reaches so far that there can never be a bird's eye view of the situation. While reverses are being suffered on one field, major triumphs are won on another. To the London International Headquarters with the news of set-backs in Kenya come facts about gains in the Congo; when the battle goes awry in Europe, it prospers in the United States and Canada. If there is silence about Salvationists behind the iron curtain, there's abundant good news from far-away New Zealand and Australia.

As noble old soldiers, scarred by the salvation war, covered with badges and the glory of their sufferings, are interred to the music of the brass band and the battle songs of the regiment— not dead, but 'promoted to Glory'—young ones, different, but every bit as devoted and good, grow up to take their place.

Like Cromwell's, Montgomery's, and all the others, the Salvation Army is, to some extent, a New Model Army. William Booth's autocratic, though withal gentle, Generalship has been modified. These days the General has an Advisory Council—an international group of leading officers from whom he seeks counsel before decision on numerous great matters. He is not

ominated, as was William Booth's successor. Every General
fter the second has been elected on a two-thirds majority vote
by the High Council, the Chief of the Staff, all active Commissioners, and Colonels of two years' standing who hold territorial
commands. In one respect the Salvation Army is more democratic
than any other army one can call to mind—all the above-men-
tioned 'brass hats', from the General downwards, any officer at all,
comes up from the ranks. He must be a private soldier before he
can be a Captain: he cannot be a General if he has not been a
good soldier.

As a lad or lassie, the candidate for officership will be trained
in a school for officers, or a college—there has been a considerable slackening of the rigidity in Salvation Army terminology:
one of numerous proofs of national autonomy within centralized
control. If he or she gets through training—about ten per cent
fail—he will be commissioned to a small corps, or institution, or
missionary centre, dependent on the country and national
method. The going will be hard; some fall out by the way.

Meanwhile, the heart of the Salvation Army, let the Generals,
Colonels and Captains do what they will, is still the salvation
soldier. Upon him and on her falls the brunt of the battle. Before
being 'sworn in' publicly under the flag, a soldier must be converted, serve a period of recruitship, be accepted by the local
corps board, and have signed a formidable document entitled
The Articles of War.

The preamble to this signifies the acceptance of largely Methodist doctrines, with the following extension into the area of
Salvationist rigour:

THEREFORE, I do here and now, and for ever, renounce the
world with all its sinful pleasures, companionships, treasures
and objects, and declare my full determination boldly to
show myself a soldier of Jesus Christ in all places and
companies, no matter what I may have to suffer, do or lose
by so doing.

I do here and now declare that I will abstain from the use
of intoxicating liquor, and from the use of all baneful drugs,
except when such shall be ordered for me by a doctor.

I do here and now declare that I will abstain from the use

of all low and profane language and from all impurity, including unclean conversation, the reading of any obscene paper or book at any time, in any company, or in any place.

I do here declare that I will not allow myself in any deceit or dishonesty; nor will I practise any fraudulent conduct in my business, my home or in any other relation in which I may stand to my fellow men; but that I will deal truthfully, honourably and kindly with all those who may employ me or whom I may myself employ.

I do here declare that I will never treat any woman, child or other person, whose life, comfort or happiness may be placed within my power, in an oppressive, cruel or cowardly manner; but that I will protect such from evil and danger so far as I can, and promote, to the utmost of my ability, their present welfare and eternal salvation.

I do here declare that I will spend all the time, strength, money and influence I can in supporting and carrying on the salvation war, and that I will endeavour to lead my family, friends, neighbours and all others whom I can influence to do the same, believing that the sure and only way to remedy all the evils in the world is by bringing men to submit themselves to the government of the Lord Jesus Christ.

I do here declare that I will always obey the lawful orders of my officers, and that I will carry out to the utmost of my power all the orders and regulations of the Army; and, further, that I will be an example of faithfulness to its principles, advance to the utmost of my ability its operations, and never allow, where I can prevent it, any injury to its interests or hindrance to its success.

Of course neither the Founder nor the salvation soldiers who came after him could win their battle entirely. As Professor Inglis says of William Booth in *The Churches and the Working Class in Victorian England*, 'Not even he had shown (in a phrase he loved) how to reach the masses with the gospel'. Yet, after a hundred years of war Salvationists fight on still, and must while wickedness, selfishness, neglect and misery are to be found on earth. They have their victories.

They do not, in St. Paul's phrase, fight as those that beat the air. There is joy in the Salvation Army, witness the 'prisoners' —the men and women won from the devil. Battle dispatches in many Salvation Army newspapers with a circulation of about 2,000,000 prove the success of Salvationist arms in many lands.

In the battle for the souls of men the words of Arthur Hugh Clough are as apt for the salvation soldier as they were when Winston Churchill spoke them in the anxiety and strain of World War II:

> Say not, the struggle naught availeth,
>   The labour and the wounds are vain,
> The enemy faints not, nor faileth,
>   And as things have been they remain.
>
> If hopes were dupes, fears may be liars;
>   It may be, in yon smoke concealed,
> Your comrades chase e'en now the fliers
>   And, but for you, possess the field.
>
> For while the tired waves, vainly breaking,
>   Seem here no painful inch to gain,
> Far back, through creeks and inlets making,
>   Comes silent, flooding in, the main.
>
> And not by eastern windows only,
>   When daylight comes, comes in the light,
> In front, the sun climbs slow, how slowly,
>   But westward, look, the land is bright.

2. THE REGIMENT OF WOMEN

What must be the effects of neglect of mental culture, and the inculcation of frivolous, servile and self-degrading notions into the minds of mothers of humanity? What endears the Christian religion to my heart is what it has done, and is destined to do, for my own sex . . . Oh, for a few more Adam Clarkes to dispel the ignorance of the Church, then we should not hear very pigmies in Christianity reasoning against holy and intelligent women opening their mouths for the Lord in the presence of the Church.

CATHERINE BOOTH.

Anti-feminist John Knox, with frivolous Mary Queen o' Scots to trouble him in Edinburgh, and fanatical Mary Tudor thirsting for his blood in London, had good reason to pen his *First Blast of the Trumpet Against the Monstrous Regiment of Women.*

Yet Knox could have written with more justice against the women of the Salvation Army. There are now more uniformed and authoritarian female warriors in that movement than there were Amazons in the Caucasus. Seventeen-year-old girls will preach on Biblical truths in public with the sincerity, if not the learning, of Dr. Billy Graham. Women officers are given full ministerial office to bury the dead, to wed young lovers, to preach, admonish and exhort the men as well as the women — a 'monstrous regiment' indeed.

All ranks and posts in the Army are open to women, and there are many women. Evangeline Booth was the fourth General. Women Captains, Majors, Colonels, Commissioners command corps, divisions, whole countries — Switzerland and Ceylon are present instances. The Leader of the Salvationist Women's Social Service in the United Kingdom is a woman, and she has counterparts in many parts of the world.

An officer's wife must be an officer in her own right. If the husband falls ill she assumes full responsibility even though half-a-dozen men are on hand who could do the job. She will

28

...ve been trained, and probably had command experience before ...e married her. If a young married couple wish to be officers, both must be 'called' and the wife normally enters the college with her husband. If she will not, he will not be accepted. An officer may not marry one who is not an officer.

In the Salvation Army a woman can discipline and command men to come or go with every expectation that they will obey her lawful orders. The idea of the equality of women in God's work is taken for granted. One woman above all others is responsible for this—Catherine Booth, wife of the first General, and known as 'the Army Mother'.

It has been said that she was William Booth's 'mother', too. That she was his wife, eight children give evidence. The 'mother' relationship arises from the fact that from the first she was his superior in education, his counsellor in error. Handicapped as he was by lack of book-learning and misgivings about his own ability, he might have given up his long, heart-breaking struggle had it not been for her love, patience, and confidence in him. He was a man of doubt and anxious mood: she had a serene and constant faith.

Catherine Booth's feminism owes much to the times in which she lived—the period of great invasion of public life by women. As one who read widely and learned to write well herself, she was influenced by the new species of literary lionesses: Jane Austen, Mrs. Gaskell, Mrs. Browning, the Brontë sisters, even George Eliot—though the author's illicit *ménage* and Biblical modernism shocked her.

Harriet Martineau, Miss Nightingale, Octavia Hill, Josephine Butler and others campaigned for good causes, most of which appealed to her. To the last named she gave friendship and support. Millicent Fawcett's fight for the female franchise, however, left her cold. As with the Army to this day she had little faith in politics as a solution to the ills of mankind. Mrs. Besant's campaign, for the right of a woman to limit her family, horrified her; and it is doubtful whether she approved of Amelia Bloomer's efforts to save women from those layers upon layers of calico, flannel, cotton, wool, velvet and other fabrics that for many centuries had smothered her.

Yet that maligned lady's efforts in the United States hardly provoked more hostility than did Catherine Booth's assertion of a woman's right not to be mute in the house of God.

Though Salvationists sometimes credit her with a more important pioneering role than she deserves, her part was historically significant, and has been neglected by writers on the subject. She by no means began it but she did take this aspect of female equality a considerable way along the long, hard road to general acceptance. The Catholics had, of course, given women an honoured place and, even more so, the Quakers, whose Margaret Fell married George Fox, and became the 'nursing mother of the new movement'. Quaker Sarah Grubb (1773-1842) was 'one of the most powerful women preachers of her time'.

When Mrs. Phoebe Palmer, a visiting evangelist from the United States, was attacked in a Methodist paper for daring to poach on male preaching preserves in alleged contravention of Biblical injunction, Mrs. Booth was at Gateshead. Her husband was a Methodist minister there and she the mother of his three children, and, it is said, in delicate health. Yet the attack stung her into publishing the first of numerous pamphlets and books which reveal her as a lucid and persuasive writer. The pamphlet was *Female Ministry* or *Woman's Right to Preach the Gospel*.

She was thirty years old now, but she had been writing that sort of thing to William Booth for almost a decade. Her love letters are full of it. Indeed, as a girl, she had complained to the preacher of the Sunday sermon because he had dared to give voice to a man's doubts about women's status.

She wrote: 'In Christ there is neither male nor female. The promise of the outpouring of the Spirit is no less to the handmaidens than to the servants of the Lord . . .

'That she is, in consequence of her inadequate education, intellectually inferior, I admit. But that she is *naturally* so, as your remarks imply, I see no cause to believe. . . . Her training from babyhood, even in this highly-favoured land, has, hitherto, been such as to cramp and paralyse rather than develop and strengthen her energies . . .'

There is no record of the reverend gentleman's reaction, but we know that her darling William was a reluctant convert to her militant feminism. He had written to her, in a love-letter from Bradford: 'Though I would not stop a woman preaching, would not encourage one to begin. Preach if you feel moved thereto: I would not stay you even if I had the power to do so. Although I should not like it . . .'

Though her love was as ardent as ever Catherine did not care for this at all, and when she struck off her chains she presented William with a *fait accompli*, in public. At Gateshead, in the chapel, on Whit Sunday morning, 1860, the minister's wife walked up to the pulpit as her husband was about to conclude the service.

'I want to say a word,' she said. He sat down somewhat non-plussed and surrendered his place. The eyes of all the astonished people were upon him and his daring wife.

One of Booth's strong points was his readiness to change his tactics when the exigencies of the battle required it — a pragmatism which is of great value to the Army to this day. Hearing dear Catherine speak so well, and noting that the Methodist congregation responded sympathetically, he announced that Mrs. Booth would preach at the service that night.

She did. The large chapel was filled to overflowing. People sat in the aisles and on the window-sills.

'I was a fool for Christ's sake,' Catherine said. In fact, she was a more polished and erudite speaker than her husband. Her entry into public life in this way was a most significant event for the future of William Booth's Army.

Today the public image of the Salvation Army is likely to be the smiling face of a lassie officer under her romanticized, familiar poke bonnet. But not too romantic: never 'soft', or sloppily sentimental. Catherine Booth took her pulpit and other evangelistic duties seriously. She was a systematic thinker and expounder on theological matters, and valuable administrative assistant to her husband as he founded his Army. She carried this practical side of the 'war' to the utmost lengths, sacrificing her own health and comfort, and training her children to be warriors in the same tradition.

'The Maréchale', her eldest daughter, was persecuted in France and prosecuted in Switzerland. Emma endured great privations in India, and was killed in a railroad accident in America 'in the line of duty', while joint commander in that

country. Evangeline, later to become the General, was arrest
for contravening police regulations against street meetings. Sh
had great charm and eloquence, which, perhaps, saved her from
imprisonment. She served as Commander in the United States
for about thirty years, becoming an American citizen. The
whole nation took her to its heart, and she left a mark on
the great and vigorous Salvation Army there which makes it
unique.

In 1878, when he was having a little trouble with anti-
feminists within the movement, William Booth wrote:

'It has sometimes been said that women preachers would be
the ruin of the mission. On the contrary, it turns out that the
prosperity of the work appears most precisely where the female
preachers are allowed the fullest opportunity. During the past
months sisters have taken a leading position in no fewer than
nine of our thirty-six stations. We have at present twenty
married evangelists, and sixteen of the twenty wives take a great
part in the services.'

With Catherine to serve as his model, how could he believe
anything else? Though the family grew, she found time to
travel far and wide preaching, presenting flags, accepting new
soldiers into the ranks. She made a national reputation as a
preacher, not only among the poor, but also the better-off congregations of shocked, curious, and genuinely interested, in
London's West End.

Perhaps it is not so much to be wondered at that a woman can
talk, even in a pulpit. Mrs. Booth made practical, far-reaching
contributions to Army strategy and tactics as women do today.
She designed the flag, helped to develop women's uniforms, and
gave the Army some of its valued principles, notably total
abstinence.

When she was promoted to Glory in 1890, something went out
of William Booth's life: he was never the same man afterwards.
There was a wistful air of loneliness. Though time and again he
girdled the earth as a soldier and prophet, hurling God's
thunderbolts against the devil and calling the sinner to pardon,
often it seemed his eyes were on the stars, and his soul already in
Heaven where Catherine awaited him.

But all over the world Salvationist women took up the sword

Catherine Booth laid down. In Castle Chillon, on Lac Léman near Geneva, of which Byron wrote:

> *Chillon! thy prison is a holy place,*
> *And thy sad floor an altar, for 'twas trod . . .*

by Bonivard of course, Captain Charlotte Stirling, an English woman Salvationist served her full 100 days in the dungeons. Her offence was to hold a religious service for children—the religious austerity Calvin enforced with stake and flames at Geneva had been slow a-dying. After serving her sentence, Charlotte was banished from the Canton.

At York, where religious freedom had been purchased by the blood of martyrs, the magistrates nonetheless sent Lieutenant Annie Bell, a nineteen-year-old girl of delicate health, to a cell in the Castle for one month. She had dared to sing about God in the streets on the sabbath. Dressed like a woman convict, as Yorkshire newspapers reported, she was treated 'worse than a thief'. She was ill and hungry, and Sir William Harcourt, the Home Secretary, advised Her Majesty to remit half the sentence.

Lieutenant Mary Fairhurst slept on planks and picked oakum in Derby jail while the Army band marched by outside playing cheerful music. She, too, had taken part in an open-air service. In 1935 the M.P.—the Rt. Hon. James Thomas, Secretary of State for the Dominions—and the Mayor, both apologized on behalf of the town. This was kind of them, but, alas, Mary was not alive to accept the apology.

And after this the deluge: 'We are sweeping through the land,' the women sang. For a time, especially in the 1880s, when the Skeleton Army rampaged, and violent mobs were encouraged by publicans and other vested interests, the marching women Salvationists needed the fierce ardour of Boadicea, and the armour of a Crusader, to be able to sustain the battle. There are records of about 250 brutal assaults on salvation sisters, and numerous arrests. At least one woman died from the treatment she received.

Abroad, Booth's female contingents played a major part in the 'export' of the Salvation Army. The first sortie in the United

States took place in Philadelphia in 1878, inspired by teenage
Lieutenant Eliza Shirley, who was an immigrant, with her
family, from Coventry, England. Her mother assisted her, and
the first citadel was a dilapidated chair factory. The official
invasion which followed two years later, was led by one man,
but otherwise comprised seven women. The work in Finland
was consolidated by a young woman. They have blazed salvation
trails in India, Africa and many other lands, giving up comfort,
home and family, often falling victims to disease, hunger
and privation. The rapacious landlord, the offender against
children, the brothel-keeper and woman seducer have often had
cause to fear these warriors as the English feared Joan of
Arc.

In war, the hands that served the tea and coffee to Tommies
or G.I.s, with the smile that sweetened it, were usually those of
a Salvation Army lassie. More than the flag or the drum this
became the symbol of Salvationism to servicemen It is grate-
fully remembered all these years afterwards.

Sometimes in war, the women gave their lives. In their own
secret and profound sense this was never by 'enemy' action. That
word is not in a Salvationist's vocabulary. They were where
need existed—need that knew no frontiers. Colonel Mary Booth,
Commander in Belgium—a grand-daughter of Catherine—was
arrested by the Gestapo in Brussels as a 'dangerous spy'. The
Dunkirk evacuation was in progress, and they found a passage
marked in her Bible—the last verse of Acts 27: 'They escaped
all safe to land'. The Gestapo could hardly be expected to know
that the Army women often marked good texts for sermon
material or private comfort. At one time Mary Booth was in
danger of being shot. Yet it is probable that her bug-infested
bed was a greater cause of distress than the fear of execution.
Major Marie Ozanne, who died in a hospital in German-
occupied Guernsey, probably felt the prohibition to wear her
uniform more of a hardship than her imprisonment.

Women officers in the Far East were lost without trace; some
came back from years of internment, gaunt like beanpoles, their
hearts devoid of bitterness, their ardour unquenched. So that
women Salvationists could go on with their work, the Japanese
extended the William Booth Hospital at Soerabaja, in what is

now Indonesia. In Britain, German nationalists conducted religious services in the Isle of Man internment blocks, convincing those who watched them that, despite Ministry of Information propaganda, not every German was a bad German.

It would be misleading to suggest that women are entirely content with their lot in the Salvation Army. In general, perhaps; in details no. Stipends, as they are termed in ecclesiastical circles, are hardly relevant, for no officer receives one in the legal sense. Yet even that 'allowance' of the voluntary worker, not enforceable by law, is in some countries less for the woman than for the man of like rank and position. The Army concedes the principle of 'equal pay', but claims, with more justification than most exchequers, perhaps, that it cannot in all areas afford to implement it.

But there would never be a Salvationist mutiny of women over money. There is more criticism by women officers of failure to maintain balance of power between the sexes. Difficulties arise for various reasons. With William Booth, most Salvationists are ready to admit that a woman is man's equal before God, but would claim that few are his equal in physical strength. The strain of high command, for example, has proved to be more than some women could sustain even though mental and spiritual ability are of the highest degree.

Then woman officers marry and, naturally, many of those with the best brain and leadership capacity as well as charm are wooed. In the early days this predilection for matrimony was frowned upon, possibly for this reason. It has always been a salutary thought for men officers in the Army that they do not take a woman 'off the shelf' when they wed, but one who could become a commanding officer, Colonel, Commissioner, or General in her own right.

Married or single the modern Salvation Army woman officer is a person to be reckoned with. As wife she will raise her children decently, and almost always without that religiosity which so often gives a child the same aversion to Christianity that school cramming gives him to Shakespeare. There will be music in the home, noise, health, laughter, and, of course, love.

Mum, the corps officer, will be mother to many other children besides her own. She will help to lead youth sections, teach Bible classes, lend a hand with the Girl Guides, assist with the women's meetings. She will be expected to do her stint as preacher on Sundays and then get home to serve a cooked dinner which she has left on mark 7 with the conviction, usually justified, that 'the angels will attend to it'.

Her own children, meanwhile, expected to be paragons, will not be so. However, they are likely to get places in grammar schools, and often win awards to universities. They do not become delinquents, beatniks or neurotics. Many of them, convinced, not by the innumerable sermons they hear, or the excessive and un-subtle propaganda, but by their parents' own lives, elect to become Salvationists and, very often, officers.

In truth it can be said of the Salvationist wife that her children rise up and call her blessed.

The spinster Salvationist officer—she would be offended by the word, because it conjures up a dour and repressive image—knows all the 'shocking' facts of life, the godless materialism amongst some of the people with whom she works. Yet all the time she is well nigh an angel who carries with her innocence, cheerfulness, and a firm belief in the possibility of personal holiness.

This latter she is expected to know of from experience, and probably does.

As a corps commanding officer, at the fraternal of local clergy, she will look with polite disapproval at the pipe-smoking parson and can give authoritative agreement to a proposal that her local Salvation Army band head the Whitsun procession or whatever. No one will be surprised that a woman can speak in this way for a group of men. She is the Captain: she is in charge.

All over the world, in far different detail, but always with the same devotion and good sense, the Army woman *is* the Salvation Army, and no one better. She may have doubts, sometimes, as to whether the Army fully appreciates her worth, or honours it accordingly. She gives her best regardless.

A woman's words epitomize the down-to-earth Heaven-powered work of all such:

One of the crowd, with hard, red hands,
With tired eyes and aching heels,
One of the blue-clad crowd she stands,
One of the lowly crowd she kneels.
For love of her Christ died to save—
For love of Christ she is His slave.

LILY SAMPSON, *The Social Work Officer*
in *The Book of Salvationist Verse.*

3. GREY MEN AND SCARLET LADIES

'If in 1851 England was no longer a Christian country she had not become one again by 1880. There were still large areas of spiritual and social dereliction, there was still gross drunkenness, brutality and vice. The accounts of the conditions against which the Salvation Army matched itself in the 'eighties seem as bad as those which the slum priests found in the 'fifties . . .'

G. KITSON CLARK, *The Making of Victorian England.*

A girl in 'a fine red dress', long, long ago; women, sitting under red lights in Amsterdam today; long lines of thin, grey-faced sad men seeking supper, bed and breakfast; children, hungry, ill-treated, orphaned . . . All these and much besides make part of the world-wide saga of Salvationist social service.

G. M. Trevelyan believed that the social extension of the Army's evangelical method was largely the reason that 'its power has become a permanent feature in modern English life'. If that is true of England it is even more so on the continent of Europe, in the United States and Canada, in New Zealand and Australia and many other countries.

With an Army of Christian romantics loose on the world it was not necessary for the General to command that bread and soup, soap and bunks should be allied to the Bible and to prayers as part of the gospel. Where Salvationists with their warm hearts and intensely practical religion were to be found experimental ventures into social service came into being spontaneously.

In Melbourne in 1883 the first Salvationist work for ex-prisoners was recognized by the Government of Victoria. It became a feature of Army operations all over the world. In the same city a 'Fallen Sisters' Home' was opened in 1884 to help girls and women involved in the moral miasma of the gold-mining boom. Here, not for the last time, the Army used the press as a weapon to arouse public conscience. The Victoria Parliament enacted a bill against the sale and smoking of opium and gave Salvation Army officers and other social workers power to 'apprehend without warrant any child apparently under the age of sixteen found residing in a brothel or dwelling with a prostitute'.

'Dive, Tenement and Garret Work' began in New York in 1889, a modest beginning to social service on a vast scale now unsurpassed anywhere in the Salvation Army in any land. Two lassie officers could not wear their uniform because of the suspicion with which the Army was regarded in those days. Today Federal and State exchequers support Salvationist endeavour as does a generous public.

The girl of seventeen, clad in a red dress, presented herself to the Army's London Headquarters early one morning. She had escaped from a brothel in Pimlico to which she had been lured by an advertisement for maidservants. She was singularly fortunate in getting away unharmed after barricading herself in a room and creeping out at 4 a.m. when the madam was asleep, expecting the girl to be starved into submission.

By this time the Army had in its care others of this kind and many not so fortunate. Before 1885 a girl above thirteen was not protected against seduction. Josephine Butler and others had been campaigning for years to bring Britain into line with the rest of Europe by raising the age of consent. In 1883, 1884 and 1885 Parliament rejected bills to this effect. The story of W. T. Stead's imprisonment following the publication in *The Pall Mall Gazette* of four articles on *The Maiden Tribute of Modern Babylon* and on a charge of abduction has recently been retold by Ann Stafford in *The Age of Consent* (Hodder). Bramwell Booth, also charged was found not guilty. As a result of the public clamour created by this and other agitation on behalf of girls in moral danger, the Criminal Law Amendment Act became law in 1885.

Now, in the United States, thousands of young people are in the Army's care: in 1888 a New York judge, with a delinquent girl before him, announced that he would 'hand her over to any suitable Christian woman who cares to take her if she will apply to me'. It was later reported that 'The ladies of The Salvation Army took her to a room in the city'.

Social endeavour by Salvationists in New Zealand began also in 1888. Today it is closely woven into the pattern of social service in that highly-organized Welfare State. The Salvationists freely exercise their religious compassion and soul-seeking zeal. No one objects, least of all the Government which provides some of the sociological know-how and financial support.

In Canada, where benevolent city, provincial, Federal and individual support is forthcoming for Salvationist social service reaching from the Atlantic to the Pacific and throughout Newfoundland, the work began when a few drunken women were taken off the streets and lodged in a small dwelling house. Now young and old, male and female; alcoholics, drug-addicts, unwed mothers, down-and-outs, abandoned, orphaned and delinquent children are cared for by the Army in Canada.

Without an industrial proletariat to provide the seedbed, and with Hanna Ouchterlony, an educated and influential woman to pioneer the work, Sweden had what might be termed bourgeois beginnings, unusual for the Salvation Army. What is said to be the highest material standard of living in Europe continues to provide the Salvation Army with an environment that challenges its capacity to cope with affluence: in the past poverty has provided the most favourable soil for its growth.

But middle-class Hanna Ouchterlony, confronted with the problem of prostitution, did not forget the Boothian dictum: 'Go for souls and go for the worst.' She opened her first rescue home in 1890, and social service in this land without the poor continues on a large scale to this day. The Government insists on socio-scientific standards: Salvationists join this to their belief that, ultimately, spiritual conversion is the only answer to the human dilemma. The synthesis produced by this amalgam is a highly satisfactory product.

A good instance of this is Kurön, 'The Island of Hope', to which, as if to prove its modernity, the Salvation Army in Sweden takes permitted visitors on its own icebreaker. Situated offshore, about twenty-five miles outside Stockholm, Kurön is a sanatorium for alcoholics. They are sent either by local temperance boards, or more occasionally by the courts. Some commit themselves as voluntary patients.

Sweden does not care for any suggestion that she has more alcoholics than average in countries where advanced technology has created ample leisure, and the means to buy liquor. Though in 1955 she abolished liquor rationing it is denied that this has resulted in any real increase of alcoholism. Strict control of 'the abuse of alcohol', following road accidents, domestic problems, and the investigations of an alert health service has brought about a rise in the number of recorded people with a drinking problem, but it is thought that this is the result of earlier diagnosis over a wider field and does not indicate increase in the incidence of alcoholism.

Owned by the Salvation Army, Kurön is about three miles long by one in breadth. Its main products, apart from rehabilitated men, are corn, fruit, vegetables, meat, eggs and timber. The alcoholics labour on the farm or in workshops, a change for many of them who come from business or professional life: Sweden has found that excessive addiction to liquor is not confined to manual workers.

About half the eighty or so patients on Kurön attend the chapel service, which is voluntary. All sit through family prayers at breakfast. Regarding religion there is some initial reserve and even resentment but much of this dissolves as the days go by and the men get to know 'what makes these Salvationists tick'.

The first week is unpleasant for a patient. There is the 'disgrace' of his committal, as some deem it; there is the physical and psychological result of deprivation of alcohol, often serious. Then some of the men regard their sojourn as a form of imprisonment, for under Swedish law if he will not take the treatment of Kurön, or some such centre, then sterner measures might be used. About half of the men on Kurön are in the compelled category; others know that if they did not come forward as volunteers legal coercion would be used.

But the Manager is an experienced Salvation Army officer with expert staff. There are ways to win hardened hearts to mellower reaction: no man lives in an abyss so deep that God cannot reach down to him. Some are saved. Among alcoholics that is the best one can hope for. All over Sweden, back in their own home, business, local church, or Salvation Army hall are men who have been helped at Kurön. On the island still are some 'failures'. They have been before, and fallen, afterwards to board the boat once more and try again.

Sweden finds, with workers everywhere, that men who are

always drinking do not eat. Many of the men are starved when they arrive on the island. Sedation, medication and careful diet supervised by doctor and nurses is essential.

All the men must have a drastic clean-up, for a superficial sign of the disintegration caused by alcoholism even among affluent men is their inability to preserve a decent appearance. After their medical check, and preliminary withdrawal treatment, the patients are sorted out for interviews and allocated to a programme suited to their case. Most fit in and after three months may be named as suitable for release on probation. Occasionally a man must be transferred to a tougher, possibly state-controlled centre, or even a mental hospital. Men have tried to escape, for in winter the lakes are frozen over. Such cases are rare. Most alcoholics who do not win nonetheless try. There is the 'no-hoper' who is of the opinion that he'll never beat the drink. He has lost his job, his home, his wife and family—everything but liquor.

Doctor Helge Knöös—Kurön's doctor—has worked with the Salvation Army for many years; he is also a psychiatrist and believes that the religious motivation is a help. He should know. Apart from his link with Kurön, and other clinics and institutions, patients considered by the Stockholm police courts to be in need of psychiatric treatment are sent to him. He shares the Salvation Army's 'out-and-out' philosophy about alcohol:

'It is impossible for a person who has once gone forward to alcoholism to go backwards to normal temperance. The alcoholic cannot again be a "one drink" man. He must give it up.'

Doctor Knöös is convinced of the efficacy of the insulin treatment of alcoholism: it stimulates the appetite and predisposes to sleep, both factors highly important as early measures. The problem with insulin is that the course can be given only under direct supervision of a doctor. Not all centres have one in residence and early solution of this problem is essential. Though he has given a lifetime to the study of the problem Doctor Knöös has no dogmatic assumptions on alcoholism. In chronic cases it seems to be incurable and the malady often has the nature of a physical disease. The alcoholic cannot use alcohol as other people can.

Just as sugar would kill a diabetic so alcohol kills the alcoholic.

This physical fact must be accepted and therefore, he says, treatment is largely psychological. Without hesitation Knöös agrees that religion is a powerful control factor. He knows many who have stopped drinking altogether but not one who has stopped being an alcoholic and gone back to an occasional 'harmless' drink. Salvationist religious faith is helpful, he insists, with over thirty years' collaboration behind him, and the Army must continue in this field when the number of conversions is not high and even when there are numerous relapses.

If proof is needed of the versatility of modern Salvationist social service Sweden's Dalarö *folkhögskola* can be exhibit 'A' with the alphabet to follow if called upon. It is a high school, about twenty miles outside Stockholm and situated in idyllic surroundings on the Baltic coast. One wonders how its Swedish teenager students, on a two-year study course at this stately mansion, can be made to work when the nearby island calls to picnics, the sea to bathing, the flowers and lawns to dreams, if not to flirtations.

But this is a Salvation Army school and, in its way, it is social service. More than a century ago, in Denmark, Grundtvig, who founded the People's High Schools, wrote lines which have been translated:

> *Is light a gift for learned men,*
> *to help them spell correctly?*
> *No, Heaven cares for everyone,*
> *and lights our way perfectly.*

From this it can be deduced that the People's High School is meant to give equal educational opportunity to the children of the poor as well as the affluent. And as poverty is ever only a relative condition the need still exists even in well-to-do Scandinavia.

There are now *folkhögskolör*, operated by most Swedish churches, and they are also numerous in Norway and Denmark. Even in such highly-developed state educational systems they are logical and important. Late developers, bad examinees, young people who have changed their minds or who for any reason now want to be educated whereas before they were anxious to be done with school—they are the beneficiaries.

The educationists in the Orwellian state must often refuse to take note of such fickleness; they are not permitted to give a second chance to the boy or girl who wasted earlier opportunities, or did not recognize them. There is then no redress. Most education authorities admit the existence of many potentially good minds, highly teachable young people, who became conscious of a desire for knowledge after the appointed birthdate, or examination had gone by.

Not only that—there is the sort of knowledge for which Grundtvig had a favourite phrase: 'The living word'. By this he did not mean holy writ alone but ideas and aspirations that helped people to live their lives more fully—including those who without extra opportunity might not truly live at all. The Army's public high school, like others of that type, tries to emphasize personality: it pays as much attention to character, moral and spiritual virtues, as to book knowledge. Perhaps more. The diploma awarded to successful pupils is highly influential not only because of any academic success but because of the maturity and reliability it indicates.

There has been a touch of condescension among visitors who have looked about them at Dalarö and remarked, 'We do not need such places in Britain'. The Salvation Army officer headmistress is too polite to argue on this, but she believes that the need for the People's High School increases in Sweden rather than diminishes even though the budget for ordinary state education constantly rises with increase in the number of pupils.

As a courteous rejoinder she tells people about Sir Winston Churchill who went to Harrow as a pupil but did not shine there. He was asked to learn the first declension of *mensa*. In due course he was examined on his progress.

'I think I can say it, Sir,' he said and he gabbled it off. The master was satisfied but the boy was not. '*What does it mean?*' he asked. The master showed no enthusiasm for this kind of questioning and when young Churchill persisted there were threats of disciplinary measures. It was impertinent of the boy to insist that he would never dream of using the vocative case of *mensa*, 'O table'. He did not become a Latin scholar. 'Where my reason, imagination or interest were not engaged I would not, or could not learn,' he added.

Pär Lagerkvist the Swedish poet would understand this. He wrote of Swedish youth:

> *I wanted to know,*
> *but I could only ask questions.*
> *I wanted a light,*
> *but I could only burn.*
> *I craved life abundant,*
> *but I only existed.*
> *I complained,*
> *but nobody understood what I meant.*

They do learn mathematics, literature, chemistry, history, music, physics, geography and much else at Dalarö. They also get solutions to some of their own personal problems. Obviously, it makes a great difference that the school staff are committed Christians even if many of the pupils are not. And even so, one cannot be two years, two crucial, formative years, in such a place without it making a mark.

The Swedish Government helps to finance Dalarö; the general public, press and most education authorities are well disposed towards the People's High School system, which has grown in late years. Anxiety for the future of the young is in part responsible for this. Sweden denies that she is the country *Time* magazine has made her out to be. She is certainly not, in fact, the land of Bergman's films, masterpieces though they are. The stream of religion still flows strong, even though it goes underground sometimes. The popularity of the People's High Schools is due in great part to the wish of Sweden's wiser parents that their children shall not have just increased education and yet lose that 'one thing needful' the Bible speaks about.

As in all lands, the morals and alleged indiscipline of Sweden's youth have given rise to fears and controversy. There is no problem of discipline at Dalarö or at any average church People's High School. Though in groups young people are reserved about religion, the staff at this Salvation Army school by the Baltic Sea discover that individual pupils are ready to talk about religion. They often learn that the girl or boy who has seemed indifferent has found an awareness of prayer, an interest in the Bible, a wish to know more about that which Salvationists reckon to be the greatest lesson of all.

Another demonstration of social service adaptability is Captain Doris Pengilly, a police court and probation officer of Melbourne. In Australia, as in many parts of the world, emphasis with delinquents is being placed on the maintenance of some sort of home life wherever possible. The young people become the responsibility of a social worker.

Any such girl is bound by the terms of her probation not to leave home, or job or school. She must report to the Captain regularly, must not consort with certain people, or frequent prohibited places. To this normal probation method Captain Pengilly adds the dimension of Salvationism, and children's court officials appreciate it. Very often crime is not the problem, but ignorance, neglect, even hunger or the deprivation of the barest essentials in a girl's life. Estranged parents, drink, loneliness or some unmentionable horror may be involved. Sometimes a girl must be rescued from her own stepfather—or even her father. She may steal from chain stores with the obsessed intensity of a kleptomaniac or place herself in sexual moral danger.

Children's court magistrates do not want to send such young people to anything like prison. They want to know about causes and symptoms. They are happy when the Captain assures them that the girl has knelt at a Salvation Army penitent-form. Years of check and double check have shown that this in numerous cases, with skilled after-care, not only saves the taxpayer's money but yields good long-term results.

Such work cannot be done in a vacuum. If a girl should live at home, perhaps the home which created her maladjustment, then something must be done about it. Captain Pengilly often accepts the task of teaching the parents how better to care for their own children. In Victoria, and this proviso is being applied increasingly all over the world, the Captain has taken the Government's course for Probation Officers. She is a member of the Probation Officers' Association and attends Petty Sessions every morning as part of the city's official concern for the weak and the wicked. But though her probation reports must be prepared with a trained social worker's skill, and though the presiding magistrate may afterwards ignore it—usually he does not—this mixture of

Salvation Army 'soul-saving' faith with the legal machinery strikes only very few people as odd or objectionable.

The Captain's failures are seen in the women's prison, and the success of Victoria's remedial rather than punitive courts is proved by the fact that there are only about forty women prisoners in the whole of the state. She is a probation officer for all Protestant prisoners and for this reason does not work on a denominational basis, even dispensing with her uniform when necessary. She holds little services but not in the prison chapel —if she did the prisoners would not attend. The gay tinkle of guitars and timbrels, the happy songs, the brief talking—not sermonizing—of the Captain attract when the formal service would not.

Sometimes, privately, there are tears in prison, regrets, prayers. A woman who had 'lived in sin' for eleven years, after her release married the man and found that her new status matched the new feeling, boosted her tattered ego. She was 'born again', as the Bible puts it. The Captain keeps in touch but even when she is on her own the woman remembers that she has found a new and very special Friend.

All this and much beside is in Melbourne where Salvationists take pride that their world-wide social work officially began. Here one finds Salvation Army officer Justices of the Peace, social workers who preside over informal courts, take police evidence on oath and remand or otherwise as the case may dictate. These proceedings, made necessary by a state law that requires a prisoner to be brought before a court within twenty-four hours of arrest, often give an opportunity for Salvationists to call on Heaven's grace while they dispense man's justice. Brigadier Allan Young, J.P., a social service officer, has presided at proceedings in prison cells, office, home and even in the X-ray theatre of a hospital.

Social ministry with so many faces also shows itself as an adjunct to the corps work of the Salvation Army—the 'church' as some would consider it. In an older down-town district of Sydney, in New South Wales, is the Glebe Amenity Project where work for the aged and lonely, though not necessarily 'poor', is carried out.

Officers and the small team of assistants provide meals and

recreational facilities—a sort of home from home—where one can gossip, sing, and feel that you belong to something—and to Someone. And as, even in Australia, a pensioner is not rich, the meal which might have cost 5s. is sold for 1s. with television gratis. Apart from funds found by the corps, markets, butchers and merchants supply some of the food at cost price while various charities and individuals also assist.

The local Salvationists also found the money and much of the labour to put up the annexe where the work could be carried out. The cost was about £6,000. A good cook was essential. The quality of the meals supplied at Glebe is proof that the cook is good. The meals are in great demand. Running costs are about £20 a week and some of the money, in true Salvation Army style, is raised in public houses, at football matches, dog tracks, and race courses. The devil's money sanctified by good use.

The local council have offered £1,000 for the installation of showers. Many of the old folk live in small rooms where hygiene facilities are poor. There is also the need to give the old folk meals on Sundays—but that is the day when Salvationists preach and sing and march the streets on their more direct evangelical mission. It is a hard gospel. All over the world the issues 'to serve' or 'to save' tend to merge into that one tremendous task —'to serve *and* to save'. There are numerous unsolved problems.

Social scientists are suggesting that boys and girls should be in homes together; as it is they are often kept apart. Work for aged men and women should be carried out by the same department, not separately as is sometimes the case. Groups of cottages, small cosy units, should replace the larger institution or home, and these should be built for the purpose. More and more professional trained Salvationist sociologists must be enlisted— 'laity' as well as officers. All this will be expensive in money and manpower.

But these changes, and many others, are in some places accomplished. The Director of Salvationist probation work in the Netherlands is non-officer Mr. J. Th. Hartjes. The Deputy Director is an officer. But the Dutch Government, which finances much of the Army's probation work, insisted on a man with university status. There is a chain of Salvationist Reclamation Centres where the rehabilitation of offenders is attempted, instead of imprisonment. In court the Prosecutor demands sentence; he or the Judge asks for the Reclamation Report; the probation officer Salvationist must at least be able to submit a report in simple socio-scientific terms. That is why professional training is usual in the Salvation Army in Holland. 'Six months conditional'—a frequent procedure—means oversight at home, or at a social centre, supervised by Salvationist or other probation workers.

Perhaps it is in great part due to this highly-efficient system, and not only to the traditional law-abiding quality of Dutch life, that the prison population of Holland is low. Salvationists regularly visit the prisons, bands and singers as well as chaplains.

The national rather than denominational nature of reclamation work can be seen at the Salvation Army centre at Lunteren where about forty per cent of the men are Roman Catholics and where the priest regularly attends to minister spiritually to his own flock.

The group system of therapy is general and 'the probation work is in the hands of professionals,' says Lieut.-Colonel Harman Lahuis, the Army's Social Service Secretary. Most of these professionals are Salvationists—but not all are officers. A generous Government, which has decided that social scientists are to be preferred to larger prisons and more prison officers, helps students with the four-year courses necessary before qualifying.

The therapy groups are of men with similar problems so that discussion and treatment are more efficient: alcoholism, sexual deviation, mental stress and so on—eight in a group. Homosexuality is encountered and given medical psychiatric treatment as well as Salvationist compassion and faith. The doctor in charge at Lunteren says of this problem: 'You have to learn how to live with it.' By that he means to recognize it and control it as the alcoholic or drug-addict can. It is also conceded by the doctors who work with the Army that religion is the mightiest weapon in the therapy programme. One doctor who works at Lunteren believes that given three to five years' suitable treatment some homosexuals become heterosexual.

Salvation Army work in Korea began in 1908 and, from the first, social ministry has been urgently necessary. The war of the

1950's created economic havoc with human suffering on an immense scale. In its alleviation the Salvation Army has played a major role.

In Seoul today the shoe-shine boy may be the *souteneur* when the teenage, unsophisticated girl comes from the country to the city.

Most countries have prostitution, or its equivalent. A difference in Seoul is that many of the girls are apt to be innocent, without the brazen, calculated indifference to morality found among street-walkers and call-girls generally. The sixteen-year-old girl down from the farmland to seek employment in the big city will have no foolish ideas about women's rights, or equality. She has been reared in a man's world, where concubinage, though illegal, still lingers; where society is patriarchal; where marriages are arranged by parents; where a woman's ambition is to marry, and where not to be married at twenty is to lose face irreparably.

Educated only in the three R's, if that, the young stranger, alighting from the train or bus at the terminus at Seoul, will be anxious to get a job quickly. She has promised to send money to her wretchedly poor family without delay.

All her life she has toiled in the fields, knowing little but the crunch of poverty. To work in a department store, or office, would be splendid, though a respectable teahouse would be best of all. There are such places, and those fortunate girls who elude the pimps and bawds do find employment in them.

But if no one respectable meets her at the station, if she has no decent job waiting, then she is in grave danger of becoming another of the 10,000 or so prostitutes in Korea.

'I know a kind lady,' the shoe-shine boy may say. 'She has a room and a teahouse. Come with me; I will introduce you.'

If the girl listens to this kind of talk, she is lost, will probably find herself the inmate of a brothel. Where scruples are awkward, ways will be found of overcoming them. One is to allow the girl to run into debt by grossly over-charging for her food and lodging while she seeks work. Another is to threaten trouble with the police—a paralysing thought to a girl from the country.

In this city, near where the 38th Parallel, policed by the United Nations, divides the Communist industrial north from the Western agricultural south, money is the magnet, the ultimate persuader. Troops on leave, with funds and leisure-time to expend, have upset economic and social equilibrium. Many Korean girls have become the players in that age-old drama of vice *versus* virtue.

The Salvation Army has a chain of homes for orphans and girls in Korea, and plays its part in the inter-denominational Girls' Welfare Association, on whose committee sit representatives of various churches including Anglican, Presbyterian, Methodist, the United Church of Canada, and other religious bodies, including the Salvation Army. Financial support is also an allied operation from OXFAM, the Christian Children's Fund, World Vision, and other sources.

Mainly, efforts aim at prevention. Korean prostitution is typical. Girls who begin it usually stay with it until they are ready to leave it, and, often, that is when age or disease have taken their toll. Some girls require treatment for venereal disease, and also acquire a police record. About forty per cent of girls are thought to engage in petty crime, being schooled in their trade by their 'owners'. Alone, the girl could not survive either as courtesan or thief.

The tragic irony with some is that while the pariahs exploit a girl's youth, she is trying to save enough to gain a dowry and be married respectably. If she remains unwed she will lose face to a degree which diminishes her even as the kind of individual a Korean girl is allowed to be. If there are hopes that she may not, in the English phrase, be 'left on the shelf', then she will have the impetus which may save her from street-walking.

These factors contribute to the marked success of preventative efforts by the Girls' Welfare Association, said to be as high as ninety per cent of all girls encountered.

The waitress who excitedly embraced and kissed a woman Salvationist in a Seoul restaurant was one of many who have cause to be grateful for protection when they were vulnerable — the day they first came to the city.

Nearly all the girls profess salvation before leaving the Army homes — some of them become Salvationists. They stay from six months to a year, learning a craft or trade before they go to a job that the Army finds.

Some, the happiest of all, go back home with their precious dowry and even that virtue which, the Bible informs them, is priced 'far above rubies'.

In Britain the 1957 Street Offences Act has cleared the streets of prostitutes but only to drive them into 'modelling', or some other euphemistic terms for call-girl activities. Salvation Army officers of the Women's Social Work still patrol London's streets at nights, succeeding most frequently in their preventive role, for the confused and relatively innocent. The girl who is an experienced prostitute, whatever name she has for it, and is 'doing well', usually stays in it until she is too old or a more lucrative pursuit or marriage offers itself.

'Amateurs' are another genus. They are more frequently met with and many can be rescued in the Salvation Army sense of that word. In Approved Home Office centres operated by the Women's Social Work of the Salvation Army, they frequently respond most favourably to moral and religious training. Some are converted and the Army helps them to find good and safe employment. Follow-up activity by Salvation Army officers and other social workers confirms that more than half of the girls who sexual delinquency may have been contributed to by poor homes and bad parents do make good after all.

The line between the 'professional' and the 'amateur' prostitute is wearing thin. On Mondays, Exchange Day in Amsterdam, 'part-timers' are available 'to meet the large demand', states Major Alida Bosshardt who works in the notorious Zeedijk area, and who has been described by Britain's *Daily Mirror* as 'The Angel of the Underworld'.

The Major knows young married women whose husbands drive them into the city at about 8 p.m. and then take them back to their children and respectable suburban houses long after midnight. In the interval the young wife and mother will have earned between £10 and £20 for the family budget—her rooming expenses are heavy. The Major tells of others who pool their resources to buy a small tavern, which they use for their trade on a three-shift system—some sleep, some work, some are soberly at home in the suburbs.

Awarded the Order of the Founder, highest Salvationist honour, for her work in Amsterdam's red light district, Major

Bosshardt sees her problem as one largely caused by men, an obvious point often ignored. The men hunt in packs in Amsterdam, like wolves: men from the sea, from military and air force bases, as is clear from the uniform of some of them. Others are students and business men. Who can tell about many, silent, obsessed, walking furtively? Some hunt alone, driving down in an expensive car, taking their time, choosing with care.

If it seems astonishing that the Dutch, a solid and righteous nation, should tolerate a red-light district the answer is, 'better the devil you know than the devil you know not'. Brothel-keeping is illegal and proven *souteneurs* are punished. The idea seems to be that the girls who engage in the business openly can be controlled. About 3,000 are known to the police morality department.

The unashamed nature of this trade in sex certainly enables the Salvation Army and others to fight it. Written up in count-less newspapers and magazines, featured on radio and TV, Major Bosshardt, who is professionally trained, is optimistic about the possibility of achieving the Salvation Army's old-time mission to rescue prostitutes. She lives among them. She knows hundreds of them by name. They will admit her to their rooms, talk to her about their problems—very often their husbands, their children, are the alleged reasons why they 'have to do this for a while'.

When late at night she marches from her Goodwill centre, 'de Ruytenburgh'—from which Captain Ruytenburgh of Rem-brandt's 'Night Watch' also marched in the famous painting, she marches to save. She has reason for hope. Safe at the hostel, guarded by one or another of her staff, are a few, perhaps more, of the girls who are attempting an escape from the red-light district and its degrading trade. Major Bosshardt claims that about fifty in a year arrive back home, or into a decent job, after giving up prostitution. She finds that it is the girl aged between sixteen and twenty-two who is most likely to be saved. The twenty-eight to forty years age-group also has a good escape potential. But the 'twenty-two to twenty-eight' girls are most likely to fail. These, the Major knows, have established clientele and experience of 'success'. Though the rent of one room may be about £30 a week the margin of profit is high during that youthful, glamorous heyday.

Though the girls welcome the Major she is bad for trade. She will station her singers and pray-ers on the corner of the little alley by the canal, just where half-a-dozen red lamps are shining, and perhaps twenty girls in business. She will go in and be received with courtesy. But the 'wolves' hold back, or go elsewhere, and competition is always keen.

She will leave the *Strijdkreet*—*The War Cry*—and renew the invitation for the girl to come to a service. Sometimes circumstances justify her in claiming that now is the time for the girl to abandon this life. Most of them loathe it. If the Major is sure of anything, it is that prostitutes have no liking for their calling for its own sake. Either they are in it because of some abnormality, loneliness, sense of rejection, or because they are supporting a man well hidden in the background. But to most the 'work' is distasteful and degrading: money is the *raison d' être*.

It is the sense of disgust in many of the prostitutes, allied to the Major's profound faith in God's love, that enables her to be 'The Angel of Amsterdam'. The fallen angels, 'her girls', she prays for. She knows that in all there is a spark of good, a capacity for recovery. Some will go back and live a new, a better life. There is no argument: an average of one a week does so.

Sometimes, as ever among women who work in the dark and alone, one is murdered. More than once the Major has been asked to bury the victim.

But occasionally she conducts a wedding ceremony. A university student, who fell in love with the girl he patronized, believed not only that she was intelligent and pretty—which was true—but that she could break out from 'the business' and marry him. It took six long years to persuade his parents to agree; to rehabilitate the girl; to help her family, whose miserable condition had helped to drive her to the Zeedijk area; to enable him to graduate and be able to support a wife. Without Major Bosshardt's help it could not have been done. But now it is. Both husband and wife attend regularly at the Dutch Reformed Church in the distant town where the couple began their life together.

If any should feel shocked at this they should try to appreciate the Major's properly tolerant attitude to this moral problem. It is not that she condones prostitution but that she regards it as part of a universal human condition—'all have sinned and come short of the glory of God'. She refuses to regard the girls as more wicked than others just because this sin is sex sin. They are certainly not more wicked than the men whose money makes the trade to flourish.

Christ, she points out, accepted the fact of prostitution. He was not, like the crowd that wished to stone the woman to death, shocked into unreasoning panic measures. But, as He accepted her with understanding and as a person, He bade her 'Go in peace and sin no more'. This is a standard of enlightenment that, in Major Bosshardt's opinion, is in short supply. Reports in Dutch papers that the Major is 'the one woman who has the confidence of the women of the Zeedijk' may be due in great part to the fact that she strives to emulate Christ's compassion and understanding.

So it must be everywhere where officers and soldiers all over the world seek to serve and save the needy of all ages. 'Our social operations are a natural outcome of our Salvationism,' as William Booth said.

4. INTO AN ENCHANTED LAND

You are old, Father William, the young man said,
And your hair has become very white;
And yet you incessantly stand on your head —
Do you think, at your age, it is right?
                                    Alice in Wonderland.

With a century's hindsight to make us clever, what the early-day Salvation Army did to its children seems to be terrible, although it was the norm for those times.

Cleaned up and unnaturally solemn, they were lined up out front, ages ranging from about six or seven, to fifteen, to sing such songs as:

> *I want to be an angel*
> *And with the angels stand,*
> *A crown upon my forehead,*
> *A harp within my hand.*

Nine-year-olds, and some even younger, would be encouraged to make little speeches—'testimonies'—regarding their religious condition. Suitably chastening Bible texts were preached at them. One used was, 'What wilt thou say when He shall punish thee?' William Corbridge, a prominent pioneer Salvationist, stationed at Barking, preached in the children's meeting on 'The pale horse and his rider'. He reported:

'This was more than ever a solemn meeting. At the close, many of the young people were anxious.'

At a children's 'Tea and Experience' meeting at Whitechapel in the 1870s, this song followed the cakes:

> *We are waiting by the river,*
> *We are watching by the shore;*
> *Only waiting for the angel;*
> *Soon he'll come to bear us o'er!*

'Two little boys engaged in prayer,' stated the report, 'and then nine-year-old "S.C." declared "I am very happy. I love Jesus. I am going home to glory when I die. I want you to accept Jesus too."' Then echoing Tiny Tim he added, 'May God bless us all,' but with an un-Dickensian final sentence—'And may we all meet in heaven.'

A fifteen-year-old lad said, 'If I should die this minute I should go safe home to glory on the heavenly train. I have my ticket. The name on it is JESUS. I do not intend to let the devil rob me of this.'

But 'B.B.', twelve years of age, differed, hinting even in his early years at the divisions which may afflict the flock: 'We do not need a train to get us to heaven. We shall get there much faster than a train can carry us—sudden death, sudden glory! I trust I shall meet you all above.'

Looking back it all seems most depressing and unchildlike. But there were reasons. Though Chadwick and other Public Health pioneers had already done much to clean up London's sewers, and though the mortality rate from cholera and other water-borne diseases had fallen, tuberculosis and other child-killers were still endemic in the East End of London, where Booth's mission was at work. Pauper funerals were every-day occurrences. The young lived constantly in close proximity to death.

Mr. Gladstone, Disraeli and others could live past their allotted span: the poor, cold and hungry found life hazardous. Brief candle, indeed. No wonder that the young would sing:

> There is a better world they say,
>   O so bright!
> Where sin and woe are done away,
>   O so bright!
> And music fills the balmy air,
> And angels with bright wings are there,
> And harps of gold and mansions fair,
>   O so bright!

There was an extensive repertoire of such hymns about death,

heaven and hell. The addresses of the missioners often took on
the apocalyptic note. The children were encouraged to be suitably serious about it all.

Yet this was one campaign the Army was to lose. It was
fighting nature, the spring of youth that could not be damned
even by privation.

At one meeting, with 300 children inside, 'Boys were outside
amusing themselves with white mice and rats to the great dis-
traction and disturbance of the service.' At Fieldgate Street
mission, 'Unruly boys turned off the gas taps and put gunpowder
in the stove.'

Indeed, keeping order at the back of the hall, or at the front
door, was a losing battle for the earnest missioners. The fact
was that many of the young folk, especially the boys, would not
always sit still to be told that they were in danger of eternal
punishment.

There was also opposition from parents. Many a mother,
though she could not have heard of child psychology—Sigmund
Freud being as yet but a child himself—felt by instinct that the
missioners were laying it on too thick. Her darlings could not
be as bad as all that.

Meanwhile William Booth was leaving this 'junior war' to
subordinates and they, colliding with the exuberance of youth,
lost heart. It was a defeat. William Booth retreated for the time
being, and forbade further effort.

'We have not any real plan for dealing with the children,' he
said in 1877. 'As far as our experience of Sunday Schools goes,
they have been an injury everywhere they existed. There are
only three left, I believe. It must be understood that no new
school must be commenced. In fact, no children's plan of any
kind must be adopted anywhere without my consent.'

It was some years before he would give consent. His missioners
concentrated on their main task—leading the drunks, wantons
and sinners everywhere to conversion. Robert Raikes style Sunday Schools—where the young were taught to read—were
disliked by Booth. He had not the staff to man them. In any
case, he had a bigger objective:

'I deny that it is any part of our work to teach the children to
read . . . our business is simply to get them converted and train

them for God and usefulness, as we do adults . . .' He took a very poor view of the fact that while there were about 6,000,000 scholars at Sunday Schools, only a minority of those children were integrated into church life.

There was, therefore, a hiatus of some years during which the Army for the most part suspended young people's work. Here and there stubborn individualists persevered, and the new idea, like much that is best in Salvation Army tactics, developed gradually at the grass roots, to be taken over later and launched officially in London.

Captain John Roberts, up at Blyth in Northumberland in 1880, made a major break-through. His local officers took the official line: children could not be admitted if the meeting was filled by adults, as meetings usually were. Roberts took pity on the youngsters and began week-day gatherings for them. As this was not Sunday School, to which William Booth objected, Roberts was allowed to proceed. Others followed suit. One of the first children thus admitted at Blyth, who later became a Salvationist, married the now famed Lax of Poplar.

When Roberts was made the first editor of *The Little Soldier* the paper did have a rather morbid and un-childlike tone. There were photos of dear departed little soldiers, with lengthy obituaries. One illustration showed a weeping couple by the bedside of their deceased son. Both were drunkards. One held the ticket for the child's boots which had been pawned to get money for beer. The lad, consequently, died of pneumonia.

Arthur James, aged twelve, was one of many versifiers whose doggerel *The Little Soldier* printed:

> If you come not to the Fountain,
> But tread the downward way,
> You'll cry for falls of rock and mountain
> On the Judgment Day.

What Booth did to change all this, was to create a wonderland —literally. Rather like that other Father William in *Alice in Wonderland,* he would do the extraordinary thing: 'vulgar' and 'shocking', people said. Though there is no record that the old man ever stood on his head, he doubtless would have tried had

it been necessary. He once told Rudyard Kipling that he would
be ready to stand on his head and play the timbrels with his feet
if it would help him to save the world.

The incredible truth, in view of the way they had boobed
earlier, was that this time Booth and his staff made the Salvation
Army an exciting, happy movement for children. It remains so
to this day as hundreds of thousands of healthy, cheerful Salvationists all over the world give proof.

Of course, the fire and brimstone did not die out at once, but
as *Orders and Regulations for the Junior War* were compiled
and enforced, a dramatic, colourful, noisy and intensely active
programme transformed the grim, grey fields. The young were
enlisted in their thousands, and this time they stayed, married
Salvationists and reared countless little Salvationists unto the
third and fourth generation.

Basically it was a kind of 'do-it-yourself' religious apprenticeship. The urge to win the souls of the young was there, but
camouflaged beneath methods that utilized the romanticism of
the time. Heroes, happy songs, happy endings; little corporals,
sergeants, cadets and captains; uniforms, flags, bands, drums.
The children of that proletariat, Marx had said, who were doped
by religion, 'the opium of the poor', who were hypnotized by the
capitalists to look for pie in the sky, now had more positive, glad
and earthy songs. Such as:

> We once lived on dry bread and what we could get,
> And when we had nothing we hardly dared fret,
> But now we have nice bread and treacle each day,
> Salvation for ever, Salvation hooray!
>
> Our bonnets were torn, and our shoes went click-clack,
> Our clothes went to 'uncles' and never came back,
> But Captain Salvation has brought them away,
> Salvation for ever, Salvation hooray!
>
> Our houses were empty, we scarce had a chair,
> And strong drink had broken our crockery warè,
> We've now chairs and tables and china so gay,
> Salvation for ever, Salvation hooray!

It was hardly poetry, but it had a catchy tune, and very often the children were fat as they sang: dad had joined the Army too, and was not spending his wages on booze. The children were getting square meals—a nice change for them.

William Booth launched his 'Junior Soldiers War' in 1888, although this was official acceptance of a spontaneous development that had been going on for some time. But now the campaign achieved victories on a world-wide front. The term 'little soldier' was rejected as being bad psychology, if that anachronism can be allowed. There was to be nothing 'little' about it. The young soldier would be of heroic proportions, and the war large-scale.

'We shall supply fun and amusement and merry times for the children, but always in the Lord,' said William Booth at the London rally where he launched his new ideal. He went on to say that the young soldiers would have their own barracks, specialist officers, their own songs and manoeuvres. He castigated the solemn ones in his Army: 'They're quite sure little Jim can be saved and go to heaven when he dies,' said the General. 'What they do not believe is that the same Saviour can keep little Jim happily alive . . .' Clearly, on this view of theology, the pale horse and his rider was a non-starter.

Yet it would be wrong to assume that Booth was about to run a holy circus at which his 'vulgar antics' were designed merely to keep children off the streets. Before being allowed to have one toot on a trumpet, one bang on a drum, the boy or girl must be converted. Admittedly it was a relative conversion. Booth conceded that a child might have a naïve grasp of the profound faith and experience involved but, naïve or no, it could be genuine. It was a beginning. The Army must have patience. More mature understanding would develop.

Now, as then, the Army begins by seeking to capture the babies. Probably more officers, sergeants, singers and bandsmen first enlisted in this way than in any other.

As soon as possible after birth the child is taken to the citadel by its parents. There, in a public ceremony, usually on Sunday morning, he is dedicated to God. Most are the children of Salvationists, but there are also many others who look upon the ceremony as the equivalent of a Church christening. In many countries the Army's register of births, marriages and deaths has legal status.

Tremendous promises have to be made. The parents undertake to keep the child from drink, tobacco, and bad moral and social influences. While the ceremony is proceeding, up on the platform in full view of the congregation, the child, blissfully unaware that its future is being thus decided, will coo happily, or stare in puzzled manner at the Captain who holds him in his arms as he conducts the ceremony. Sometimes the infant will shriek in annoyed or shocked protest. He has even been known to try to eat the bright yellow-red-and-blue flag of the Salvation Army that always hangs over him. The ceremony proceeds regardless.

Children, of course, can have too much religion. Salvationists guard against this. The average child in the Army is a healthy young animal, free from the melancholia and neurotic maladjustments often presumed to be the concomitants of an evangelical Christian faith. Though often assailed by such ditties as 'Salvation Army, all gone balmy!', Salvationists are not, in fact, mad.

They have certainly learned that children cannot thrive in a passive role. That same 'kidnapped', unconcerned infant will probably be keenly involved in the Army by the age of eight or nine, if not before. He will have his own religious experience. Salvationists are not with the cynics on this, rather with Wordsworth:

> *But trailing clouds of glory do we come*
> *From God, who is our home:*
> *Heaven lies about us in our infancy.*

William Booth's people could produce a million 'case histories' to prove the truth of that assertion. They would concede the truth of those other sadder lines, too—

> *Shades of the prison-house begin to close*
> *Upon the growing boy . . .*

But by that time they try to have him so woven into Salvation Army life that it is hard for him to escape. At adolescence he is often in love, or thinks he is, with a lassie Salvationist, looking forward with equanimity to a lifetime as a soldier in the Army.

'Full' is an apt word for the kind of life a boy has, and will continue to have. By the age of ten, or even earlier, he will probably be in a band. Girls join the singing brigade. Sometimes boys and girls join both. There are the Boy Scouts and Girl Guides, Wolf Cubs, Brownies, or their equivalent organizations in countries outside the United Kingdom. There will be drums to bang, trombones to blare, guitars to thrum and timbrels to beat. Holiday camps, music schools, youth clubs, classes and courses galore . . .

Briefly, religion of that common-sense, practical kind, combined with fun and games, as William Booth decreed. The Salvation Army has even found a way to make the Bible an exciting, attractive book. At about thirteen years of age many of its young people join the Army priority youth section—the corps cadets. In it they will mix Bible study with a cheerful, useful social life. They will receive training in public speaking, and tactics of open-air 'warfare'. They do lessons and sit exams. It is from this aristocracy of Army youth that most candidates for officership come forward—very good officers, who can be found today at the far outposts of the Army empire—wherever sacrifice, know-how and ardent missionary, social-service, or evangelical faith is required.

Almost all young people in the Army acquire musical knowledge, not as listeners but as participants. The Army does the teaching and provides the music and instruments, the young folk must find their own uniforms.

In the company meeting, that substitutes for the Sunday School, a religiously functional, rather than a theologically academic line is taken. In this respect, William Booth, who was shocked by Jeremy Bentham's lack of Christian faith, was all for utilitarianism but of a Boothian kind.

The young are taught not only that prayer is wonderful, and essential for them, but also how to pray. They are exhorted to be salvation witnesses, then given some training in how to speak up in public and in private. Relatively few Salvationists are at a loss for words. The young must 'fight for God' at home, school, work, and in their leisure time. It is not just what is in the

Bible—but how to do what the Bible commands. Not the collegiate method but the training system of an army.

All these years afterwards, William Booth's tactical inspirations are seen to be inspired. In the parlance of today, they pay off. The Army's main source of new recruits is now from the young people's war. Adult conversions are still sought after, still numerous. But it is from the sons and daughters of the regiment, schooled and well-drilled in Salvationism, that the Army gets most of its *élite* of officers and local officers.

Not only in numbers do the young people aid the Army. There is the quality of youthfulness itself. Like any similar military-style machine the Army has a quota of Colonel Blimps.

> *Old soldiers never die,*
> *They simply fade away.*

So the song goes. Salvationists of any age do not die—they are 'promoted to Glory'. Some, understandably, are most reluctant to fade away. Retirement age for a man Commissioner is 70; for other men officers 65; for a woman 60. Even in retirement most of them continue with their life work.

On an average the longevity of Salvationists is good. They do not drink, smoke or womanize. If they are what they should be they do not even get tensions, for they believe in that Bible which enjoins them to take no anxious thought for the morrow —to know always inner peace.

Excess of tradition, undue reverence for the past can injure any movement and has sometimes hurt the Salvation Army. Very heavy prejudices sometimes develop. The rising generations of youth help to keep this within bounds. Though much of the Army's nomenclature, system of government, music and tactics were borrowed from the American Civil War, the Crimea, and other military campaigns, the young cadets in its training colleges, the legions of youth in its bands and brigades, regard 'Theirs not to reason why' as old hat. The modern Salvationist is still ready to obey orders but he likes to be told why, and usually is.

Springing as it did from a somewhat puritanical nonconformity, it was perhaps inevitable that the Army should acquire a highly-shockable attitude about sex—sometimes not so much the pitying compassion of the Salvationist towards a transgressor, but a sort of unreasoning horror.

In one of the first set of rules for 'the junior war' it was laid down that the boys and girls, however young, should always be kept 'quite separate'. But this stern decree did not long survive. In these days the Army is less stuffy about sex than one might suppose. The average social service lassie officer, though unmarried, morally meticulous, is no Mrs. Grundy. The gamut of sex offences is known to her. Her case histories may include rape, lesbianism, promiscuity, girls assaulted by fathers or other male relatives, and venereal disease in children. Even that will not exhaust the list.

Though requiring that the New Testament code of chastity before marriage and fidelity afterwards shall be observed, the 'good mixer' religion of the Salvationist makes it impossible for anyone in the movement to live in any monastic or nun-like atmosphere, ignorant of what goes on in the wicked world.

Celibacy is not a rule in the Army. Captains, Colonels, Commissioners and Generals live with their own sons and daughters —there is no more effective corrective of a reactionary stance.

An instance of common-sense enlightenment stimulated by youth can be seen in one or another of the Army's co-educational colleges for the training of officers.

In the old days a girl might incur official displeasure for looking at a boy cadet, leave alone talking to him. Now she may walk about the lawn, or sit by him on the bench under the cherry tree. It is not unknown for her to accept a dinner date, although it is usually, of necessity, a frugal dinner.

Steady courtships can begin during the second year of training. Many romances do, in fact, blossom in Army colleges, though the engagement must usually wait until after the 'passing out' ceremonies before it can have official sanction.

Agreeing generally with the Biblical injunction against being unequally yoked with an unbeliever, the Army girl usually marries the Army boy to live happily ever after.

The Army lassie at the factory bench, or at the typewriter in the office, or even walking with *The War Cry* in the pubs, is in truth a very human and desirable girl. The young man behind a pint who succumbs to her charms, and many have, knows

C

others he can flirt with, or more than that. Such pretty painted ladies sometimes hardly know the words of the Lord's prayer, leave alone how to teach a child to pray. Such a one would do for an affair of some sort—for Saturday night, but hardly for Sunday morning. The average Army lassie has high marriage potential.

The Army has even gained new recruits in this way, when the patron in the pub follows the lassie to the Army. William Booth, a one-woman man, who loved his darling Catherine from time of meeting until his last breath, would not disapprove even of this somewhat unusual mode of winning a soul.

Salvationists also hear when in springtime—the season of youth and love—the voice of the turtle is heard in the land. To them 'respectable' and 'romantic' are quite apposite ideas.

The Sunday afternoon gathering at many corps, the praise meeting, known as 'the free and easy', is often made raucous by the shrieks and cries of a horde of infants. At some centres special 'parking places' have to be found for prams, and nurses are provided so that mum can sing in the choir and dad play with the band. At some richer corps sound-proofed, glass-fronted rooms are provided where the infants can bawl and not be heard. But in general the baby grows its first tooth at about the same time as it learns to join in the chorus of 'Amens' and 'Hallelujahs', the hand-clapping and timbrel playing which make sleep impossible at an Army meeting.

The 'natural increase' is large, especially up to teen years—when losses can be serious. In the old days, of course, families were larger: mum, dad and numerous offspring. Salvationist social patterns, in the Western world at least, agree with the general trend towards fewer children. This may be bad for the Cradle Roll, but it is good economic and social behaviour. The average Salvationist home is a very happy one.

Numerous Salvationist children win music awards and scholarships, having had the stuff dinned into their ears from birth. There also may be something genetical in this since grandpapa probably played a cornet in the early-day brass band. Quite naturally, also, Army youth often shines at religious knowledge at school, and develops a sense of vocation when the time comes to consider a career.

Many of those who in the old days would have made officer-ship their first choice, now turn instead elsewhere. Young Salvationists are numerous in secular social service for one or another of the public authorities, in probation or welfare work, the police force, teaching and nursing. From infancy young Salvationists are exhorted to 'Do something useful with your life'—'Have a sense of responsibility'—'God first, others second, yourself last.'

So it must be admitted that the Army is itself responsible for this 'wastage' of its youth, if that is what it is. In fact the enrichment of the professional, social, welfare and public service by Salvationists is another contribution the Army makes its mission. All over the world within the Army loss of better educated young people is being halted by the establishment of university level standards in theology, sociology and in other fields. This policy is already bearing fruit.

Meanwhile, astonishing as it may seem to some who cherish the legend of the grey and grim Salvationist, the Army's regiments are filled with happy soldiers, many of them young. The idea of the ranting, perpetually disapproving street-corner preacher, obsessed by sin, and ridden with neurosis, is born of inadequate knowledge.

The young legions of the Army have enough religion to live by, and to die with when the time comes, but, meantime, not so much as to cause them to wither as if deprived of humanity and the rich and proper joys of existence.

5. SALVATIONIST IMPERIALISM

Now it is not good for the Christian health
*   to hustle the Aryan brown,*
For the Christian riles, and the Aryan smiles,
*   and it weareth the Christian down;*
And the end of the fight is a tombstone white
*   with the name of the late deceased,*
And the epitaph drear: 'A Fool lies here
*   who tried to hustle the East.'*
                                    RUDYARD KIPLING

The old man who had built an empire for God, as he lay blind and dying in 1912, was restless because of conquests not yet made: 'Bramwell,' he said to his son and successor, 'I have been thinking about China. Promise me that you will get together a party of officers and unfurl the flag in that wonderful land. Promise me that you will begin the work in China.' Bramwell did promise and the work was begun.

By that time the Army had invaded many countries outside England. A reckless man might argue that the first such missionary venture was to Scotland where a corps was opened in Glasgow in 1879. Obviously, the Scots would take a poor view of this: they have always been notable for being at the giving, not the receiving end of missionary endeavour.

Traditionally, 'a missionary country' is one in which, as Bishop Heber puts it,

> *The heathen in his blindness*
> *Bows down to wood and stone.*

The idea, in Heber's sense, would no longer be valid, let alone tactful. When it was, the wood and stone were symbols of the only God 'the heathen' knew—an expression of a religious instinct sincerely expressed, as such works as Frazer's *Golden Bough* have shown. From the first, most Salvationists regarded missionary service without the patronage and superiority that became so objectionable in a world where the under-privileged refused to continue in their role as the inferior man.

When the first Salvationists went to Glasgow, the United States of America, Ireland, Australia, France, Switzerland and Sweden in that order, and then in 1882 to India, it was all part of the same imperial vision—the world of God. There was to be no distinction between white or black, no fish of one and fowl of another. There is not, and there has never been, a Salvation Army missionary society or department. Salvationists sent from London were not expected to be the British Salvation Army overseas. The Army belongs where it is. It is indigenous. The word 'foreign' is banned from its terminology. William Booth declared that he objected to the phrases 'Christian countries' and 'heathen lands'. He divided mankind into two groups: those who were for God and those who were against Him.

The working class background of most of the 'invasion' contingents, their marked ability to live on the country and be absorbed by it, helped the Army to avoid some of the pitfalls existing where hunger and nationalism prompt the Indian, African or Asian to ask, 'Why should these people be so wealthy when we are all so poor?' 'Why are they so fat and well-fed when we are so hungry?'

Part-creator of Salvationist strategy for conquest abroad was Frederick St. George de Lautour Tucker, an exception to the rule that most early-day Salvation Army officers were working class. One of a famous Anglo-Indian family, Tucker was educated at Cheltenham College to become a magistrate and Assistant Commissioner for the Punjab. He was a Greek scholar and also knew Hindustani, Urdu and Sanscrit.

But he became odd man out with his family and the Indian Civil Service when he was converted in a Moody and Sankey Mission, at the Royal Agricultural Hall in London. Eaten up with zeal to convert India's millions for Christ, he was often admonished for holding open-air services and other attempts to evangelize the natives. This not without cause. A magistrate's efforts to proselytize were bound to give rise to embarrassment in a land where religious strife was rife and the Indian Mutiny a recent memory. That had been sparked off by religious agitation.

Tucker was not daunted. He wanted to present Christ to the Indians in an Indian way. He reasoned that Jesus was a man of the East, not of the West, and that the attempt to make the gospel an English export could not succeed. He had read much about St. Francis Xavier who lived among Indians as an Indian —a policy which reaps a great harvest to this day. Tucker wanted a chance to do likewise. William Booth said, 'Get into their skins,' Tucker was to prove adept at that powerful form of psychological warfare.

Opportunity knocked through the Christmas number of the Army's *War Cry*, four pages, one ha'penny. It told of soul-winning effort: 'An Army with its sleeves tucked up, doing its work on its knees, stooping to conquer, going out to fetch the people in . . . making themselves fools for Christ's sake . . .'

These are the people I have been seeking, Tucker told himself, and sailed for London where he offered his services to William Booth as an officer.

The General smiled. He knew about these middle and upper-class people who delighted to go 'slumming'. 'You are one of the dangerous classes, but we shall see,' and he refused to accept Tucker until he knew more about the Army. In his own West Country the Indian magistrate put a Salvation Army ribbon round his hat, shocking his family and distressing his wife. For six months he studied the Army then resigned from the Civil Service, and was accepted as an officer with the rank of Major.

He was going to be poor. His father threatened to disinherit him; his officer's allowance was ludicrously small. But poverty would help him in India. He would dress in native clothes, walk barefoot, live in the poor villages—just like Francis Xavier, Brescia and those others who endured privations for Christ's sake.

While Tucker waited for his invasion party to be assembled, he completed a Hindustani hymn book. He arrived in Bombay with three assistants on Sept. 19th, 1882. The police were there in force, believing, naturally enough, that all the advance publicity and talk of 'capturing India' meant invasion by hundreds of troublesome Salvationists, and consequent public disorder. Tucker's little Army marched away to the noise of tambourine, cornet and drum. The Indians were delighted, and many marched behind. But the Governor, Sir James Ferguson and the Commissioner of Police banned all street processions by *Muktifauj*, the Indian name for the Salvation Army, and Tucker was in trouble before he had really begun.

A tent was erected, meetings held, and open-air processions continued despite police prohibitions. At first some of the Indians thought the Army was a circus. The police seized the flag and forbade the drum and trumpet to be used on the grounds that they would provoke fanatical opposition. When the Army of four, one of whom was the ubiquitous lassie officer with the tambourine, refused to obey, all were marched off to jail and later fined. *The Times* correspondent wired London: 'The attempt, however honest in intention, to proselytize the natives of India by clothing the solemn tenets of Christianity in an unseemly surrounding of vulgar buffoonery can but end in defeating its own object.'

He was wrong. The drum and other noises are every-day occurrences in Indian religious life. The Army gained firm hold, and religious freedom won a famous victory. What could stop people who even made the proceedings in the magistrate's court into favourable publicity? Captain Henry Bullard, Tucker's chief assistant, had a gift for copy-writing. With grand disregard of contempt proceedings, he announced in *The War Cry* that a forthcoming court hearing would be as follows:

LOOK OUT!

GRAND HALLELUJAH

Free and Easy

On Friday, 23rd Feb., 1883, at 11.30 a.m.

BY SPECIAL INVITATION

of the

COMMISSIONER OF POLICE

at the

GIRGAUM POLICE COURT.

Mr. Dosabhoy Framjee

WILL PRESIDE

Addresses will be given by
THE PUBLIC PROSECUTOR,
The Deputy Commissioner
Of Police
and Several other Police Officers
On the Work of The Salvation Army.

The Famous
BLOOD AND FIRE BANNER
will be presented to the Audience.

A Large Body of Police will be present
and will suppress with a Strong Hand any
ATTEMPT AT RIOT.

Everything will be done decently
and in Order.

Admission Free!   Come and See!

NO COLLECTION.

Despite the most unusual and generous concession in the last line, Major Tucker was sentenced to one month and served it, refusing to promise not to march or hold open-air meetings in return for a suspended sentence.

Prison was a blessing to him: he used the time to plan and pray. He came out to take up the fight where he had left off. Soon he had the Bombay authorities as tolerant towards the growing Salvation Army as were those of Allahabad, Delhi, Benares and Calcutta, although he did give a written promise not to march singing in strictly Mohammedan quarters, if the police so wished.

He found that when he and his people were 'European' in appearance and method, progress was slow; but if they were shod with sandals, or walked barefoot, and wore the saffron-coloured garb that denoted poverty in God's service—if they dispensed with chairs, tables, beds and other un-Indian luxuries and, most of all, if they begged like the local priests, their acceptance came more quickly. Indian names helped. An officer named Paynter became Jai Bhai—'Victory Brother'. Tucker became Fakir Singh, and soon everyone was being renamed.

Today, though proselytizing is forbidden in India and Pakistan, a large Salvationist force exists. Converts are won. People are free to join the Salvation Army if they wish, and thousands do. There are about 3,000 officers in India and Pakistan and tens of thousands of soldiers, with more in adjacent Burma and Ceylon.

There is no need of proselytizing. The 'Army with its sleeves rolled up', the Army on its knees, wins and keeps the people—the Army that teaches children to read, that cares for orphans, nurses the sick, buries the dead, whose doctors heal the lepers . . . these make the more eloquent appeals.

And in response to these sermons without words people surrender their hearts. There are about 5,000 centres of work, mostly in the villages, where the poorest people live. It was to these that gentleman Major Frederick St. George de Lautour Tucker made his way.

They found him sleeping under a tree and his bare, uncalloused feet were bleeding from his long walks along the dusty roads. 'This man is one of us,' they said, and so must any Salvationist be to this day who goes to India.

SOUTH AFRICA

When the *Warwick Castle* docked at Cape Town on Saturday, February 24th, 1883, a newspaper reporter demanded to see the 'invading host', for he had an earthy idea of statistics, making no allowance for the heavenly legions often counted in Salvation Army publicity.

He was received by Mrs. Major Simmonds, the young, newly-married wife of the officer-in-charge, and told that the whole invasion force consisted of herself, her husband—a most inconspicuous man—and a girl Lieutenant. It was nonetheless a formidable confrontation. The woman officer, as Captain Rose Clapham, had won a notable reputation in Britain by her management of mass meetings, unruly mobs and drunks. W. T. Stead reported in *The Northern Echo* that she 'turned Darlington upside down', winning some of the worst riff-raff to the Army, and making 'blackguards into converts'.

Something had gone wrong in London so that there was no money in the bank at Cape Town. They sold old copies of *The War Cry* to get money for food and lodging.

'We'll raise our Army here,' Mrs. Major Simmonds told the

reporter, and did just that—a less expensive method than that of the British Government when it had transported large numbers of troops there for the Zulu war shortly before.

In the first meeting in the drill hall, roughs turned out the gas, set fire to a bundle of copies of *The War Cry*. The meeting ended in disorder, yet one man remained behind to be converted. The next Sunday 112 people knelt at the penitent-form. As usual, some Salvationists were arrested and kept in jail all night, but this sort of persecution was not long continued in the Cape Area. At Simonstown a policeman who, while the worse for drink, had unjustly ill treated the Salvationists, was fined and dismissed from the force—justice indeed.

Mrs. Simmonds, who seems to have been the officer-in-charge —despite her husband—with two children, one a baby three weeks' old, sailed the five-day voyage to Durban to open a corps at Maritzburg. Forbidden to sing in the street, she led silent marches of protest. These were even more effective than the noisy ones.

At Port Elizabeth an officer had been locked up on a charge of 'shouting and screaming', on which count most Salvationists in the world could be imprisoned. Yet the work advanced. Fifteen sailors who knelt at the penitent-form at Simonstown later sailed for St. Helena where they held Salvation Army open-air meetings and conducted services in a room lent by a resident. The flag still flies over the Army's forces at St. Helena.

At Weltevreden Major Jim Orsborne, who had heard of Major Tucker's work in India, learned native African languages, walked barefoot, slept on the hut floors, ate African food and otherwise identified himself with the people he sought to save. As a result of this, Chief Ntshibonga became a Salvationist. The work spread . . .

In 1891 William Booth, in Africa, dispatched a party of five to conquer the Zulus whose King Cetewayo, in 1879, had defied the military might of Britain. The party was led by J. Allister Smith, a Scot later to become a Commissioner. The others were Isaac Marcus, who spoke Zulu fluently, could build a house and was otherwise a typical South African colonial strong man; Sovereign Bang, a Norwegian; Stephen Nikelo of the Fingo tribe, an interpreter; and Richard Joslin of Colchester, England.

They had twelve oxen to pull the trek cart, and about £50 in cash, some food, a tent, tools, and, of course, Bibles. All were men of prayer. They were also able to eat mealie pap, the porridge made from maize that is a test to the fortitude of the uninitiated. None drank anything stronger than tea.

Nine hours a day they journeyed, praying at three-hour intervals, and secretly often in between times. The long rests were necessary while the oxen grazed. When they came to the Umvoti River the tired oxen were quite unable to proceed so they knocked at the door of a native who owned cattle. When the door opened they saw framed on the wall the words from the Bible: 'When thou passest through the waters I will be with thee . . . the rivers shall not overflow thee.' This was encouraging and with the loan of ten fresh beasts they passed safely across and presently came to the great Tegula River.

'There, at last, is Zululand,' said Marcus. Companies of Zulus greeted them. These had been told: 'Salvation teachers are coming to teach you to love God and learn the way to Heaven.' Before their war the Zulus had a heaven of their own: blood and spears, strong physique, graceful women, good food and many cattle which were used as barter, dowries and status symbols. They conquered 300 tribes, exterminating about 70. As they attacked the British squares at Ulandi they chanted:

> *Amazulu! Amazulu!*
> *Who is as great as we are?*
> *White men, yellow men, black men tremble*
> *When they hear us! When they see us!*
> *So! So! Gleam ye spearheads!*
> *When we shout the eagle trembles*
> *When we chant the rain clouds lower;*
> *When we charge, whole nations perish,*
> *So! So! Gleam ye spearheads!*

But it was the Zulu nation that perished, their blood-tipped spears no match for Maxim guns.

Crocodiles abounded in the Amatikulu River, and the black mamba, the puff adder and other snakes in the veld. Malaria was rampant. The first meeting for the Zulus was in the height of the rainy season. Few appeared and everyone was drenched and depressed. But the next Sunday there were many Zulus in the congregation—far more women than men because of the decimation of war. All over fourteen years had reeds through a hole in the lobes of their ears. The reeds were full of snuff which the Zulus passed to each other during the meeting.

The singing was not good, to put it mildly. There seemed to be as many different tunes, all at the same time, as there were singers, and all extremely loud. At first the Zulus were taken aback by the content of the preaching. Allister Smith spoke of God as being 'a Loving Father'. The Zulus knew differently. Had they not suffered the vengeance of an angry unpropitiated God? Had not their witch doctors described him so, and rivers of blood slaked his thirst?

Two converts were won in that meeting, and many later. Some were men who had to leave for the gold-fields 'to get money for the tax man'. When they came back a year later, it was with eight other converts won while they were all working in the mines at Johannesburg. Many Zulus became Salvation Army soldiers and local officers, and gave life-long proof of understanding of the gospel the missionaries brought. Today there are two divisions of Army operations in what was Zulu-land. The work includes farm-training at Salvation Army settlements. Some Zulus have become officers.

RHODESIA

From South Africa, on Rhodes' imperial route, the Salvation Army moved north to Fort Salisbury with one trek-cart pulled by eighteen oxen. In charge of five men officers were a Salvation Army major and his wife. After a six months' journey they reached Fort Salisbury, 1,000 miles away, on November 18th, 1891. Rhodes, and Jameson the Administrator, were there to greet them. Rebellion, fever, and marauding lions played havoc with time-tables and health.

Matabele raids often made the Salvationists take refuge in Fort Salisbury. While Captain Edward Cass was helping to convoy women to safety he was killed by the Mashonas. Cass Avenue, in Salisbury, is named in his honour, but the thousands of African Salvationists, the missionary officers from many lands, the schools, hospitals, with men's and women's social centres, are greater memorials to pioneer devotion.

THE CONGO

Openings in Nigeria, what is now Ghana, Portugese East Africa, Kenya, Uganda and Tanganyika, with other areas of 'the dark Continent' followed. One of the most striking series of advances took place in the Congo. In 1934 Henri and Paula Becquet, Belgian officers, 'opened fire' in Léopoldville—they had a flag, a violin, a great faith and hardly anything else. The war began when Henri Becquet borrowed an old chair and Paula stood on it in the market place to sing:

> '*I have a message,*
> *A message from Jesus.*'

The march away from that first open-air service in the capital, which has since staged some of the largest Salvation Army processions in the world, consisted of Henri, playing the violin, and Paula carrying the flag as she went. Seven hundred Congolese followed them into an old fish store used as a citadel. Twenty Congolese knelt at the penitent-form in that first meeting.

The Becquets felt awed, smothered by the immensity of their task. Up river for 1,000 miles to Stanleyville was their parish, with countless square miles of jungle and bush at either side—14,000,000 souls in all. 'But God has led us here and God will guide us,' said Paula, whose eyes were blind to difficulties.

From the first, there was no problem about gaining an audience. Blackboards, with chalked verses from the Bible to sing; guitar, concertina, harmonium and violin music attracted huge crowds even at six o'clock in the morning. In the rush to get in, doors were sometimes knocked off their hinges. Within a year the Belgian couple could speak Lingala and were beginning education work. Reinforcements were sent from Europe. The salvation war leaped across the river into French Equatorial Africa.

There are now two vast areas of Salvation Army work, each side of the Congo, with one Headquarters in Léopoldville, and the other at Brazzaville. About 300 officers and 750 centres operate in them. Most of these are corps, evangelistic centres in city and bush. There are about seventy-five schools in the Congo; one in Léopoldville, built in 1963 with the help of the Congolese Government and UNESCO, provides secondary education to university entrance level. Another, provided by Sweden, is one of the all too few secondary schools for girls only. Over 200 teachers have been trained at the Army's Kasangulu college. At present about 16,000 young Congolese are in Salvation Army schools.

Obviously, the Army could not do this great work without revealing its evangelistic aims. From the first, the Becquets taught 'under the flag'. There has been no pretence otherwise ever since. Youths and some girls who take a commercial course, for example (typewriters supplied by the Salvation Army New York Headquarters), are also 'infected' with Christianity. Some become Salvationists, and when they marry send their children to the Army. Many join 'The Association of ex-Students of Salvation Army Schools'. Tens of thousands of Congolese regard themselves as Salvationists although they are not on the soldiers' roll. Men in Government offices and business life state proudly that they were 'educated Salvation Army'.

It has been found well-nigh impossible to learn your letters at the Salvation Army without also acquiring something of a reputation for hard work and trustworthiness. Of course some of the students become 'out-and-out' Salvationists, wearing uniform and becoming officers or local officers.

Only lack of money and men prevents medical work from being extended. There are dispensaries staffed by European nurses, but some patients have to walk up to twelve miles.

The present Army leader of the work in the Congo believes that 'given peace and time and the necessary technical assistance, the Congo will become a prosperous country'.

He points out that the Congo has vast quantities of minerals that man needs: copper, tin, iron, coal, gold, diamonds, radium . . . Cotton, rubber, tea, cocoa, coffee, quinine, and palm-oil are produced. He also agrees with other Congolese missionaries, Catholic and Protestant, that early successes with conversions were so rapid that necessary consolidation suffered. There were so many conversions that there was too little time to teach and train converts in the basic truths and behaviour that should follow conversion. He is careful to add that in this the Congolese are no different from any other man and woman to whom Christianity comes as an alien faith.

When the Becquets mentioned 'eternal life' some of their hearers thought this meant that conversion would prevent them from dying. Even their witch-doctors could not guarantee they would live for a thousand years, so the idea appealed very much. Salvation Army converts from Léopoldville went home to their bush villages which had been zoned into 'spheres of influence' by the various denominations. With characteristic irrepressible Salvationist zeal they preached and held meetings. This, naturally, gave rise to indignant protests about bad faith from the missionary groups whose area was being poached. In a few instances Congolese Salvationists were sent to prison and Army halls were burned down by the police.

Things are different now. Hardly a month goes by without the present leader being asked—as Becquet was—to open new centres of work. Most of these he must refuse for lack of funds and officers. Extensions are made regularly but at a pace that allows for careful supervision within his sadly meagre means.

Meanwhile, the Army's place in the Congo astonishes United Nations observers and others who remark, 'I had no idea the Salvation Army did this kind of work . . .'

A strength of Salvation Army missionary endeavour is seen in the international composition of its officer personnel. Whatever country might be in or out of favour at any particular time, Salvationists invariably avoid official or public displeasure because they are not involved in political or other idealogical tensions. At Léopoldville are officers from Belgium, France, Italy, Switzerland, Sweden, the Netherlands and the United Kingdom: their soul-saving mission transcends the turmoil of the Congo.

GERMANY

Although the opening in Germany was not missionary in the conventional sense, it proved to have its hazards when a start was made in 1886. Numerous German newspapers were hostile, and mobs broke up meetings while the police looked on passively. One indignant German advertised:

To avoid any possibility of mistake I declare that the souls saved by The Salvation Army are not to be found in my family and among my relatives, but that under the firm of Gottlieb Angerbauer, shoemaker, they may be found and known.

Jacob Angerbauer,
Gross Assbach, Feb., 15th, 1889.

Soon there were converts, even 'martyrs'. The German building the first hall because no one would rent or sell suitable buildings, fell to his death from the roof. Commissioner George Scott Railton from London was expelled from the country. All in all, *Die Heilsarmee* had a slow start. Yet growth was sure. Jakob Junker, a Rhineland industrialist, was so impressed by what he read in *Der Kriegsruf, The War Cry* of Germany, that he became an officer, giving not only his money but himself to God's service in the Salvation Army. Many other Germans followed as the work spread throughout the land. They exist today, not only in West Germany, where a large-scale evangelical and social work is carried on, but also, silent and patient, in the Eastern Zone, where public Salvation Army operations have been closed down by the Government.

THE WEST INDIES

Very often the missionary image is one of colour, so that the West Indies, 'attacked' on December 15th, 1887, conforms to that type. The pioneer officer there started on the wrong foot by writing in a magazine published by the Salvation Army in London that there was—'. . . a marvellous lack of love among the majority of the black people we have met.' He went on to state that they did not care for their children, that they had no conscience, that modesty and shame were in short supply, that the blackest of lies could be told without a blush and that seventy-five per cent of the children were illegitimate. He said that rum was 'liquid damnation'—a statement a Salvationist might make to this day—and asserted that tobacco was an evil too, for it grew wild and 1,000 cigars could be bought for fifteen shillings.

If the officer thought that the Jamaican 'heathens' would stand for this, he had a rude awakening. A local editor brought the article to everyone's notice, and the fat was in the fire. West Indians could bleed, just as Shylock could. Incensed mobs broke all the windows of the citadel, besieging the forthright writer and his family, who were kept captive inside for three days. Later, a family violin had to be sold to get money for food, for the criticized West Indians closed their hearts and their purses towards the Army—for the time being. The tactless officer was recalled to London.

But something remained: if tactlessness or other error could destroy Christianity it would have sunk into oblivion long ago. One of the West Indian comrades, Brother Raglan Phillips, seeing his too-outspoken leader depart said, 'I will be the Army.' He soon had many converts and numerous officers. The colour, gusto and joy of Salvationism suited the islanders very much, especially when it was their own.

Having no favourable response to requests for aid from London, Phillips donned a long ministerial coat, a hat with the words 'Salvation Army' printed upon it, and set sail to demand it. He caused something of a stir at I.H.Q. in Queen Victoria Street. Some of the staff thought the man to be a hopeless oddity. One called him a 'freak'.

But William Booth decided otherwise. After several long interviews he became convinced of Phillips' sincerity, made him an Adjutant and sent him back with reinforcements to extend the West Indian operations.

Today the Army is spread far over what it terms the Central America and West Indies Territory, operating in British Guiana, Barbados, Trinidad, Panama, British Honduras, Cuba, Surinam, Curaçao, the Bahamas and Haiti. Social work among the young, and especially the friendless and homeless, is a major feature.

SOUTH AMERICA

Argentina was the first objective of Salvationism on the South American mainland, 1889, and one of the familiar revolutions gave the pioneers a chance to show the cautious people how helpful *Ejèrcito de Salvación* could be. With people dying in the streets of Buenos Aires, Salvationists went to the rescue although they had frequent and narrow escapes from death. The officers were so poor that they had sometimes to live on after-dinner leavings sent to them from one of the good hotels. But since those days the work has spread to six other American republics among which Paraguay alone is 'missionary' in the familiar meaning of the word.

RUSSIA—CHINA

Though the Army is now in seventy-one countries, and uses 147 languages, it has had its failures, or perhaps it would be fairer to describe them as reverses. But it still sings 'The World for God!' and believes what it sings. It had to withdraw from Russia shortly after the Revolution, and its links with China, where it 'opened fire' in 1916, were broken in 1951. But prayer remains a bond and Salvationists in many lands are one with their far-off comrades when they sing:

> *The sun that bids us rest is waking*
> *Our brethren 'neath the western sky,*
> *And hour by hour fresh lips are making*
> *Thy wondrous doings heard on high.*

All over the world, as this book offers evidence, the grand imperial vision of William Booth to win the world for God is still the Salvationist objective.

6. 'A LITTLE NOVELTY'

You must stir it and stump it,
And blow your own trumpet,
Or trust me, you haven't a chance.
W. S. GILBERT

One way to disarm the Salvation Army would be to take away its music. By far the largest group of men and women in its ranks are the musicians, about 200,000 of them. Without its songs, brass bands, guitars, timbrels, concertinas and drums, the Army would be paralyzed.

Yet anyone knowing William Booth could hardly have foreseen the musical emphasis that developed in his Army. For him a service was an occasion for a sermon, in which he was lengthy, passionate and highly effective. The prayer meeting which followed was the climax in which 'souls were saved', when men and women knelt at the bench out front, the penitent-form.

There is little evidence that William Booth was fond of music: the musical incidentals forced upon him he regarded as diversions. Some of his supporters suggested that they were irreverent and superfluous.

But that was nothing to the shocked distaste with which Victorian clergymen, press and local councils regarded the Sunday morning disturbances caused by the Army's bands and hand-clapping singers.

Up at Bradford, where the officer-in-charge had been 'Fiddler Dowdle', a holy man but not a skilled violinist, the city fathers breathed a sigh of relief when Booth sent him elsewhere, and one Captain William Pearson succeeded him. They had the worst of the exchange. Pearson was the first of a galaxy of writers; he wrote the first notable Salvation Army song at Bradford. It went at once to the top of the Victorian 'hit parade'.

Charles Dickens had found that the absence of copyright agreement between the United States and Great Britain was distressing: Captain Pearson, of the newly-formed Salvation Army, found the absence convenient. He simply took an American ballad tune, 'Ring the bell, Watchman', and made it into the 'Song of The Salvation Army'. One verse went as follows:

> *Come, join our Army, the foe must be driven;*
> *To Jesus, our Captain, the world shall be given;*
> *Foes may surround us, we'll press through the throng;*
>   *The Salvation Army is marching along.*

As his noisy band sang this up and down the streets of Bradford it was all the more hard to take because Pearson learned his tune from the Town Hall clock which pealed it out at regular intervals. Soon it was being sung in the streets, the mills, and in the crowded Pullen Theatre used as barracks by the Army.

Pearson was called to appear before the magistrates and ordered to cease holding such meetings in the streets. But, like Peter in Jerusalem, Pearson in Bradford felt that he had to do what he did. He said, 'I went out that same night, and every night. The summons did not come, and the work rolled on gloriously.'

Though Church of England clergymen and others have in times past shown their displeasure at the stunts of Salvationists, and their raucous Sabbath morning brass band music, the ironic truth is that the Anglican church probably contributed to this development of 'corybantic Christianity' as Army-baiting Professor Thomas Huxley termed it.

After the Puritans had banished church organs and music as being 'worldly baubles', unfit for the house of God, the restoration of less bleak conditions was spread over a considerable time and took varied forms. Sometimes, where funds for a new organ were lacking, the method favoured was a small group of musicians, who at other times played at the village inn, or on the green, for the May Day festivals.

A Thomas Hardy hero, Gabriel Oak, the farmer, always carried a flute in his smock, 'on which he could pipe with Arcadian sweetness'. On the evening of the day he married Bathsheba the village band provided 'a hideous clang of music' on drum, tambourine, clarionet, double bass and other 'venerable worm-eaten instruments, which had celebrated the victories of Marlborough under the fingers of the forefathers of the men who played them now'.

William Booth, as a small boy, almost certainly heard his first religious 'band' in Bleaseby parish church, near Nottingham, where on week-days the parson taught him his letters, and where, on Sundays, he and his mother and sisters worshipped as Anglicans. Behind them, high in the gallery as they sang, was a musical group that led the hymn-singing: a flute, cello, fiddle . . .

So the idea of bands in places of worship was familiar to him when at Salisbury the Fry family, father and three sons, all of whom played brass band instruments, joined his Army and later accompanied him on his evangelistic campaigns. Earlier, up at Stockton-on-Tees, he had allowed a cornetist to lead the street procession, noting: 'Last Sunday we had a little novelty which, apparently, worked well. Among the converts are two members of a brass band. One played the cornet . . . He certainly improved the singing, and brought crowds all along the line of march, wondering curiously what we should do next.'

When Booth left Methodism, to become a free-lance evangelist, many of that denomination's churches were closed against him, just as Anglican churches had been closed to Church-of-England clergyman, John Wesley. Wesley had used the cemeteries; Booth hired tents and theatres, any old building procurable, provided the rent was not too high.

For this kind of venue, and with the unchurched semi-literate audiences who flocked to hear him, music was a problem. If it were not lively, the congregation would sit dumb, or, when they caught on, would run ahead or lag behind—uncontrollable.

The Fry family, the Stockton cornetist, the first Salvation Army band proper, at Consett in Durham, with the musical legions which followed all over the world, solved the problem. The drum would give a strong beat, and the blare of brass would lend heart to the musically inept and faint-hearted. Indeed, as Professor Inglis has recently written. 'Like a heavenly anthem, a Salvation Army band drowned all music but its own.' But the bands attracted men to Booth's meetings.

Often they came out of curiosity. but the visit led to their

conversion—that, to Booth, was the crucial factor. The secular
brass band movement was by this time firmly entrenched among
industrial communities, especially in the North of England.
Besses o' th' Barn and other famous combinations had been
formed by colliery and factory managements, and some by the
workers alone.

A marked degree of alienation had been taking place between
working men and the church. In part this was due to the
depressed, inert condition of religion in England.

Jane Austen's huntin', shootin', fishin' parson was not merely
fiction, and such men knew little of the proletariat. Booth knew
a great deal. In Westminster the apathy towards reform by some
churchmen, Members of Parliament and bishops had widened
the gulf. Booth was one of those eminent Victorians who bridged
it.

Many men who had drifted away to mechanics' halls, working men's clubs and institutes, became keen brass band fans.
From them Booth recruited numerous band trainers and players.
Of course, all had to be converted first—any Salvationist musician must sign on the dotted line a 'contract' of spiritual
profession and Army service that would give a prelate cause to
search his heart.

Booth laid down strict rules, accepted with that same Victorian ardour which sent men of the time to the Sudan, the
Afghan Frontier and the Zulu wars to die for empire. Today
the *Orders and Regulations* for Salvation Army musicians totals
sixty-one pages of closely-written type.

Army musicians may not drink or smoke, on pain of suspen-
sion. Jewellery is frowned on. The sisters should not dress in
'flashy', worldly manner. In uniform, at least, they should be
sparing with cosmetics. The men may not belong to other bands
or orchestras (except as professional musicians), and must not
contract debts. All must buy their own uniforms, and pay
regular sums into Army funds.

Bandsmen or singers get no fees or honorariums. If the parks'
committee, entertainments' officer, NBC or BBC, or whoever, pay
a fee for a band's services—of course, they often do—then that
fee is handed over to local Army funds.

Besides which, the bandsman must be the perfect husband:

the singing sister the good wife. They should know their Bible from cover to cover, and heed it too. Most train themselves, or are trained, as public-speaking evangelists. If either were divorced or separated, the Army would, under its orders, be forced to take serious action. In fact such lapses are extremely rare.

Among the neighbours, at work, and in his leisure pursuits, the Army musician is thought to be a paragon. His Christian light must always shine, not least because his Army brand of extrovert, rather ostentatious religion focuses attention upon him—even the irreligious are watchful of another man's religion. The Salvation Army bandsman is looked upon as a common-sense sort of holy Joe. Most pass the test.

If any man can have too much of a good thing, he might be that man. On his day of rest, Sunday, he may not lie a-bed because the band will be marching early, playing for outdoor and indoor services. In the main, because of the way they lend themselves to good open-air meetings, it will be down a long, closely-built working class street, where hundreds of thousands of householders have become accustomed to the Army band's hymn tune with the morning tea and *The News of the World*—strange mixture indeed.

The Salvationist's musical chores will go on until late on Sunday evening—nine o'clock or after is not unusual. Many bandsmen find the Sabbath to be their hardest working day— but a very, very happy one withal. The band will play in the streets for the children, for the passers-by, for those who gather regularly on Sunday night at the market square or town hall, and who declare: 'This is my church. I do not attend any other religious service.'

Very often the band will visit hospitals, old people's homes, and play on the promenade during the season, by request of the entertainments committee. It is often pressed into service by the Mayor, the Free Church Council, and may sometimes play at the Cathedral, by invitation of the Dean. A far, far cry from Victorian times.

Socially, of course, today's bandsman is in a different state from his Victorian ancestor. Musically he is much more sophisticated, being aware not only of George Frederick Handel, some of whose music is very brassy, straightforward and 'Salvation

Army', not only of the 'Father of Salvation Army Music',
Richard Slater, but also of modern trends in music—the 12-
note scale, Bela Bartok, and the flood that followed after. Salvation Army bands are presented on television and radio
programmes the world over. Vaughan Williams wrote music for
the International Staff Band of the Army in London; Sousa for
Army bands in the United States. Today bands in those countries
and in New Zealand, Australia, Sweden and elsewhere are near
the top of the brass band firmament, bar none, 'sacred or
profane'.

Religion tends to agree with business, which fact Booth, Wesley, and perhaps Professor Tawney have seen as a devilish trap.
Salvation Army bandsmen, non-smokers, non-drinkers, non-
gamblers without the option, and thrifty, steady spenders by
choice, are inclined to prosper. Some of them drive to the cita-
dels in Jaguars, Thunderbirds or, at least, the newest Volks-
wagen. Some own substantial businesses, are well advanced in
the Civil Service, are insurance tycoons or in one of the professions. One, at least, is a don at Cambridge; another is influential
on the National Executive of the TUC. Some become rich. There
is, of course, spiritual peril in all this, but peril the Salvationist
is expected to overcome. Many do.

Apart from the aforesaid sixty-one-page book of rules, which
applies to all without regard to social status or affluence, the
bandsmen will be regularly admonished as to their spiritual
state from the platform by the Corps Officer. The Band-Sergeant
—a sort of chaplain—will carefully watch and counsel on morale
and religious condition. The Bandmaster will also maintain
discipline, sometimes severely, if needed. Men have been sent
home for appearing on duty without a uniform cap, suspended
for one month or longer, for disobedience, insolence, or cigarette
smoking. Such infractions are the exception.

The musicians of the Army are more than a pool of music,
they are a wonderful reservoir of spiritual power. Thousands of
Army men have put down their trumpets, given up home, job
and kin to enter one of the Army's colleges for training as
officers; some, while young, have died on some 'corner of a
foreign field', sanctified by their sacrifice and made 'a richer
dust', as Rupert Brooke put it. But they made their sacrifice for

the Kingdom of God. 'Every land is my fatherland,' they say with General Bramwell Booth, 'because every land is my Father's land.'

Salvationism does not go to the head in the same way as another sort of religious pursuit might: it is a warm, emotional faith. Though a growing number of Salvationists are reasonably well educated, the heart rather than the mind is the focal point of activity. As yet, the Army has not produced a scholar of national renown in theology, for example, although it places great emphasis on the Bible. There are a few eggheads. Tradition may be responsible for this.

Salvationism is 'vulgar' in the old, literal sense of that word — 'of the common people'. It does not foster culture, and its scholars sometimes find the romantic fervour of the aggressive, ever-campaigning Army hard to take. However, this situation is being modified in the Army's favour by recent developments in popular education.

Though William Booth preferred good old Methodist tunes, with occasional Anglican ones, he found that many of his un-churched audiences could not sing them, either because they did not know the tunes or because they could not read. So Pearson's 'Come, join our Army', as already mentioned, with 'Amen for the Flag' to the 'Union Jack of old England' quickly caught on, with many other 'catchy' tunes from the music-halls. Farrar said, 'These people will sing their way round the world.'

The poor, weary after long days in mill, mine and kitchen, sang 'Champagne Charlie' with tonic effect. Though not the words, of course.

A host of amateur versifiers met that need. To this day 'Champagne Charlie' is sung as 'Bless His Name He sets me free'. 'Pretty Louise' became 'Living beneath the Shade of the Cross'; 'I traced her little footsteps in the snow' became 'O the blood of Jesus cleanses white as snow'.

This policy produced results. There were no ritualistic traditions to flout, no liturgy to destroy. There were some difficulties. In New York a Salvation Army bandsman walked down Times Square whistling blithely. Next day a newspaper columnist with an inch to spare reported: 'These Salvationists get around and sound quite chirpy. Today I heard one of them whistling better than moma's canary. The tune was "The Pink Lady Waltz".'

Rather hurt at this inference of worldliness, the bandsman wrote in to correct the journalist: 'You are mistaken. Though I was whistling the tune you mention, the words are our own, written by our General Albert Orsborn, and known all over the world as "Let the Beauty of Jesus be seen in me".'

Next day the writer referred to the matter again briefly: 'I have heard from the Salvation Army canary. He admits that he was whistling "The Pink Lady Waltz".' Fair enough, even though a little hard on the bandsman.

All this music-making is big business, though woe betide that Salvationist who forgets that it is sanctified business. The words and spirit of William Booth haunt the Army's International Music Editorial Department in London. The words, like Calais on Queen Mary's heart, are written on every Salvationist musician's purposes: they are:

> *Soul-saving music is the music for me.*

About sixty new band pieces are published annually in the United Kingdom, and about one hundred new songs. Others are published in the United States, Scandinavia, Canada and elsewhere. Many of the items are broadcast; some are recorded by commercial record companies.

The standard of composition and performance has improved greatly, and has been favourably commented on by George Bernard Shaw in his brief term as music critic, by Elgar and many others in recent times: Sir Arthur Bliss, present Master of the Queen's Music, Sir Adrian Boult and Ralph Vaughan Williams are among them. The Army now has its crop of musically qualified men, Doctors of Music, Mus. Bac., ARCO, ARCM, FTCL. The leading trumpeter of the BBC Symphony Orchestra is a Salvation Army Bandmaster, while the leading trombonist of the Hallé Orchestra, for many years, was a Salvationist bandswoman. These are exceptional, but the general standard is surprisingly good.

Though the Army's musical idiom changes with geographical location and the passing of time, the soul-wooing strategy must not. All Army music is written or arranged by Salvationists, who do it as part of their religious faith. They do not get paid for it. Like the Army banker, journalist, doctor, Commanding Officer of a large corps—it is all part of a vocation: money is beneath consideration.

When the Music Board in London, a select group of officers and laymen, meets regularly to consider new music, the criterion of choice is mainly soul-saving potential. A smaller number of other types of pieces are allowed for domestic use—the war song, the jubilant strains of fighting soldiers seeking to win the world for God. But heard above all must be the note that calls the penitent to prayer.

Literally thousands of true accounts have been recorded of men and women, and young people, who have been converted and have become Salvationists because they 'listened to the band'. Even in the modern evangelistic hard times of the mid-twentieth century converts are still being won all over the world through the Army's ministry of music.

The faith of the Salvationist is audacious; some would call it ludicrous, or even blasphemous. In its quest to win converts, especially among the young, the Army is now producing the beat music of the pop fans—as ever to the dismay of the reactionaries.

Scandinavian Salvationists have over a long period used the guitar for their women's bands. In India the one-hand harmonium, the little drums, the one-string fiddle and the flute are used by Salvationists. In Africa Salvationists beat tom-toms and make their timbrels out of coca-cola bottle tops and animal skins. They also have British-style brass bands. All over the world indigenous music is used for that same great purpose of saving souls.

If a Mersey-sound, or any other sound, will make the young stop and listen, so that the Salvationist can speak a word in season, then that is the way the Army fights its battle for the souls of men. Booth would not have regarded the Beatles as damned, or their music as worthy only of the papal index. 'Take it, consecrate it and use it for God,' he would say.

Our bands are to work for the salvation of souls and for

nothing else. We are not going to stick them up on the platform or march them through the streets for them to perform and be admired.

They are to go there and blow what they are told, what the Commanding Officer thinks will be best for the good of the Army and the salvation of souls. If they don't play for that object then let them stop playing.

The man must shut his eyes and blow his cornet, and believe while he plays that he is blowing salvation into somebody: all his beating of the drum and blowing of the cornet is to get the people first into the barracks and then to the penitent-form.

So there! It is the grand old man speaking. And let no Salvationist forget it.

7. THE SINEWS OF WAR

Up and down the City Road,
In and out the Eagle,
That's the way the money goes . . .

The public image of the Salvation Army is sometimes that of a lassie with a collecting box. If begging for the needy is a crime the Army pleads guilty. Emmott Robinson, the great Yorkshire cricketer, during a 'War of the Roses' match, turned on wicket-keeper George Duckworth and exclaimed, 'George tha'rt t' best appealer I've iver 'erd since t' days o' General Booth.'

One hundred years ago, as his Army was being born, William Booth was be-devilled by money troubles. Those of his bankrupt father caused him to be taken from school to work in a pawnshop. Later, the poverty of his widowed mother, who kept a poor little shop, made his own miserable pittance as an apprentice help to keep the family from actual want. When, in 1849, at the age of twenty, Booth left Nottingham for London, it was not with any high sense of mission. He was out of work and could only find a job back in pawnbroking, in a shop near the Elephant and Castle. There he learned more about the poor, and there he personally suffered hunger and loneliness.

When he became 'rich' it was with other people's money. He raised millions for the homeless, the betrayed, the underprivileged. He bought tents and pubs to convert to tabernacles, old warehouses to make into hostels for the down-and-outs. He wrote books that were best sellers—social documents that helped to stir the conscience of a nation. *In Darkest England and the Way Out* was a blueprint for much of what is now Britain's Welfare State. He launched two weekly newspapers that sold half a million copies a week, and still do. He acquired The Salvation Army Assurance Society, founded the Reliance

Bank, the Fire Insurance Corporation, the Salvationist Publishing and Supplies, Ltd., and his own printing works, The Campfield Press, St. Albans, and the musical instruments factory.

There was money in all this, but none for him. He was normally in debt, inhibited from doing much that urgently needed to be done, because of lack of funds. He equipped hospitals, orphanages, sent missionaries to Africa, India. Converts were made who became his children—hungry, needy children. When he made a highly successful land investment at Hadleigh, in Essex, that was merely incidental—the purpose was the establishment of a land colony where misfit men could be trained for work on the land, helped morally and spiritually meanwhile.

Empire-builder Cecil Rhodes went down to see this place. He admired Booth, and Booth returned the compliment. The men had much in common. But when Rhodes bought land on the Rand, he made millions from it: the highly valuable development potential at Hadleigh has never been fully realized because, of course, there is no money in helping the poor. The Hadleigh Colony for the rehabilitation of needy men is still being subsidized from Salvation Army funds.

Booth died a poor man having lived on the interest on £5,000 which had to be divided among a numerous progeny. Royalties on *Darkest England* amounted to more than that, but the Founder reckoned all such money to be Salvation Army money. It was not for him. Rich Rhodes envied him: 'I would give all I have,' he said, 'to be able to believe what that old man believes . . .' Christian charity consumed the Army's funds more quickly than replenishment could be found but, of course, there were insinuations that William Booth was feathering his own nest.

Normally irascible, a chronic dyspeptic, he kept remarkably philosophic about it all. Only those who could comprehend 'a burning love for souls'. one of his favoured phrases, could believe in his indifference to personal gain. Yet, as the General, he often had to cease from his redemptive labours to answer such charges. The great Professor Thomas Huxley, when not harassing the anti-Darwinian evolutionists, was often sniping at the Salvation Army, which he disliked, and William Booth in particular.

After an attack in the columns of *The Times*, a Parliamentary Committee was set up to enquire into Army finances. The verdict was unanimous: though money had flowed into the coffers of the Salvation Army, it was properly spent: none of it had adhered to the fingers of the grand old man who was its benevolent autocrat and none had been diverted to causes other than those for which it had been given.

In 1865 the movement that was to become the Salvation Army was still only an East London Mission. Its running expenses for the year were under £100. William Booth's small stipend was not included, though numerous gifts to the poor were. (To this day the General is modestly supported, independently of Salvation Army funds, with £1,000 a year from a trust established many years ago by a number of wealthy friends of the Salvation Army and now controlled by the Charity Commissioners.)

Today, though the hundred has become millions, the Army is still short of money. Domestic income, in about eighty countries, is nationally controlled and varies from the richest of all, the United States, to the very poor, newly-independent African republics. These latter are supported from the Army's international Self-Denial Fund and other gifts from the richer territories.

Main item in the international income is the Self-Denial Fund. This appeal, held on a world-wide basis, yields more than £1,000,000 each year. Much of it is used for missionary work. In late years the Army's overseas work has been aided with great enlightenment and generosity by OXFAM.

'Company profits' are those of the Salvation Army Assurance Society, Ltd., the Fire Insurance Corporation, Ltd., the Salvationist Publishing and Supplies, Ltd., in which are included the Campfield Press, and the Reliance Bank, Ltd. William Booth's idea for the Assurance Society was not only that it might give him money to 'carry on the war', as he put it, but that hundreds of Salvation Army agents would be house-to-house agents for God, as well as salesmen of policies for the Salvation Army. So it has proved. Men who have made a modest living in agents' commissions have made far greater impact as Christian counsellors in countless homes where the visit of 'the insurance man' in his Salvation Army uniform, is the visit of a friend, a pastor, a man to advise on the children and a hundred-and-one social, domestic and religious problems.

The annual income of the Society in recent years has been in the £4,000,000 region. Apart from the necessary professional assistance: actuarial, legal, medical and audit, the business is run by Salvation Army officers; almost all its staff are Salvationists. They believe that business can be holy—even insurance business. This might raise eyebrows in the City, but evidence is overwhelming that the synthesis of hard-headed business with warm-hearted religion is achieved. There need be no affront to tender consciences.

The net profit is paid by the Society into Salvation Army funds, together with the sum recovered from the Tax Commissioners. There are no directors' fees. A Salvation Army officer who works for the Society will be appointed to it in the line of duty. Whether he be Managing Director on the Board in London, or a district superintendent up in Glasgow, he will not be paid other than as a Salvation Army officer.

Perhaps because William Booth bought it from the Methodists, the Salvation Army Assurance Society has not been the same cause of anxious doubt by religious purists in the Army as has Salvationist Publishing and Supplies, Ltd., which is a London department store in Judd Street, W.C.1. It exists, with a number of branches in the provinces, for the sale of bonnets, brass instruments, flags, timbrels, guitars, uniforms, books and other of the paraphernalia of Salvationism. This is mere trade, and there have been those who have seen it as the realm of mammon into which the Army should not venture.

But Booth always believed that the bad can be sanctified, the secular made sacred—the devil's tunes, the brewers' money, the trade in the market-place. With the subsidiary printing works at St. Albans, the Salvationist Publishing and Supplies Ltd. pays an agreed sum from its profits into Army funds.

There are prayer meetings at Judd Street, and at all the Army's 'Company' buildings, not only for employees, but for executives, most of whom are Salvation Army officers. Even in the best of years the officer directors, secretary, departmental managers, get no cut of the dividends, no bonus on profit—nothing but the meagre Salvation Army officer's allowance.

Probably the most dangerous commercial venture taken by William Booth, a Methodist preacher by inclination and training, was into the quicksands of newspaper production. There were many forecasts of doom when he established his *War Cry* in 1879, and the beginnings were ludicrously primitive.

Yet he made it a marked success, both for his purpose of making the newspaper into a medium for his evangelistic propaganda, and also, incidentally, for making profits to be used for his Salvation Army work. Reginald Pound and Geoffrey Harmsworth in their life of Northcliffe state that the great man was influenced in founding the *Daily Mail* by the layout and contents of Booth's *War Cry*.

Also successful is *The Young Soldier*, the children's weekly which has the largest circulation of any Salvation Army paper in the world. It has claimed to be the biggest children's paper published by any Christian movement and, at 260,000 weekly, this is probably correct. The two papers sell above 500,000 weekly in the United Kingdom.

These are the London editions. There are four editions of the *War Cry* published weekly in the United States—New York, Atlanta, Chicago and San Francisco. There is one in Canada, Australia, New Zealand, Sweden, Norway, Germany, France, and others in almost every country where the Army is at work.

Though none of these papers accept advertisements, they keep their heads well above water financially—something Fleet Street deems to be impossible. William Booth took a poor view of the advertising ethics of his day. That same Salvation Army which some people assert is 'always cadging', turns down thousands of pounds of advertising revenue every year because of Booth's scruples; a fact which makes most Salvationists feel proud, though probably, in these days, ample advertising exists of a kind that can be accepted by Christian movements.

There is also a literary department. This publishes Sunday School lessons, *The Company Orders*, 25,000 copies yearly; a manual of devotion titled *The Soldier's Armoury*, also 25,000; a *Year Book*, 10,000. All of these, and numerous other manuals and educational and theological textbooks, show modest profit.

D

About twenty book titles are also published yearly by the Salvationist Publishing and Supplies Ltd. As a rule, sales are not large; 3,000 would be about average.

It is all small stuff by ordinary publishing standards, for normally religion is not a popular commodity to market, and the Army lacks know-how in this highly competitive publishing field. Yet the number of books sold totals millions, and William Booth is doubtless content. His people, not markedly literate or book-loving in his day, have learned their ABC and are reading books written, printed and published by the Army. Some even read other more learned and more expensive books and their bookish tendencies grow.

The Army also publishes books abroad in many languages, and from London recently produced the first titles in a series planned for African and Indian readers. These publications are sold at half the cost of production, so that the subsidy called for is considerable.

The Army's bank began without capital. Many early deposits were in the form of saving stamps sold by Salvationist agents all over the country—they were in varied colours, blue being for one penny, and mauve for ten pounds. The only security was Booth's good name. This seemed impertinent, but it was enough. The title, Salvation Army Bank, was registered in 1891, but later changed to Reliance Bank. By 1900, deposits were £200,000 of which £125,000 was loaned on property mortgages. It was 1922 before the bank paid a dividend on its 60,000 £1 shares. Deposits now total about £3,000,000. The account is handled by the Bank of England. Dividend paid to the Salvation Army from its bank is modest, about £6,000 yearly. There are years when there is no dividend. Mainly, the bank serves the Salvation Army and as with other companies, it is administered by Salvation Army officers who receive no fees or gratuities for their services.

Legacies and donations are a main source of income in most countries. In the United Kingdom the annual yield from this source may be as much as half-a-million though it must be kept in mind that much of this will be for specific purposes to do with women's or men's social service, children's work, effort overseas. One trust in London is to maintain reasonable street lighting, so that the band can play at the open-air meeting in the High Street.

Another is for the provision of Bibles for circus and variety artists. It owes its existence to sea-lions which had to be fed on Sundays, even when the circus was not performing. But William Booth, who had rented the tent, was a great Sunday worker. The trainer of the sea-lions, out back feeding his animals, heard the General preach. Hence the legacy.

At Heywood, in Lancashire, years ago, a shy, unknown man listened regularly to the open-air meeting at the corner on Sunday nights. Occasionally the Salvationists passed the time of day with the stranger. It would be the officer's duty to get to know any listener, if possible, and invite him to attend the meetings in the citadel. The man was probably asked that old and somewhat embarrassing question put by Salvationists: 'How are you in your soul?' Whatever was said, a good impression was made. The unknown man on the corner left the Salvation Army £120,000.

The Men's Social Work of Great Britain maintains a large chain of hostels for working men and down-and-outs, operating on under £1,000,000 a year. There are also a number of boys' homes, and places for the aged, and other centres including a clinic for alcoholics. The Missing Persons' Bureau costs the Army about £10,000 per annum; work for discharged prisoners, over £5,000; the Labour Bureau, £1,000; and these services are subsidized from Self-Denial and social funds.

Income in this arm of endeavour will come from the small amounts vagrants or poor working men can pay: some pay nothing. There are some grants from government and local authorities. The buildings used in this 'Darkest England' work are, for the most part, old and expensive to maintain. Yet they are crowded every night with thousands of homeless, hungry, cold and lonely men. Rising public health standards have made it necessary for large amounts to be spent on improvements in accommodation, sanitation and hygiene to William Booth's old Victorian shelters. About ten million pounds would be needed to rebuild to modern standards the buildings of the Men's Social Work of the Army in Britain.

The work for women, girls and children in Britain, which

includes prison, police court and midnight patrol service, costs the Army about £600,000 in any one year. There are numerous maternity homes, hostels for unmarried mothers, children's homes, hostels for women, approved schools and probation homes. There is a chain of children's homes and homes for the aged. There is an affiliation section whence the Army tries to get putative fathers of illegitimate children to accept their responsibility; there is a Family Services and Enquiry Department.

Much of this work for men and women might be thought to be superfluous in a Welfare State. Prostitutes are not now allowed to bargain on street corners; girls of tender years are not now purchaseable. In fact, the Salvation Army Social Work in the United Kingdom functions admirably within the Welfare State legislation, and has, in some fields, provided case work and know-how of great value to hospital boards, Home Office and Ministry of Education officials and others. *Laissez-faire* or state control, there is always need. That is where the Army comes in.

In the old days the Army's Migration Department chartered its own ships for the thousands of emigrants it accompanied to a new life overseas. The volume of such Salvationist-sponsored migration is now much smaller—most of it is done by governments concerned—but the Army still sends, meets, and sometimes accompanies migrants. This work has to be subsidized.

Hugh Redwood, in *God in the Slums,* put the Army's Slum and Goodwill Department on the map. Here again, social changes that might have been expected to create redundancy amongst Salvationist social workers have not in the event done so. Some people are as irresponsible in new houses as they were in old hovels. Children can be neglected on council estates just as they might have been in slum tenements.

On a budget of about £70,000 the Goodwill Department operates a chain of posts in most of Britain's large cities. The lassie officer, so brilliantly described by Redwood in a best seller that sold 400,000 copies, still tends the sick and aged, visits the lonely, takes gifts to the poor, Shaw in *Major Barbara,* Runyon in *Guys and Dolls,* many others in novels, radio and TV scripts, have romanticized the 'Angel Adjutants' of the Salvation Army who go like nuns in bonnets, prayers in hearts, and help in their hands. The real thing is not so romantic, nor so glamorous, but it is acutely necessary even in the affluent societies.

People who are sometimes irritated by Salvation Army money-getting tactics, the Self-Denial appeal, the street corner box or kettle, the lassie selling the *War Cry* in the pubs at the week-ends, do not all realize that the soldiers of William Booth's Army give as well as get. There are no shares from the collection, no free hand-outs; the highly-expensive uniform that the officer, bands-man, singer, must have and must pay for, is for cash only. The Army does not allow credit terms. The man who tootles in the band gets no fee, even though he be a virtuoso. The collectors, the lassies who sell the papers, are not paid, not even for their shoe leather or for the wear and tear of their expensive bonnets. It costs money to be in the Salvation Army.

That will not be all. There's your cartridge—William Booth's name for the gift envelope that all soldiers are expected to put into the collection plate on Sundays. The citadel will have cost anything between £10,000 and £50,000. Mortgage repayments, light, heat and other running costs, including bread-and-butter for the Captain and his lady, may amount to anything between £20 and £50 per week.

This is domestic money; the local Salvationists must find it. Most of it and much besides, they give themselves. In the old days they would give pennies; some of them now give pounds, covenanting their gifts so that the Army can recover tax from the Commissioners of Inland Revenue.

Many Salvationists give their tithe in the Biblical sense—ten per cent of their spendable income. One girl office worker in Australia, as related elsewhere, gives £5 per week, and there are many other such generous givers.

A boy in his first job after high school, began his giving with 10/- a week. When his Commanding Officer questioned him as to whether he could afford this the lad said:

'Major, I get all my pleasure at the Army—the band, the singers, my friends. Because I am a soldier I am not allowed to drink. Because I am a bandsman I am not allowed to smoke. In truth, I am happy to forgo both. In consequence I save a lot of money, and am better off in other ways. I am glad to be able to give this much and one day, when I can afford it, I will give more.'

Stewardship appeals, similar to those made in churches, have greatly increased the Salvationist's sense of financial responsibility. Like the schoolboy, many of them realize that as non-smoking, non-drinking people they are better off than in their 'worldly', wicked days. They are encouraged to 'count their blessings' and then pay. Wesley used to worry lest his Methodists should become proud and forgetful in the thrift and affluence that followed their conversion. It is a danger that attends on soldiers of the Army. They are often warned of that danger.

Officers are not paid in the Salvation Army. As stated earlier, they get an allowance, and have the legal status of voluntary workers. This allowance varies from country to country according to the economic climate of that country, but it is always relatively small. For officers, as for St. Francis, Christian poverty is part of their Christian vocation. The top rank and responsibility in the Army, apart from the General (whom the Army does not support) is that of Commissioner: his allowance in the United Kingdom would not be half that of a provincial bank manager. Yet as there are about 25,000 officers, their bed and bread-and-butter, their rice or mealie cake, makes a large hole in Salvation Army budgets. National officers in India, Africa and elsewhere, where standards of living are rising, have all had increases in their allowances in recent years.

The training of officers is very costly. The United Kingdom budget is about £100,000 per annum. In the United States, with four colleges, it is much more.

The Army also has a college for officers, a kind of Camberley, which costs £10,000 a year. It has an Education Department, for schools and adult education feature in its operations: cost £5,000.

Obviously, the winds of change blow also through the exchequer of the Salvation Army, creating new problems—most of them deficits. One new African republic recently stopped all subsidies on teachers' salaries. As the Army has a group of schools in that country, a large sum of money was required quickly.

Another newly-independent African state stopped the payment of part-cost of school fees. The Army that sends a man to Africa with his family must see that the children are educated. In this instance, fees became payable even on primary and secondary education—including African children. The additional money called for was £15,000.

Lepers can be healed by Salvation Army doctors—up to eighty per cent of cases—but drugs and equipment are costly; and the doctor must be brought home for rest every third year. His qualifications make him a £2,500 a year man or, if he has consultant rank, £4,000 or more. In fact, he gets an officer's allowance, about £10 per week, and needs a free ticket for self, wife and children, if he is to get homeland rest.

Missionaries become tired and must be replaced or given sick-leave. That means training and transportation—all very expensive. Sometimes currencies are devalued, as in one Far Eastern state where missionaries of other churches had to take part-time jobs or starve. This would not please the ghost of William Booth who regarded officership as a full-time job, on a twenty-five-hour-a-day basis. So the Army's Chancellor of the Exchequer had to find the extra money. The extra cost in that one territory is £12,000 per annum, and there are other like contingencies.

Even if it were true that 'the Salvation Army is always cadging', which it is not, there still would not be enough money to meet the need with which it is confronted all over the world.

Part II
THE WAR

8. PUTTING MEN INTO ORBIT

Though the Salvation Army is said to have begun under William Booth's top hat, many people contributed to its foundation. The first General was not reluctant to adapt, beg or borrow other people's ideas and innovations. The benevolent dictator, rock-like on principle, was fluid in method.

By 1888, when the world growth of the Salvation Army made it so complex that rules and regulations were required against the many contingencies that arose, William Booth's eldest son, Bramwell, had already given proof of his gifts as an administrator. To begin with that watchful care and control was exercised which a wise mother has over her young. But children grow up and the Salvation Army outside of Britain has grown up. Supreme strategic control is still vested in the General, whose International Headquarters is in London, but the terms of reference for the Territorial Commanders he appoints to national commands all over the world allow them considerable freedom of action.

The wide tactical variations which soon developed in the Salvation Army, or were forced upon it, did not occasion William Booth any loss of sleep for he had no particular reverence for tradition, was allergic to ritual, and highly interested in experimentation. He encouraged his officers when in Rome to do as Rome did—sought to make the Army indigenous, in fact.

Former Indian Civil Service Judge, Booth-Tucker, sent by Booth to India as a missionary, walked barefoot, and wore the garb of a fakir, because it identified him with the poor and oppressed, and not with the British Raj. This willingness to be Indian among the Indians, and Bantu among the Bantu, is still a great weapon in the Salvation Army. It has won to it a large native force in all lands, which has matured and become influential to the third and fourth generation of converts, soldiers and officers. Inevitably, though these share the universal Salvationist vision of 'the world for God', they wish to pursue it in methods suited to their own lands. They do this, sometimes, in ways that London wots not of.

The North American continent is far less devoted, of course, to the idea of State control, economic and social planning, than is Britain. There is no national health service and other adjuncts of the Welfare State are lacking. What is in its place is excellent 'free enterprise' social service and in this the Salvation Army plays a very important part. Generally speaking the American people prefer the voluntary agencies to do their relief and welfare work; they give generously to make this possible. This obviates the need for much intervention by Federal or State authorities.

Americans consider that theirs is the better way when compared with Welfare State systems. It certainly agrees with the Salvation Army in America.

There were soon differences between the Army in the Old World and the Army in the New. As early as 1884, four years after invasion by William Booth's first detachment, Major Thomas E. Moore, having exchanged British nationality for American, broke away from the parent movement to launch the Incorporate Salvation Army of America.

In 1896 William Booth's second son, Ballington, refused to accept London's discipline, and formed his own Army as 'The Volunteers of America', an organization that still exists. The Mayor of New York, Congress, and even President Cleveland displayed American partisanship all the more keenly because feeling between Britain and the United States was running high at the time on account of the Venezuelan Boundary Dispute. American Salvationists recalled the Boston Tea Party, and the defeat of General Burgoyne at Saratoga.

But like fate was not in store for General Booth. Neither of the splinter movements flourished. Cut off from Booth's genius they languished, while the Salvation Army went marching on.

Commander Eva Booth, William Booth's fourth daughter, who was a brilliant commander of her father's forces in the United States, was a lady with a mind of her own, and a sister's disposition to stand up and argue with her elder brother. This she did even when he became the second General. There was a resultant high tension, but not another splinter movement. Instead, there was a greater degree of autonomy. Commander Eva Booth set the Army in the United States on a route that, though parallel in principle, is divergent tactically from the Army in Britain.

In the rich profusion of men and methods in the United States, consider Captain George Duplain, in charge of the Social Service Centre in San Francisco.

Here, of course, the frontier spirit still lingers. Lieutenant-Colonel Peter Hofman, Duplain's immediate superior, is a frontier type whose arrival, struggles and survival did not fit him to be a stereotyped executive. He holds Duplain on a loose rein, giving him much scope for experiment. When this is allied to American hard work, hustle and financial resources, the results are dramatic. It is not to be wondered at that universities of California send numerous students to do social work at the San Francisco Centre.

It has its own staff of doctors, a psychiatrist available for consultation, and there are half-a-dozen professional social case workers. There are hundreds of men being 'processed'; many in clinics, some in hospital, or otherwise being rehabilitated. The Chaplain is a Baptist minister, while a Professor of Pastoral Psychology conducts a Bible Class and leads group therapy. But Captain Duplain pays the salaries, and Captain Duplain is in charge. No one is in any doubt about that. Whenever 'outsiders', State or Federal subsidies, and indirect and secular methods are used in the Salvation Army, there are prophets of woe who foretell Salvationist loss of control and purpose. This need not, and usually does not, happen. Consider Duplain.

There are no brass bands or big drums at the centre. Many of the men are Catholic, some will be Jews or Mohammedan or other non-Christian religions. Many will be unashamedly atheistic. It is possible that one or two of Duplain's social workers are not Christian, but, at best, agnostic. Clinical Psychologist Dr. Lawrence Katz is Jewish. He confesses to being intrigued by the penitent-form, or altar, as the Americans call it. Certainly he is not blasé about this. Perhaps he remembers that the Temple altar of his own people was also the place of forgiveness. It was golden, and that man died who touched it; the ordinary man might not even approach it. Katz's work at the San Francisco Centre has made him familiar with men who have knelt, penitent, at the wooden form which is the altar. Whatever he believes, he knows that many of these men are profoundly changed afterwards.

Modern psychiatry confirms many time-honoured Salvation Army methods. It is not strange that the Army finds a helpful resource in applied psychiatric social work. William Booth, recognizing the difficulty of work with alcoholics, early made the point that we must 'bring to bear upon it every agency, hygienic and otherwise, calculated to effect a cure'.

Doctor Katz, under Duplain's supervision, is in charge of a five-year research project financed by the Federal Government to the tune of 360,000 dollars. The Salvation Army adds large sums to this. It is expensive. Not only drug-addiction, alcoholism and vagrancy are in the scope of the enquiry, but also homosexuality.

Duplain and his staff talk with pity and understanding of the homosexual and comment that Tchaikovsky knew about that kind of hell. Let them all come—they try to help the worst. Duplain insists, 'The homosexual is also a child of God'.

He has been warned of the dangers of trying to help such men. But Salvation Army social work officers must take risks. Duplain insists that the homosexual confess his condition. Many seek to hide and deny their problem. Yet when they trust the staff, much can be done to help them. Sometimes the treatment is akin to the treatment of alcoholism, and many homosexuals seek escape in drink. And, as with alcoholism, though clinical cure is hard to achieve everything is done to assist the victim of homosexuality. 'There is evidence,' writes Dr. Katz, 'that some homosexuals, through psychotherapy and other means, do become heterosexual.' Others must accept that they are different and live with their condition. They can take comfort in the fact that they are not alone. Many, many of them live useful, law-abiding lives.

'I'm like God made me,' said a man with a case history of homosexual conduct.

'Not so,' said Duplain. 'There are numerous factors arising after you were born that could have contributed to your condition. What is sure is that God can help you now.' That was a new beginning. Neither the homosexual nor the alcoholic is encouraged to excuse himself from responsibility and the need for self-discipline. He is taught to believe and act on the firm conviction that God has delivered him from his curse—not, perhaps, the latent homosexuality, but from the committal of any homosexual act.

Every private room in the San Francisco Centre is a *private* room. All of the heavy book of rules falls on the man who breaks that Duplain commandment. The man who visits the private room loses the right to his own private room. The man who receives him loses his, too. The private room is a privilege. It is not gained easily. Normally, a man advances from a six-bed dormitory to a five, then to four and then to three. There are no two-bed rooms.

The Salvation Army, which has in the past made the usual unenlightened and horrified noises when encountering this problem, now has among its trained social workers in many parts of the world those who can consider it calmly without having to consign the offender, or victim, straightway to hell. The man in charge, or others among his staff, is, as always, the key. If he can be objective about it, he can help the man, and often does. Numerous clinics for homosexuals are being operated by the Salvation Army, and understanding and the degree of aid increases.

THE ELECTRONIC COMPUTER

'What happens,' asks Katz, 'when a man kneels at your altar as a penitent? Is he really penitent? Is he helped?' The doctor feeds this research data into the electronic computer of the University of California, at Berkeley. William Booth would be puzzled by this, but Katz is accepting no one's verdict but his own and that of his team of social scientists. 'Who are these men? Why are they inadequate? What triggered off their alcoholism? Do they make permanent recovery after being "saved"?'

'It doesn't matter to me that it is the Salvation Army,' he says. 'Any organization would have done, but it does seem to me that yours is an effective agency.'

It can be seen, the Doctor agrees, that some men make considerable headway after religious conversion. Behaviour improves. They often make restitution to friends they have wronged, and are restored to their wives and families. Many hold down decent jobs. After six months to a year Katz tracks down men who have been through this 'salvation mill' at San Francisco. Already there is considerable material on which to base a verdict.

'Emotion takes some of the penitents farther than the facts,' says the Doctor with a scientist's caution. He has heard many of the 'testimonies' which Salvationist converts are encouraged to make. There can be little doubt that alcoholics in particular, but also many other converts, indulge in verbal exhibitionism when speaking in groups about their conversion. Some take delight in washing their once dirty linen in public. A few make premature claims that salvation has washed all away.

But Duplain knows about this. Time will confirm or deny. Let the convert say what he will. He is sure, alas, that some who say they have been transformed, have not. But William Booth knew that 100 years ago. It is a hard lesson that all Salvationists learn. The first Christian encountered pretenders. Of a large group of men who had been helped in health by counselling, by religious persuasion, and by social rehabilitation, Dr. Katz's team found that forty-three per cent showed 'fundamental upgrading'.

There are, inevitably, the missing men. Not all wish to be labelled, followed and questioned afterwards. They prefer to drop out of sight, some of them, doubtless, back into the dark pit whence they came. But, also, by the law of averages, some of the anonymous men make good.

The Rev. Frank Tierman, the Chaplain, made his way up to the pulpit as a preacher, then found that his true vocation was among those whose lot he knew from personal experience, in the armed forces and while training as a prison chaplain. He had graduated at a business college, but later entered the Berkeley Baptist Divinity School. After eighteen months as a Church Pastor he heard that the Salvation Army in San Francisco wanted a chaplain at their social service centre. Duplain hired him.

Tierman likes the Army's certainty. Alcoholics Anonymous,

he knows, speaks of 'God as I understand Him', which, with the follow-up work and know-how of which they are masters, suffices for many men. But he prefers it as William Booth and the Baptist Billy Graham would put it: 'God as I know Him—in Christ my Saviour.'

He likes Duplain and found himself surprised at the modernity of the centre. He had, with many others, vague ideas that the Salvation Army would know about St. Paul and bowls of soup but not about daily shower baths and psychiatric analysis.

The Chaplain, eminently qualified to judge, considers that the pattern of reclamation of the down-and-out is something like this:

1. *The needy man must get himself sobered—really sobered.* Drugs, doctor, clinic, or even hospital treatment may be needed before he is dried out enough to think clearly again. With the chronic alcohol-saturated man this may take three to twelve weeks. He cannot even think properly until this process is complete.

2. *You can start him towards religious experience, but he must go forward under his own steam.* Help him; you must not carry him. If he goes too slowly for your liking and you rush him, he'll probably miss the goal.

3. *When he is on to that practical and plain evangelical religion which Salvationists proclaim he will know it.* Also he will probably give proof of it. The problem then is how to hold it.

The twentieth-century Salvationist has moved a long way from the rather narrow terms of reference of Victorian times. At San Francisco men are asked about their religious faith and told: 'Please state your own beliefs. Do not be swayed by what you feel others believe, or would like to have you believe. Your replies will not affect your stay at this centre.'

The man is thereupon allowed to say that he does not believe in the Bible miracles, or life after death. He can contend that the Bible consists of legends and myths, and that a man has within himself some of the characteristics of God. Perhaps the latter point is not heretical, but one would expect the Salvation Army roof to cave in on the assertion which some make: that 'Christ ended His life in defeat and failure'; or that 'Christians are weaklings who merely try to get their problems solved for them by an imaginary "God"'.

Duplain and his team are not shocked. When they know what a man believes, or will not believe, they have a better chance of helping him, pagan though he be. After all, that Salvationist social worker, though fastidious and, to a degree, puritanical, is not easily shocked who knows that some men entering the centre in San Francisco need treatment for syphilis and that others are homosexuals.

William Booth, one hundred years ago, was fond of leading his congregation in the singing of 'To the uttermost He saves'. They sing it in San Francisco and believe it with all their hearts.

Present at the regular case workers' conferences will be Duplain, Dr. Katz, the Chaplain, college students, counsellors and case workers, a secretary, a nurse, the Resident Supervisor, a doctor, and various other persons.

Item—'J.', a patient or 'beneficiary' wants to borrow forty dollars. He has good reason. He is doing well. Request agreed.

Item—'K.', ditto, has been violent again. He is not responding. Decided he must go. One of our failures.

Item—'L.', suitable for transfer to Lytton Ranch, annexe of the centre, where a much improved man can have a transitional period before going out to begin work and fend for himself.

Item—'M.' This man not suited to the centre and not likely to become so. Argument on this, with some of the team demurring. Decision postponed.

Item—'N.' This man has homosexual tendencies, and has attempted suicide. Decision, to continue trying to help him.

Item—'O.', extreme hypochondriac. In trouble over payment of his labour union dues—card withdrawn. Chaplain's comments: 'I don't think he's finished yet. He does try and is sincerely anxious to get on his feet again. We'll be able to get his union card back.' Decision, to continue treatment.

Item—'P.' A Mexican. Isolated man, sullen; drinks in almost continual state of anger. Persecution complex, probably based on rejection in early life. Agreed that group therapy might help him.

Item—'Q.' 'This man,' the Doctor comments, 'has proved that he can give up drinking. He doesn't really need us any more. We've had his varicose veins taken care of. We can let him go. . .' So decided.

And so on—there is a pile of papers on new admissions to be considered.

BALLINGTON BOOTH'S 'WAR OF INDEPENDENCE'

What of the man who makes this centre function so efficiently? There is irony in the fact that Duplain is a Salvationist as a result of Ballington Booth's American 'War of Independence'. His mother was converted in the Volunteers of America before becoming a Salvationist and leading her son into the Army. When he was eighteen he went to Long Beach, California, to work in the Douglas Aircraft factory. At twenty-six he had his pleasant home paid for—in that part of the world this needs something like the wealth of a Morgan or Rockefeller! He was a Salvationist, but of that new breed of affluent ones, oft encountered nowadays, who find that religion is good for business, and that sobriety and strict morality tend to get one promoted into the executive class.

He and his wife were willing to consider officership, but he felt that he had little qualification for evangelical work. Now if he could be a social work officer . . .

In those days, the candidate for Salvation Army officership had to give unrestricted mortgage on his life—'unconditional surrender'. Any assignment, anywhere: no bargaining.

'You'll probably have to do five years of evangelical work, at least,' they told him. He joined the United States Army instead, fought in the Philippines, and contracted malaria so badly as to write finis to any chance of his being a Salvation Army officer. Or so it seemed . . .

Chastened, he offered himself to the Salvation Army with a new-found discipline worthy of a trooper with Stonewall Jackson.

He entered the Army's college in San Francisco, taking his wife and infant son and daughter with him. He reconciled himself to the near certainty that though God wanted him to be a social worker, the Salvation Army would appoint him to a corps with a preaching and pastoral ministry, for which he felt he had no 'call'.

In training, he was a restive colt, but the Americans are used to that. He came out of the pipeline tidied up considerably and ready to accept orders to become a square peg in a round hole. He was surprised and delighted, however, to be sent to the Fresno, California, Men's Social Centre—the first time in the Salvation Army on that West Coast that a married couple had received such an appointment directly from the officers' training school.

It was soon manifest that he was likely to succeed in social work. He had drive and aptitude. Though he is still inclined to argue, he knows when to stop argument and get on with the job. For that virtue much is forgiven in the Salvation Army. When the huge San Francisco Centre was being planned, his superior called him in, a mere stripling of a Captain and told him he was to run it.

He argued then and authority was not pleased.

'This is a complimentary appointment for you. Senior officers have been passed over . . .'

'Thank you, Sir,' Duplain said. 'But I would not wish to be party to building and operating a flophouse.'

Instead of putting him on a charge for gross impertinence, Authority handed over the plans: 'Here, study these, and let me have your considered reaction.'

Duplain by now had ideas on how to build and operate a West Coast social centre. The cost, estimated at 300,000 dollars, he upped to 600,000. Most irregularly he consulted friendly professional social work experts and builders. All but the architect donated their services.

He stood out for privacy and dignity for the drunks or otherwise misfits who would use the centre. Small rooms, private rooms, rooms with radio and television: standards of hygiene and convenience hitherto not reached, and very, very expensive. As a crusader he was hard to deny, for he was willing to invest his own young life and promising future in his vocation. The Army found the initial 650,000 dollars, and much more afterwards. San Francisco, with Duplain in charge, is now one of the most remarkable social centres in the world—in the Army or out of it.

Modern ideas in furnishing, streamlined building and other

'luxuries' horrified old hands who foretold dire depredations. When Duplain stood out for costly Danish modern furnishings, he was told that the men would ruin such good material.

'We must make them come up to us, not go down to them,' he insisted. More than five years later the furniture is as good as new.

Duplain studied sociology, and is often invited to lecture before conferences of social scientists. In all, he says, he is going by the book, a very old book, William Booth's *In Darkest England and the Way Out*.

When many of the men, even most, will not come up, he searches his soul for that Boothian—Christ-like—quality of being patient, compassionate—forgiving seventy times seven, as the Bible says—and so on *ad infinitum*. Men go absent without leave; they get drunk and try to hide it; they buy a prostitute; they carry liquor into the centre, drugs even.

If caught, they are disciplined, but given another chance, and another . . . Even when Duplain and his team must eject a man, they do not give up hope. The man may come back if he will, and sometimes does, and makes good at last.

With any American Men's Social Service Centre, Duplain is in business—big business. He operates twelve stores, maintains a fleet of twenty-eight trucks, runs a factory and employs a staff of about 120 truck drivers, clerks, clothing sorters and so on. There are also the 130 men receiving treatment who are given work therapy. The highly skilled or professional man might be found a *pro tem* position in the city. All Duplain's trucks are fitted with walkie-talkie radio. The California Highway Patrol can hardly have tighter control of its police cars than Duplain has of his collection trucks.

His income from the collection of the throw-aways of the generous citizens around the Golden Gate is about a million dollars a year. Housewives in this affluent society change their fridge, or furniture, simply because they have grown a-weary of looking at it. Sometimes Duplain is asked to collect the furnishings of a whole home.

Most social work officers in the United States can give substantial assistance to the needy, and there are instances of imposition and misuse by the insincere or confidence trickster, but it is not easy for the scrounger to get on to the gravy train at the San Francisco Centre. In the initial interview, if there are indications that a man is ill or otherwise in need of help he will be asked:

'What do you want?'

'A job,' he may reply.

'We don't give jobs,' he will be told. 'We give treatment. If you come here you will be a "patient" or a "beneficiary" and you will have to accept our programme. It is not easy.'

So the man will start again, and frequently persists in evading the issue. Great effort is made to get an honest answer from him. 'What is your problem?' He is accepted for treatment only when he admits he needs help with his real problem, when he stops inventing alibis.

He enters a kind of 'open prison'—a place of compassion, profound faith, and tremendous patience. Very often the man is so low that the doctor, psychiatrist or hospital consultant will warn Duplain of suicidal tendencies. One such man, who had more than once tried to take his life, who had wasted 45,000 dollars on drink, who had lost his wife and children—they were ashamed of him—said to Duplain one morning: 'This is the first time I've come down sober in three years.' He had been a school teacher. Four 'attempted suicides' had been admitted to the centre in one week.

The programme seems hard, but it works efficiently and kindly. Food, clothes, health, hygiene, hospital or clinical treatment, visits to the Chaplain, chapel services, work, group discussion, interviews, house regulations, add up to a rule almost monastic. But it works.

'You agree, or you don't come in,' says Duplain. 'You can walk out any time you like.' He is a realist. He expects a high ratio of casualties. It is the residue he is after—those will be reclaimed. They make all worth while.

As he puts it: 'It's like the Government space probe. There are some misses. Some missiles do not get off the ground—others go wrong after launching. Those that get into orbit justify everything. Some of our men "get into orbit".'

For the first thirty days a man is on probation. Sometimes, after sticking it out for a year or more, he will be asked to come back 'for evaluation'. The Salvation Army in America uses a lot of psychological jargon. By now, the former patient may be in a regular job and may complain that he would lose his wages by returning.

'We'll make that up to you,' they say, and do. Sweet are the uses of financial security!

Linked with the San Francisco Centre is the Lytton Ranch, where men with aptitude, or special need, can work among the hogs or cattle in the country before being returned to the cold, hard world. This place has its own officer-in-charge, its own chaplain and staff.

Big business helps to rehabilitate some of the men who have been dried out and 'saved' in the San Francisco Centre. Standard Oil, Remington Rand, the Douglas Aircraft Corporation, might be asked: 'Will you take one of our men? He is an alcoholic, but has not been drinking for the past eighteen months. We believe he can be of use to you. It will help us. We'll continue to keep an eye on him.'

The man is provided with the tools of his trade; his union dues are paid. It is not a simple matter. Because of union rules any firm that keeps a man on the payroll for ninety days must keep him on afterwards. Alcoholism is a disease. Medically it is not curable. *Ipso facto* a sick man who is a regular worker cannot be dismissed.

Duplain insists that it is no use giving a man a Bible, and teaching him to pray, unless one also helps him in his mundane affairs. He must be respected as an individual, though an inconvenient one. When a man had ambitions to learn IBM data-processing, Duplain sent him to college, provided him with two new suits and advanced the necessary spending money. All this adds up. The aim of the centre is to put Heaven into a man's heart, while planting his feet straight and firm upon the earth.

To hear the men who regularly pack Duplain's chapel sing, 'Holy, holy, holy, Lord God Almighty' to the soft music of an organ, is worth a long journey. Mere youths, hardened in delinquency, now mellowed by the infectious and warm Salvationism of this place; old men, who have spent twenty or more years in the penitentiary; tough, big bruiser types, and emaciated wraiths; drug-addicts, alcoholics, men convicted of armed robbery; confidence tricksters; these, and many besides, are singing: 'Holy, holy, holy, Lord God Almighty . . . All the saints adore Thee . . .' Some of them have the shining faces and bright eyes of saints.

But not all are on the salvation band-waggon, though it is not easy to get away with insincerity, or to remain unaffected by the Salvationism here. Even the kitchens sparkle, the rooms and corridors are air-conditioned, baths are as obligatory as Bibles. No one is allowed to bark, 'James! Johnson! Jones!' as if the place were a jail. The fact that a man has been pushed down or let himself down, does not deprive him of his right to courtesy and self respect—if he can find it. Duplain is sure that the worst offence, the most dire wretchedness, need not estrange a man from God. Like the Prodigal, who lived profligate, and worked among the swine, many men at the San Francisco Centre rise up to re-trace their steps from the far-off land, across the wilderness of loneliness and despair. Some come with true penitence and prayer. They find that God is waiting to give them a welcome.

9. THE SUN SHINES BRIGHT ON ROTO ROA

Chalmers fidgets nervously in his chair. 'Of course, I'm not really an alcoholic, Major . . .'

This familiar line will get us nowhere. I interrupt him, 'Roto Roa is for the treatment of alcoholics. If you're not an alcoholic, why come to me?'

He knows he has to come. If he cannot find what he wants on this island, he is lost.

'There's no point in accepting anyone who does not honestly admit that his drinking is out of control,' I continue.

His head droops, eyes glued to the floor in unseeing dejection. His clothes are too large for him, for malnutrition is one of the marks of alcoholism. He has the lot—ulcers, chronic anxiety, loss of appetite, insomnia, the nervous condition that makes his facial muscles twitch. He drinks before breakfast, drinks alone, he is not able to stop drinking all day and far into the night.

He looks up. 'O.K. Major, have it your way. I know I'm licked. I am an alcoholic. Now can I come?'

Under Section 7 of the Treatment of Inebriates Act, 1909, I admitted him to the Roto Roa Island Colony. This section allows for a man to commit himself as a voluntary patient, though, even so, he must obtain a Court Order, for this place is largely financed by the Government.

Roto Roa is about thirty miles off Auckland, one of a chain of islets spread across Hauraki Gulf, deep into the north-east coast of the North Island. It is an agricultural settlement, owned by the Salvation Army. Many men who come here with a drinking problem that seems hopeless, go away sober and stay sober. As alcoholism is a growing problem in New Zealand the Government is highly interested in our programme and helps to support it financially. At the moment we are planning to erect new houses for ninety men, and we make our own building blocks. The Government is finding about £40,000 of the needed funds, their

Public Works Department undertaking the building programme.

Staffing has always been a headache; the settlement is rather
isolated; the boat to the mainland is dependent on tides and
weather. People have even compared it with Alcatraz, the former
penal centre for the toughest sorts of prisoners, in San Francisco
Bay. Both are islands, but there the resemblance ends.

Roto Roa is not a prison. When men come to me and say,
'Major, I'm leaving,' they can leave. More often than not they
come back. I find that alcoholism gets a man down, beats the
life out of him. When this happens and he knows it, God—and
we—can help him to live again. We are not interested in keeping
men here whose hearts are not with us in the intention to defeat
alcoholism.

Years ago, the National Council on Alcoholism, with the New
Zealand Government, magistrates, the Salvation Army, hospital
officials and other interested parties, met to decide on the future
of Roto Roa. We were confronted with depressing statistics and
a poor record of progress.

The Salvation Army had to learn that time demands changes.
Great advances had been made in the scientific study of alcoholism. The doctors had recognized it as a disease. We were faced
with the fact that all is not over when a man kneels down to
say his prayers, and declares that he is saved. The thirst is still
there.

We needed new buildings, a modern power plant, better
drainage, many renovations and additions, costing many thousands of pounds. We could not find all this money.

But we've got our new chapel! The Logan Campbell Trust
helped with this and the Sargood Trust put in £1,000 for an
organ and hi-fi equipment. If the men must go through a sort
of hell while they suffered their painful dehydration by being
deprived of alcohol, then at least let them have good music as a
palliative.

It has long been a Salvation Army principle to 'set a thief to
catch a thief'. I, Major Robert McCallum, was born at Invercar-
gill on the tip of the South Island of New Zealand. My father
was an alcoholic, and so am I. Naturally, seeing I am a Salvation
Army officer, I never taste alcohol, I would be dismissed if I did.

But I subscribe to the medical theory that, in the clinical sense, there is no cure for this malady. Therefore, seeing I was once an alcoholic, I am still an alcoholic. An alcoholic can stop drinking, thank God. Yet alcohol remains a dreadful ghost at rest only while I taste it not. Let me take one drink, then the ghost is raised again and there's the devil to pay.

Someone could write a book, probably someone has, on the special relationship of the sea to alcoholism. Perhaps it is the loneliness, the monotony; maybe the calls to port, the good companions, free spending, the strong social pressure to have another.

My mother died when I was eleven, from neglect and misery I dare say. My father and my grandfather were heavy drinkers. I began my working life while still a child as little more than a serf on a farm, sleeping on straw, covered by sacks, not allowed to live in the house with my employer's children, but kept outside in one of the barns. One job I had was as assistant to a baker, pay five shillings a week. My working day began at three o'clock in the morning.

Often I would see the ships go by. They called me to a dream-life of freedom and wonderful adventures. My life was ugly, cold, cruel. More than once I ran away from the jobs where I was ill-treated. If there was such an agency as a Child Welfare Department, I never heard of it. In due course I got myself taken on to a three-masted barque, a 700-tonner, ferrying explosives across the shark-infested Tasman Sea from New Zealand to Australia. Farther afield I sailed in steam ships. Once in a troop ship *en route* to Egypt, I saw forty men consigned to the deep, all victims of a 'flu epidemic.

Graduating to the Royal Navy and later to the Royal New Zealand Navy, I shone as a boxer, welter-weight, and found myself mildly famous, being sent from duty on the China Station to South America, a navy representative champion at the world fair. For some time I served in submarines until I developed a smoker's cough. Then they sent me back to the surface.

This intrusion of my own affairs into this story is to come to my own problem. I want to indicate my qualifications for being able to help alcoholics. My boxing came to an inglorious end because I began tipping the bottle. I lost control of my alcoholic intake.

Though an alcoholic may not be able to control his drinking if once he lifts the glass to his lips, he can learn to live without the glass. The best way I know of doing this is to find an interest, a passion greater than the craving for alcohol. In my case this was religion. It has been termed 'the expulsive power of a new affection'.

When I was invalided to shore duty, drink having played havoc with the physique that had enabled me to become a boxing champion, I found myself at Devonport Naval base where the Salvation Army had a corps. As my personal problem grew worse I became interested in religion and found the Army meetings very much to my liking. The spiritual transformation had taken place, conversion, which is the best recovery programme for any drink problem or most other personal problems for that matter.

With me the results were dramatic. A girl said to another, 'Remember Bob McCallum? He's sober.' To anyone who knew me, that statement was incredible.

Later I became an officer of the Army and came here, competent, more or less, I hope you'll agree, to help this poor wretch now in the abyss into which I fell myself.

Officially we call them 'patients' and all is very respectful— 'Mr. this' and 'Mr. that'. When a man arrives, saturated in liquor, we send him to hospital, whether he likes it or not. Our regular doctor gives us all the authority we need. Three or four weeks are needed to build them up physically before they can even listen to religious argument—a modern slant on old William Booth's crude but cogent principle: 'Don't waste your time preaching to a man with an empty belly or cold feet.'

I want to know what's behind the craving for the bottle. The thirst is usually a symptom, not the malady itself.

They tell me that no two sets of fingerprints are alike. I'd say that every alcoholic is different from every other. I've learned to consider a man as an individual; the merits and demerits of his case; his background, family, conditions of employment, temperament, childhood—everything.

You need a strong stomach, too. When they come here they

are so run down, so past caring, that they are often filthy, verminous and unwashed. On the other hand, some who come are well groomed, dignified members of the professional classes —a doctor, or lawyer, or one of that ilk, maintaining a façade of sobriety with the aid of a distressed family.

On this island of hope and achievement, there are often tears and misery; sometimes failures. Men go away cleaned up, emptied of alcohol, 'dried out' as we say, and then, with the wages we give them, on the very first day back among their old companions on the mainland, they decide to take 'just one drink'.

It is well-nigh inevitable that 'one drink' to an alcoholic will trigger off the old explosion, the uncontrollable binge that ends with empty pockets, or drunkenness, or unconsciousness, and more of the same the next day and the next. This pattern about alcoholism is sickeningly familiar.

Yet even this helps in the complex process by which many drink-slaves find liberation. Ignominious failure must be rubbed in; a man who has been away and begs to come back and try again is often nearer to the final solution by reason of his breakdown.

Sometimes when my patience is running out, and it must, for there are some who cannot be saved and whose malingering and insincerity only takes up the space, time and effort needed for the genuine cases, a man will say: 'Major, please take me back. Give me another chance.'

He's already had six chances and I have declared that he must have no more. Sometimes I change my mind. Now and then, M. L. G. H. Sinclair, the Chief Magistrate, will intercede for the men I have written off as failures:

'Give him another chance, Mac,' he says, and I do. Best of all, of course, God does. There's no limit to the number of times *He* will forgive. He gave me very many fresh starts, and of this I remind myself when I run out of forgiving spirit.

Did I tell you that I am a J.P.? Some people think that results in the Department of Justice having undue sway here. Naturally, we work closely with them, but there is no attempt at coercion. We are encouraged to do our own work in our own way. Recently I asked the Government for a bigger and better boat. They gave us the *Mahoe* which, incidentally, is part of a Salvation Army navy afloat in Alaska, Holland, Sweden, Britain and other places.

Though the crew and myself as skipper are alcoholics, we keep a straight course, or, at least, a safe one as we twist in and out of the various channels on the trip from Auckland. And just as I am the man in charge afloat, so I am on Roto Roa. The university professors who come here, the sociologists, the students from college, the members of Alcoholics Anonymous, parsons, Roman Catholic priests and many other interested parties are studying how the Salvation Army tackles this great problem. They do not tell us how to do the job.

We, of course, are willing to learn from anyone. We keep open minds and we are happy to be judged by results.

Two-thirds of the men here attend religious services where the pressure is unashamedly towards religious conversion—but not towards conscripting soldiers for the Salvation Army. Some of the patients are Catholics, others are Jews; most of no religious profession. But to all it is the religious experience we emphasize, not the creed or sect.

Sixty-five per cent of the men sent to Roto Roa for up to three times, do not return. We have reason to believe that a large number of these make the grade in normal life on the mainland. They have learned to cope with their problem. I know men in good jobs, doing well in the professions, happily married, re-married, restored to their wives after estrangement, sober men, new men, all as a result of coming to this island of hope.

Men have been able to win back the respect of their children and hold down influential positions in the community because they now know their problem and, by God's grace, have con-quered it. Many who come here but once, never come back—they have no need to do so. Many an alcoholic is so disgusted with himself that when he learns that he can stay dry he stays dry for ever.

This is a good billet except, of course, that there's no booze to be had. The sun shines bright on Rota Roa. There are sharks out at sea but in the idyllic coves surrounding the island the fish abound in deep blue water above which a man can sit, quiet and thoughtful, planning his new life as he waits for the next tug on the line.

There's a cinema, and well-equipped leisure facilities, but the chapel is the focal point. We generate our own electric power and the place is as bright as can be even when the sub-tropical sunshine gives way to night. We have modern houses for our staff, mechanized farm equipment.

We preserve the names of the 'old boys' happily married and making good—as if this were an old public school in the old country. Normally, alcoholics are divorced, about to be divorced, or at best, legally separated from their long-suffering wives. The number of men who go away from us, make good and then send me invitations to the wedding is a constant source of astonishment.

Men here kneel at the penitent-form in our chapel convulsed in agonized repentance and remorse. Remember that if alcoholism is hard on the drinker it is hell for those who love him. But incurable alcoholics can be lifted up by God whose arms can reach to the lowest. A man sent here because of chronic alcoholism stole a boat and escaped only to be arrested in Wellington and sent back. He tried again and this time made good. He's a personal friend of mine now and a good sober man.

A doctor, who committed himself because his drinking was out of control, was converted here. He is now a very competent and sober G.P., who is not afraid to witness for Christ.

I must confess, as is well-nigh inevitable, that my own first marriage was wrecked by drink. Of course, that was before I became an officer, in my unregenerate days, and learned that faith and prayer and self-imposed discipline can do miracles for a man.

My present wife is my 'right hand man' now, my children the great delight of my life. Remote on this voluntary 'prison', to which our Army appointment and willing service commits us, there were years when my good lady had to be their schoolteacher, supervising the excellent system of Correspondence Schooling devised for a country with many rural communities and isolated farms. Because of the wasted years of my benighted youth and early manhood, I could not possibly make up all the ground I lost.

When I have been preparing a sermon, my own brand of simple, straight-from-the-shoulder talks for these rough diamond men on Roto Roa, or elsewhere, I have heard my daughters praying, knowing of my agonized strivings with English grammar and Biblical theology: 'Lord, help dad. Help our father.'

God did. God does. He helps us all. Sometimes I ponder on the wonder, the unbelievable privilege I have. Former drunk, Bob McCallum, Major in the Salvation Army, J.P., M.B.E. But, come to think of it, God has always used the likes of me to seek and save the likes of them.

If angels were allowed to save the world, so I read, Heaven would be empty in five minutes. It takes a sinner to understand sin. The grand old man of the Salvation Army, old General William Booth was right. Set a drunk to save a drunk!

10. THE WATERS OF LETHE

Gloucester House at Highworth, about six miles from Swindon, is in the charge of Auxiliary-Captain Robert Baldwin, himself an alcoholic with twenty-three convictions to 'his credit', as he put it. This refuge for men with drinking problems, is next door to the Saracen's Head public house, and facing a most inviting country inn on the opposite side of the street. It is axiomatic with regard to dried-out alcoholics that restraint or isolation does not meet their case; they must learn to live with their temptation while not yielding to it.

Sometimes, Baldwin speaks of a 'cure' for alcoholism, but talk with him reveals that he means the arrest of the disease, the cessation from drinking, not the final destruction of its terrible potential. He admits that the man who comes to Gloucester House with a chronic drinking problem has taken out a mortgage on his future and the well-being of those he loves. Let him fail the terms of his 'contract'—a religious one, says Baldwin— let him omit prayer, worship, and the rest of therapy from his regular 'payments', then he will be foreclosed. The first drink will trigger off a catastrophe; the last state of that man will be worse than the first.

His own story is powerful illustration of this. It is in great part the story of Sylvia. She was brought up by her aunt because her own father had committed suicide: her mother died when she was five. As a child she began attending the Salvation Army at Swindon and in her late teens became an officer.

She was home on furlough when she heard about Bob Baldwin. It was as a meeting of an angel with a son of darkness. Bob was notorious for his misdeeds; she was a sheltered and pious Christian social worker, an officer in the Salvation Army. But just as cats can look at kings, so the wicked can view the saintly: there is, indeed, a psychological principle of compensation in such aspirations. Baldwin did not only view from afar, he fell in love, he courted the angel just as Faust did Marguerite. But Bob did not drag Sylvia down with him, she, with God's help, lifted him up.

Baldwin has tried to analyse his own drinking problem, while being cautious about placing too much weight on his amateur conclusions. He was in trouble with the police before his fourteenth birthday, was drowning his youth in alcohol, at an age when most other boys were at school learning how to live. He broke into the sports pavilion of the local gas company 'just to get at the wine'. He had strong suicidal tendencies, once trying to throw himself under a train because life was hell when he drank, and worse hell when there was nothing to drink.

His own mother, a good woman, thought of her boy as a kind of monster. 'He should be put away,' she cried, in the agony of shame his escapades had brought to the family. She had no understanding of what ailed her son. He now asserts that he was afraid. Life was too difficult. He was incapable of living it. If he could be drunk—or if he could die— he'd not have to face it. The river of forgetfulness, Lethe, that ran through Hades, fascinated him.

At Salisbury Quarter Sessions, though he was the youngest in a procession that came up from the cells, he got the stiffest sentence—four years. By this time his record was as long as his arm. Basically he was sick, superficially he was insolent and violent. His four year sentence could be appealed with good chance of reduction, so his lawyer told him. But he was too proud to appeal. He found a twisted kind of delight in imagining that by serving a stretch for which he did not legally qualify he was putting the judiciary in the wrong, hurting it in some way. Baldwin was acutely hypersensitive. At school he was a 'foreigner', from the country, never gaining the boon of acceptance by other schoolboys. He was bullied, until one day he made the explosive protest that has been found in him many times since, and defended himself so well that he gained a reputation as a fighter. After that he had to fight to keep on top.

When his parents refused to allow him out at nights, knowing the risks he ran, they diminished him in his own eyes and in the eyes of the gang of boys who looked upon him as their leader. He had to be a liar and braggart in the streets: a 'good boy' at home. This duality of personality made havoc of his character that showed itself in the Merchant Navy.

As with Long John Silver, and many another, the sea completed his downfall. When the boat put in at Swansea, it was amusing for his crewmates to put Bob on show as if he were a circus act. His performance was to prove how much he could drink. Six pints was considered good. Drink was 'making a man of him' and his fighting powers became legendary. For his prison sentences he gave 'Salvation Army' as his religion: his sister was a Salvationist. Prison was in some ways good for him: he learned to read and write and even studied psychology. In the back of his mind was the wish to know himself. Emptied of ale he was not a madman. Some who had heard of his shocking temper and record for drunken assault, could not believe that he was also the quiet, studious model prisoner. In jail he wore the red band, the mark of a 'trusty'.

His ironical attestation of his religion as 'Salvation Army' brought an unexpected complication: he was visited in his cell by a Salvation Army prison work officer and close proximity to a Salvationist proved to be significant to Baldwin as it has been to many others. On the day of his release from prison, he knelt, for the first time, at a Salvation Army penitent-form. It was not the final victory: it was a beginning.

At nineteen he was thrown out of the Merchant Navy, classified as 'chronic alcoholic'. He went into the R.A.F.—they found him expendable also. He was drinking all he could get hold of, living rough on building sites, barns, deserted huts. He was barred from the pubs in Swindon, which was the same as to forbid the Sahara oasis to the man dying of thirst. Like an outlaw he crept in at nights to beg drink from those who had kindness but not discretion.

He found himself in a strait jacket in a mental hospital. Later he attacked a policeman with a broken bottle for which, not surprisingly, he was given six months in jail. Here, again, he mended his ways, advancing to G.C.E. 'O' level in a number of subjects in the prison school. Trouble was, he had to go out again into that alien world where the dark water of oblivion was in every bottle he drank.

Yet, as related, he met Salvationist Sylvia, and knelt at the

penitent-form at the Salvation Army in Swindon, becoming in
due course a candidate for officership. Because of the officer-
must-marry-officer rule, he could not marry Sylvia without this
qualification. But Mephistopheles and Bacchus are not inevitably
defeated by one essay at the penitent-form, or the most sincere
prayers. Bob was sincere in his religious quest, and he was in
love but, as an alcoholic, was sitting on gunpowder. It blew up
about six weeks before the date of his entry into the International Training College. There was a difference of opinion with
an official of the Army: Bob's reaction was to go on a drunken
bender.

Though he was quick to repent, the damage was done: a
certain sense of responsibility is required of would-be officers.
Bob's acceptance for training was ruled out for the time being.
But now his angel reached lower to lift her despairing lover,
withdrawing from officership. They took two rooms at Swindon,
and celebrated a 'real Army' wedding. Bob hung on, though
racked by agony of unquenched thirst. His bride was sure that
all would now be well, having excess of confidence in the anchor-
age of connubial bliss and an under-estimation of the ravages of
alcoholism.

Old cronies from pub and club called upon Bob as one of their
fraternity of the bottle. The couple were poor. Sylvia, though
still in a job, was expecting a baby. But with the domestic
impracticability of men, Bob would have kept open house if he
could have afforded it. As it was he offered excess of hospitality
and was given notice by an indignant landlord who, not unnaturally, objected to his rooms being used without permission
as a hostel for down-and-outs.

It was hard on Sylvia who petitioned God regularly for the
salvation of her darling husband. He remained sober but now
wanted a larger house where his amateur efforts at aiding the
needy could have fuller scope—'it's always the poor that helps
the poor'. With Sylvia he appeared before the local council as
applicant for a mortgage, being questioned as to his character
and prospects. Either the questions were superficial, or the council were men of unusual acumen and optimism, for they granted
the mortgage, court convictions notwithstanding.

The couple moved into their new house just before the baby

came. They had as their total furnishings: 1 table, 4 chairs, 2 sets of curtains, 1 small carpet, 1 bed. There were eight rooms, not counting attic, cellars and bathroom. Into the empty spaces moved the homeless alcoholics, who were tearing at Bob's heartstrings.

It was hard on Sylvia, yet she had the idea that Robert found this work to be a therapy for his own drink problems. Helping others to keep away from the bottle was part of his own salvation. They were both regular in their attendance of the Salvation Army meetings at Swindon.

Bob's unwonted term of dryness, and worthy activity as a Salvation Army soldier, brought him publicity in *The War Cry*, the Army's weekly paper. This was excellent for Bob, but trying for his wife who presently found herself with two babies and ten alcoholic lodgers. But some of the men forgot to pay their dues after having been given bed and board from the Baldwins' hard-earned and meagre resources. Robert was an idealist: even the routine for claims on the National Assistance Board was beyond him.

Letters came from far and near, particularly from jail where former good companions of the tap room wrote hard-luck stories of imminent release into a cold, unfriendly world. Bob must take them in. Soon he found that he was working in close liaison with the probation officer, the doctor, the welfare people and the county psychiatrist. It was somewhat irregular, but the men were responding under Bob Baldwin's régime. Problem drinker Baldwin, now not drinking, was good for them.

All this, though Baldwin did not know it, was original Salvation Army tactics—almost everything worthwhile about that movement springs from the grass roots: spontaneous, experimental actions by enterprising members of the rank and file. But Bob's private war of salvation became too big for him to manage. The business details became involved, the local council forbade further extension of the eight-roomed house, which was already much too small. The doctor and others who were helping with the good work, told Robert about Gloucester House and suggested that the Salvation Army, as such, take the place over.

In such situations people have an unfailing recipe for action, they 'write to the General', which, as he is constitutionally the autocrat, seems reasonable enough. In practice, however, such letters are filtered through to the officer directly responsible and this one found its way to the Governor of the Men's Social Work of the Army in Britain. Fortunately for Robert Baldwin he is a man of wide experience and deep compassion, and not inclined to let grass grow where his mandate runs. He lost no time in going to Swindon to view Gloucester House and he was interested. He saw its possibilities, and the possibilities in Bob Baldwin—it is always people, not bricks or concrete on which Salvationist endeavour depends.

The Army bought Gloucester House and the Harbour Light Corps was opened with room for twenty men, and numerous apple trees in the garden. The Army made Bob Auxiliary-Captain, and provided him with the financial and administrative oversight and aid he needed. The place costs £3,500 a year to operate. Together, Robert and Sylvia seem just right. When a man falls, as some alcoholics will, they both know from personal experience what the hell of backsliding means. Sylvia knows about the hair-trigger temper that is part of the make-up of most thirst-wracked men. Bob has one.

Everything is worthwhile. Wonderful events, miracles, take place at Gloucester House.

HE RAN THE SHIP AGROUND

Let Charles Forbes tell his story:

The less I say about my home life the better. I ran away to sea and went to hell, or near it. My theme song might have been

I care for nobody, no not I,
And nobody cares for me.

One day, properly sozzled at the wheel, I drove the ship aground and was put ashore: 'If you can get yourself a cure we'll take you back,' they said. I might as well have tried to fly. The £35 pay-off I spent in three days, mostly on booze—rum in coffee allows you to go on drinking when other potations would put you under the table.

When I'd had it, and was reduced to begging, somebody at the L.C.C. told me to go along to the Salvation Army—'They'll help you.' I was unemployable now: my sea-record, otherwise good, was made shocking because of my inability to stay sober at due times. Of course, when I went to the Great Peter Street place of the Army, I was not interested in any of the religion. They took me in and I couldn't grumble, but there was no future in it for me. I wasn't a bloke who needed a doss-house: I was an alcoholic.

Top marks for them—they spotted this and sent me down here to Gloucester House. I'm acting foreman now, and dry as a matchstick. Now and then I read the notices that the Captain puts up. One of them is—

> *Factors that keep alcoholism*
> *from being controlled are:*
> SELFISHNESS
> FEAR
> RESENTMENT
> LACK OF HUMILITY
> *These are matters for which you*
> *have responsibility.*

I get it. Though I don't know all the answers, and wouldn't qualify as one of the General's top officers, I have been to the penitent-form. I understand what it is about.

MY NAME IS FRANK, AND WE'LL LEAVE IT AT THAT

I began working at 17, and by the time I was 22 I couldn't live without drink. While I am to blame the fact that my parents kept an off-licence did not help. When I was 34, I found that if I did not have a bottle by me I could not sleep. My nerves were shot to pieces.

My drinking schedule began at 7.30 a.m. I was working at a brewery. Believe it if you can, I got to be so thirsty that I began to get up at 6 a.m. or earlier so as to have time to drink before I went to work. I went through about fifty jobs in ten years and cost the National Health Service a pretty penny in barbiturates to help me sleep, and drugs and treatment to keep me alive.

One of the County Medical Officers sent me to a place for the treatment of neurosis. I knew what I had, for like most alcoholics, I was acutely interested in my ailments—an amateur psychologist—hypochondriac. According to my diagnosis I had:

1. anxiety neurosis.
2. psycho neurosis.
3. enlarged liver.
4. alcoholic neuritis.

5. loss of reflexes.
6. occasional D.T.s
7. the after-effects of hypnosis.

I had three terms in mental centres where I received vitamins for nutritional deficiency, with E.C. shock therapy and enough drugs to knock out a regiment.

When they let me out 'cured', I needed money fast. Liquor is expensive in Britain—what with taxes and prices for good Scotch. Even low-grade booze needs some financial status. I could put away thirty pints of beer or cider a day. But whisky or brandy is much to be preferred. I add up that I've spent about £6,000 on drink, not counting what I've cost the taxpayer through the National Health Service and the National Assistance Board. My friends and relations and any other soft touches I could find, added their quota.

But I began to crack up and that's how I got to this place, Gloucester House—'Harbour Light'. I'd been in hospital and they'd done a good job on me, when H.M. tax inspectors sent me a rebate of £15. The doctors had said that another bender might kill me, but with £15 nothing could keep me out of the pubs. I had a glorious binge, and still cannot remember all I did. But I know I smashed up a British Railways booking office, including a large plate-glass partition. I ended up in a cell, appearing in the police court next morning. The police doctor and probation officer knew all about me, and the magistrates acknowledged that sending me to prison did not meet the case. I was remanded and told to see the probation officer.

On rock bottom now, I was taking sodium amytal. I got the idea that if I could hold enough of it I could kill myself. A doctor prescribed it for me and I went along to a pub. I was going down for the last time, as do drowning folk. After a cider or two—all I could afford—I took the lot and woke up in hospital three days later. They'd used a pump on me, and spent another small fortune of taxpayers' money, though why they should have wished to preserve my life I could not understand. I expect you will be puzzled about that also.

They gave me the works—threw all the psychiatric books at

me, so to speak. I was in hospital for eleven weeks. The probation officer was distressed at what had happened to me while under his wing, but a top-drawer man of the Freudian school went into court and testified: 'This man will not respond to medical or psychiatric treatment.' So they sent me to Horfield prison while they considered what further might be done for me—perhaps the money was running out.

To my astonishment, Captain Baldwin came from Swindon and tried a little religion. Admittedly that was cheaper than all those experts and drugs, but I was an agnostic and had as little faith in prayers as I had in the Alcoholics Anonymous and all the hospitals, having tried the lot. But Baldwin was very persuasive and did get me to consent to go to Gloucester House for a trial run. Handcuffed, I was taken back to court, and there I told the magistrates that I agreed to go to Gloucester House. I laughed when I saw the pub next door. What simpletons these Salvationists were!

It must seem ludicrous in cold print, but I went to the penitent-form the next Sunday evening. If you knew Baldwin and some of the other fellows who were at the place, you might understand better. Remember, that if I were not here I'd be dead—there is no doubt about that. I can walk past pubs now—keeping my fingers crossed, you understand. You must not get to be a big-head when you're like I am.

I have the feeling that I am not the same man at all. The Captain says that's O.K.—it's in the Bible—'Old things have passed away. All things have become new.'

THE NERVOUS DRUNKARD

You might call mine The Case of the Nervous Drunkard, but there's no need to call in Perry Mason. Captain Bob Baldwin and the Salvation Army have dealt with it.

My depressions go back to before World War II. I was invalided out of the Army and spent six years in various mental hospitals, mostly in locked wards. Why was I nervous? Why depressed? As a rule people like me always blame other people and even now I am not quite sure . . . but I know much of the fault was mine.

I was in one of those locked wards when I heard my wife was leaving me, 'to save our daughter from your bad influence' as she put it. I broke out and walked through the dark night to find that not only my wife and child but even the furniture had vanished. Frightened, terribly alone, I searched one room after another, crying. The sound of it echoed through the deserted house, my feet thumping on the bare boards where the carpets had been; the T.V. set, the toys, the places where the child and I had played together . . .

They never came back. I was on my own now, and nothing could be worse for me. Sleep was impossible without drugs. I was given hypnosis and electrical shock treatment, but when released just slipped back to something worse than before. I drank methylated and surgical spirits, and drifted from one employment to another, keeping none for more than a few weeks. In this period I had seventy different jobs.

Suicide began to obsess me. My first attempt consisted of swallowing 220 prescribed tablets of various kinds. My physical appearance was as wretched as my health was bad. I could not be served in public houses for patrons objected even when the publican did not. I bought what I could at off-licences, consuming it in deserted alleys, on benches down by the river, even in public lavatories. Food did not matter, it rarely does to an alcoholic. There were times when I ate scraps from the litter bins.

My watch, which I had clung to because my wife had given it to me, and which seemed to be my last link with love and happiness, I sold to get drink. The doctors at the clinics regarded me as hopeless. At this time I could not cross the road in safety. I was sleeping out. Inevitably, I was charged, and hoped that by refusing to pay my fine I would find refuge in a cell. But the law would not co-operate. A station officer phoned the hospital:

'We have a man here who is in a bad way.' But when he gave them my name, they replied:

'We know him. There is nothing more we can do for him . . .'

'Nobody wants you, John,' the copper said. I went down by the river. I had a razor, but I am distressed by the sight of blood. Drowning did not appeal to me. Slowly, calmly I worked out a plan. I remember that laughing children were playing nearby. The sun was shining.

They had told me in hospital that I had not much expectation of life, and I saw myself passing on from a mental hospital or from a gutter. This bench by the river would be better. So I went to a doctor, concocted a story which resulted in his prescribing fifty sleeping tablets, and went back to my bench. After this attempt at self poisoning I woke up in hospital where they were using a stomach pump on me. Alas, I did not die. When they released me I tried again using the rest of the tablets, which they had conveniently left in my possession. Perhaps they were not lethal: the stomach pump again saved the situation.

Someone at the hospital told me that they had found a place for me, near Swindon, where I would receive the 'most advanced treatment in the country'.

After the E.C.T., narcotics, drugs and what-have you, I expected such a place to give me the works. It was a Salvation Army centre, and what I got was talk and prayers!

Naturally, I took a poor view of this. Me, with all my experience of doctors, drugs and hospitals! Yet it turned out to be right, what the almoner had said. This was 'advanced treatment'. After a while I got the idea and I was able to stop drinking for the first time in all these years.

More important, I began to be less afraid. Captain Robert Baldwin has the human touch, and he had been like I was—an out-and-out alcoholic, yet he had stopped drinking.

He taught me how to pray: that was something new and it seemed to work better than the revulsion treatment. He and Mrs. Baldwin were friendly, and so were the other chaps, alcoholics like me. The good thing about this place was that we were all in the same boat, if you know what I mean.

You know by now that I am a sleepless man. Only those who have been through it can understand what it means to lie awake night after night, although you are weary nigh unto death. I think that was why suicide fascinated me—the deep, long sleep.

Now, at Gloucester House I found I could sleep like a child and without drugs or drink. And I don't wake in sweat and fear as I used to do. I've learned a little song from the Captain: 'Get the touch of God on your soul.' They read to me the Bible,

'Come unto Me all ye that labour and are heavy laden and I will give you rest.'

It was my fault those wasted years, and the pain I caused those who loved me, although I did not know it at the time. But God has forgiven me. This is all the truth that I've told you.

11. CRIMINALS NO MORE

In India, the Salvation Army encounters different problems. In the days of British rule, an official of the British Colonial Service said to a missionary officer: 'I don't know how you live and work among these people; to us they are cattle, just cattle.'

'Sir,' the officer replied, 'to us they are immortal souls.'

He shook his head and there was some justification for his scepticism. The Doms, the Nats, the Sansias, Bhatus, Karwals and other tribes had terrorized India from time immemorial, living outside the law, born and reared in utterly amoral traditions, professional thieves, gangsters, even rapists and murderers.

Their children, upon registration at birth, were automatically classified as criminals. Their skill at crime, nurtured from one crooked generation to another, made the efforts of the police ludicrous. In the manner that a burglar would 'case the joint', make an innocent call at a home to find the lie of the land, so they would visit a village selling baskets or some such handicraft. Or they might beg, and frequently be received with compassion and aid. Yet they would return at night to steal everything from the homes of the villagers. Watch-dogs would be strangled, cattle would vanish, the few valuables of the people would disappear as if by magic from their poor rooms in which they slept.

The immensity of the country and the density of the population made the task of law enforcement impossible.

One man wrote to a police official:

'Sahib, you are a very strong and clever police officer. You have suppressed crime mightily. But, tell me, what has happened to your two good horses? Are they now in the stables? If they have gone have they been stolen? Then how could that be seeing they are so well guarded? You are such a clever policeman and you sleep near where they are stabled. Where are your horses now?'

The thief had wrapped the horses' hooves in blankets, and walked the animals out almost literally from under the official's nose. They were never recovered.

Sometimes crime was on a communal scale and had a comic opera air about it.

At Gorakpur, city of about 60,000 souls, large numbers of Doms, one of the criminal tribes, were taken to work in gangs during the day then locked up in *domrakhanas* at night. After roll call the police locked all doors, posted sentries and went wearily to their quarters. But locks, bolts and high walls were as nothing to men steeped in the lore of centuries of banditry. Moving silently as ghosts, with the keen night vision of the great cats in their jungles, they were busily engaged during the nights in the homes of the sleeping citizenry of Gorakpur.

In the morning they would be wakened by the gong, all present and correct. Naturally the crime rate for Gorakpur was highly inconsistent. The police spent many anxious hours, made many fruitless journeys, trying to find the thieves who reaped such a rich harvest in the city. Meanwhile they kept close guard over the Doms.

Asked why they must thieve they would say that it was because their ancestors had been dispossessed of their land, yet when they were given land they let or sold it.

'We have no bullocks with which to plough,' would be their complaint. When they were given bullocks they sold them and pocketed the money.

'The bullocks are no use to us, we have no seed to sow,' was their excuse. Provided with seed they ground it for flour, made it into bread and continued with a way of life that appealed to them—terrorizing large areas of the country and resisting all efforts to make decent citizens of them.

In 1908 the Salvation Army was given the task of rehabilitating as many as possible. A chain of agricultural settlements was established all over India in which farming, weaving and various other employments went side by side with schools for the children and Salvation Army halls where it was hoped the 'crims' would be persuaded to listen to stories from the Bible and perhaps also learn to pray.

In some cases drastic remedies had to be taken, including the founding of a 'Devil's Island' kind of establishment. One group of criminal tribesmen, with their wives and families, were transported to the Andaman Islands in the Bay of Bengal. The men were in chains and Major Edwin Sheard, the Salvation Army officer in charge of the party was advised to carry a gun. He was a man of only moderate stature, quiet and peaceable in disposition.

Of course it would be unthinkable for a Salvation Army officer to be armed, except with faith in God. Sheard, who carried no gun, ordered the manacles to be struck off the legs of the convicts as soon as they arrived at their destination after a 2,000-mile journey. There were dangers, outbursts of anger, threats from the 'crims', but there was something about the Sheards, their self-forgetting ministrations, that disarmed the gangsters. The missionaries remained on the Andamans for five years, developing the colony from scratch, for when they arrived not a spade had pierced the soil, not a tree had been cut, not one site surveyed.

In time, the settlement, in Sheard's words, came to be 'not unlike three peaceful English villages'. Sheard and his wife trusted God—and the convicts. Sometimes, when the 'crims' had axes in their hands, the Salvation Army officer could not help remembering that the known crime record of his 'family' stood at 300 robberies and fifty murders. Eight of his men had been sentenced to death. His cook was a murderer, three of the village policemen were convicts, the headmen of the villages had crime records longer than Major Sheard's arm.

Yet, as the days went by, the 'crims' responded to the simple and transparent Christian love of the Salvationists. On Sunday, when the bell tolled its call to worship, groups of orderly, smiling Indians would be seen going in family groups to the Salvation Army hall where the Major would lead the service. What all the might of law, what two centuries of British rule had failed to achieve, a soft-spoken Salvationist had achieved—without a revolver.

Sir John Hewett, Lieut.-Governor of the United Provinces, first approached the Salvation Army with a request that it attempt to carry out redemptive work among the criminal tribes. Afterwards he said: 'I am, however, convinced that in time the Salvation Army will succeed in the object it has in view, namely the absorption of the criminal tribes into the ordinary population. When that has been done, Commissioner Booth-Tucker and those who work with him will have combined to achieve one of the greatest moral reformations the world has ever seen.'

Succeed it did. But the Criminal Tribes Act was rescinded almost immediately India assumed control of its own destinies in 1947. Then when is a 'crim' not a 'crim'? Can he be redeemed by act of Parliament?

Congress thought so. Certainly there were social causes: gross poverty, injustice, maladministration and numerous other reasons why crime became a way of life for so many people. Social historians will long argue it out, while those who are freed from the heredity stigma of crime by legislation are still people.

At Stuartpuram, near Bapatla, for example, one of the Salvation Army's largest agricultural settlements, members of the Yerikulas were established on a criminal tribes colony in 1914. The land was swamp or poor sandy soil, 3,000 acres of it at the foot of the Eastern Ghats. Much of this was reclaimed and, as one generation followed another, as the day schools and Sunday Schools achieved their aims, as literacy increased and the Christian programme of the Salvationists bore fruit, there came into existence a huge and fertile communal farm. The desert rejoiced, the former 'crims' learned the way of holiness, the rice crops flourished where the wilderness had been.

The Salvation Army does not work by law enacted. A soul is a soul, whether it resides in a burglar or a solid, respectable member of the community. The people who had descended to the plains like the hordes of the Great Khan, and then fled to the mountain with their loot, were Salvationists now, or at least law-abiding citizens, born into Salvationist communities.

What any self-respecting social agency dreads had happened. The residue of Yerikulas, the one-time 'crims', had become 'institutionalized'. They were free to go, but they chose to stay. They had no place in modern times, the poor needy outcasts, the 'crims' of 1914. Congress said that they were free, just like any other Indian national and that the British Raj had sinned in labelling groups of people as wrong-doers.

Maybe so, but the Salvation Army could not wash its hands

of the people at Stuartpuram because they are reformed and, in many instances, Christianized. It, too, must demonstrate that it can move with the new laws, march on with the times.

The thousands of acres of land at Stuartpuram had become expensive—about 3,000 rupees an acre (£230). It was worth about 2 annas an acre when the Army acquired it: eight acres for one rupee. Everyone was misled by the discovery that the water beneath the surface of the sandy soil, and in the marshes, was brackish.

Then a Salvation Army officer, a former Straits Settlement planter, proved that below the superficial salt water level was good fresh water, plenty of it. The land rocketed in price. Where peanuts had grown rice was made to grow, and potatoes, tomatoes, coconut . . . The place prospered so much that it had its own railway station and villages sprang up like a wild west town after a gold strike. The men who had been 'crims' became policemen, postmen, builders and farmers.

Those who had been watched by police while they worked in groups akin to the chain-gangs of Mississippi, who had been compelled to go to services at the Salvation Army hall, now attended the corps by choice. They were given travel permits to leave the settlement, or cottages of their own. Men were asked if they would accept employment in the settlement factory and were paid the rate for the job. Then they began to believe that times were changing.

They read the Bible and liked it, something that millions of 'Christian' people find difficulty in doing. With that love of story-telling that characterizes the Indian, one man of the Yerikulas earned renown as a story teller, always from the Bible.

'You take your Bible with you?' an officer asked him, when he returned from one long journey.

'Oh no,' he replied, 'I know them all by heart.' This was not strictly speaking true but he is a diligent student of the great book.

There is a fairy-tale element in this story, a happy-ever-after quality that might make those wary who are versed in gloomy newspaper headlines—yet the most fantastic feature of the tale is still to come.

The valuable land at Stuartpuram is being given away to the

one-time 'crims'; parcels of irrigated, good farmland. There are brick houses now, surrounded by fertile fields. In these live today's farmers who are descended from the terrorists of yesterday. The people who were compelled to go to the Army meetings or risk police displeasure now go because they enjoy the meetings: they want to worship that God of the Christians whom they have accepted as part of a new way of life. There's brass, string and reed music of the sort beloved of Indians, and gay choruses for all to sing, hand-clapping all the while.

More often than not the leader of the meeting is an Indian, a Salvation Army officer most likely. Speakers are Indian and the intervals are taken by neatly apparelled young people's singing groups.

On Monday these same children will go to school, unlike Shakespeare's schoolboy, neither greasy nor unwilling. They wash fastidiously, though their 'crim' ancestors loathed water and were normally verminous. They want to go to school: not to be schooled is the new social stigma in India.

As the children walk they pass rice pools where the plants bend over in the breeze from the Bay of Bengal. Sometimes the children hail men high up in the coconut palms, reaping the highly profitable harvest of those prolific trees. Now and then the boys and girls move aside from the dirt road to let the bullocks go by with their load of hay.

Some are singing the chorus they learned at the Salvation Army meeting yesterday. The language is Telugu:

> santōsha maina ātma nākun-nadi
> nākun-nadi, nākun-nadi.
> santōsha maina ātma nākun-nadi
> stōtram yēsuku.

> I've got the joy, joy, joy, joy
> Down in my heart,
> Glory to his name.

You may feel it is all very odd. The British of the time of Clive and Hastings would hardly know what to make of it. Even our own Commissioner Booth-Tucker, who began it in 1882, a man of great compassion, who believed all things were possible in God's name, would doubtless be surprised in his genteel way at the dramatic metamorphosis of the 'crims'.

As for those Yerikulas, the old-time rogues and vagabonds who believed that India owed them a free and easy living, they would be most astonished of all. If their ghosts are up there in their ancient strongholds, those hills far back from the seashore, then they must marvel as they look down.

Their flesh and blood, honest, hard-working and educated. Those barren acres, fruitful and owned by their descendants. Those Sahibs, the feared and hostile regime, now accepted as friends and brothers. Most unbelievable of all, many of the Yerikulas in *Rakshana Sainyamu*—the Salvation Army. Some of them, Captains, Lieutenants, Majors, drummers, students of the Bible. It is as well that the 'crims' are safe up there with their ghostly ancestors.

12. THEY SING FOR THEIR SUPPER

Ernest Hemingway, who knew Skid Row and the bums who live among its trash cans, saloons and flophouses, once wrote of men who 'take a nose dive' at the Salvation Army in order to get free supper and board for the night.

It does happen. Every night, still, hundreds of men in American and Canadian cities pretend penitence, kneel at the penitent-form, pray, weep, and sign on the dotted line in a parody of being 'saved'. They do not mean a word of it.

But the social service officer of the Salvation Army is not as naïve as that. He knows his drifter even better than Hemingway did. 'Let them all come—*some will be saved*,' he reasons. The Salvationist programme can separate the sheep from the goats.

Probably the most remarkable operation of the traditional, direct, soul-saving sort now being carried out by the Salvation Army anywhere in the world is that undertaken for the vagrant type of man in the Bowery of New York and the Skid Row districts of other United States and Canadian cities. Thousands upon thousands of the lost and hopeless endure terrible existence in these slums. The men are often verminous, racked by disease, poisoned by rotgut spirit, unemployable, and without a friend in the world—until they go to the Harbour Light.

For many people it would be like going back in time to Moody and Sankey, Charles M. Alexander and old William Booth. Yet it is up-to-date, it costs hundreds of thousands of dollars every year, it is efficiently run and it does rescue men from despair.

It can be said to have begun with Boozer's Conventions in New York—a mass Salvationist effort to round up, capture and convert drunks in the pre-prohibition days before World War I. One of the men roped in by these efforts was a 'hopeless' alcoholic, one-time newspaper editor, Henry Milans. He had recently been discharged from Bellevue Hospital, New York,

as being an 'incurable dypsomaniac'. Milans believed he was
going to die and thought it not improper that the condemned
man should have a hearty meal. Hence the Salvation Army.

Outside the building where the drums were banging and the
lassie Salvationists were seeking to tempt drunks to drink coffee,
a large placard read: 'FREE EATS ALL DAY!' Milans went along,
ate the food, drank the coffee, but did not believe a word of it.
When he remarked to a lassie officer, 'I am a doomed man,' she
didn't believe either. She retorted, 'Jesus can cure you. He can
make a good man of you. We will pray for you.' To the average
lassie Captain such faith solves everything.

Milans did not surrender—but he did continue to attend the
services. One day the girl said to him, 'Please, don't go away
without saying goodnight. We have been praying for you. God
is going to do something for you. Come back tomorrow night.
It is better than those hard benches in that dark old park. God
bless you.'

She got through to the sick and friendless man. Some time
later, about Times Square and the roundabout newspaper offices
it was news that 'Milans got religion'. Bets were laid on the
duration of his sobriety. In fact, he remained teetotal until he
died, which, despite the doctors' death sentence, was nearly forty
years afterwards. He became a prominent lay Salvationist, winning others from alcoholism and despair, as he had been won.
His dramatic story is told in Clarence W. Hall's *Out of the
Depths*.

From this great work of uplift for the drunkard, stemmed the
Harbour Light chain of centres which began in Detroit, Michi-
gan, in 1939. There a Salvation Army officer opened a building
in the city's Rum Row. He told the 400 social misfits who
gathered: 'This is to be your church. We want you to come here
every night. Come sober if you can, but drunk if you must.
Come anyway.'

That help, in Detroit, and dozens of Harbour Lights throughout the world, is comprehensive. It includes food and lodging;
medical and psychiatric treatment; showers, delousing, clean
clothes; hospitalization if necessary; personal counselling; Christian indoctrination; group discussions; lectures on the problems
of social readjustment; a job when rehabilitation is sufficiently

advanced. There will certainly be invitations to become converted and, in many cases, these invitations will be accepted.

The Harbour Light is the Boozer's Convention of the nineteenth century restyled to the twentieth century. The mod. cons. are added, but the Bible, prayer and conversion are still the main furnishings. What Milans was to the Boozer's Convention, Tom Crocker is to the Harbour Light. This man drank himself out of a good business as a real estate agent and had to be admitted to hospital for treatment of alcoholism on more than one occasion. He is yet another example of the Boothian adage, 'Set a thief to catch a thief.'

Crocker slept under cardboard in back alleys, commenced his hunt for a livener at 6 a.m. He began to have D.T.s, lost the use of his own limbs; his health collapsed. He was a dying man when he stumbled into Detroit Harbour Light, quite uncomprehending when he knelt at the penitent-form. He was given a bath, put between clean sheets and, next morning, sober and in torment from thirst, he began to pray. 'How I prayed, no one will ever know. I wanted to live and be clean and decent again.'

Somewhere someone heard. Crocker became a Captain in the Salvation Army and, by strange irony, was required to go to the Courts to speak on behalf of men charged with drunkenness and the allied offences. In Chicago and Detroit thousands of men were placed on probation in his care. Many of them experienced religious conversion and were restored as decent citizens to their wives, families and communities. In 1952 he was acclaimed 'Chicagoan of the Year'—the city's outstanding man. It was estimated that he had helped 5,000 men to climb out of the gutter, back to self-respect. (He was also awarded the Order of the Founder, the Salvation Army's highest honour.)

'WITHIN A YARD OF HELL'

Vancouver's Harbour Light is in the Milans-Crocker tradition. Major William Leslie, who leads a remarkable work in the city, worked with Crocker in Detroit.

Vancouver is such a new, clean, busy and prosperous city that it is hard to credit the existence of its sordid social problems. Prostitution and alcoholism abound there, and the city is a focal point of the trade in heroin. In Canada's fast developing North

Pacific port seamen and lumberjacks with fat wallets frequent the saloons, and are ready victims in the old game of Samson and Delilah. Wherever prostitutes are on sale, where big money can be earned at hazardous jobs, there are bound to be social problems.

The Harbour Light work began in a small way, conditioned not by the amount of money, or the intensity of the public relations drive, but by the religious quality of the man in command. It is axiomatic in the Salvation Army that the work accomplished (or failed) depends entirely on the man (or woman) in charge.

Leslie, a dynamic man, sounds arrogant but isn't. His stock in trade includes a simple fundamentalist faith, his Bible, his evangelistic fervour, and string music. To hear his converted alcoholics strum on their banjoes and guitars, crooning a gospel song in St. Louis jazz style, is to learn that Presley, Adam Faith and the Beatles have no monopoly of music with a beat. Leslie is the leader of the band.

Although he respects Alcoholics Anonymous, and works with it, Leslie insists on more than its limited objectives. 'In this place there will be no talk of "Higher Power"', he declares—a reference to A.A. terminology, which he considers to be ambiguous. Instead, his message is based on a text such as, 'If any man be in Christ, he is a new creature. Old things are passed away . . .'

That means the drink, the dirt and despair. It works. The evidence is at the Harbour Light where the useless human flotsam and jetsam is salvaged to make twice-born men: old and lonely men, men without women, almost always men without God. Of many of these in Vancouver it can truthfully be stated after five, ten, or more years of confirmation—'All things have become new.'

Tunic off, shirt sleeves rolled back, Leslie perspires as he leads his class of converts—up to fifty of them, all with open Bibles in hand. In Leslie's harbour the Bible is the chart and compass; his men must read it. Some learn to love it. Numbers of them become Bible scholars, an incredible transformation when one remembers whence they came. 'God so loved the world. Jesus died for it. Therefore He died for you,' Leslie proclaims. He then challenges them to find documentary proof in the Bible. They do this. Woe betide the man who cannot because he has not done his homework.

In one respect Leslie is a fortunate man. He is a prophet in a land that needs his prophecy. The men make rotgut from stove polish; 'contacts' supply heroin, morphine or cocaine at a price; the Health Department notices advise where confidential treatment for venereal disease is obtainable. There are sinners right, left and centre.

'Being converted means a right-about-turn,' the Major tells them. 'I was going one way—down to hell. When I am saved I turn right-about and go the other way—to Heaven.' It all has to be checked against the Bible, and his studious alcoholics make notes as he talks.

These literary accomplishments are for the 'insider'. Later that evening the mass meeting is for about 500 'outsiders', many of them on the scrounge for supper and a bed for the night. Some of them get more than they bargained for.

The atmosphere of the place is electric. There is a Russ Conway type strumming at the piano, with rippling fingers that make hundreds of feet go tap-tap-tap. There's a violin, and Major Leslie's guitar, the 'hottest' contribution of all. When the string group sings, it becomes evident that Leslie can sing as well as he can preach, and he is a good preacher.

By the huge floodlit painting of Christ is a clock on which the minutes beat inexorably towards decision: be saved or damned. 'A man must accept the Bible. Not interpretations of it. Not scholarship about it. Forget the Dead Sea scrolls, archaeology, the highbrow literary opinions. The Bible as it is . . .'

So Leslie tells his men who listen with a dazed respect. Ten years' outstanding success in Vancouver confirms the Major's simple faith. When he came to the city he began in a small dilapidated shop premises. But he had big ideas and confidence that what he demanded of God for the outcasts of the city, God would give him. Leslie needed money, hundreds of thousands of dollars. He asked the city for it. Headquarters back in Toronto considered that he was going too fast. But Leslie said that God moved swiftly, that He was a millionaire and that the money would be forthcoming to prove it. Of course it was.

In the jam-packed meetings men stand up to testify. Their good clothes, spick and span appearance, sober demeanour is plain to see. Their lives are open books. Most of those listening have knowledge more deadly than a lie-detector machine.

No. 1: Hopeless alcoholic. Stopped drinking twenty-two months ago, been dry, non-stop, since. Takes coffee, reads the Bible regularly. Holds down a job of honest, hard work.

No. 2: In Salvation Army uniform. When he came to the city, he was in rags, verminous, with a police record. Now well dressed, healthy, quotes book of Romans. Sober two years.

No. 3: Man in grey suit. Seven-week apprentice-Christian. Yet his short term of sobriety is the longest dry period since his twenty-second birthday, many years past.

No. 4: A youth who looks rather like a beatnik, wearing suit from salvage given to the Salvation Army for the poor. Not yet in the clear. The Major interviews him regularly and reports progress.

No. 5: 'Nine years, one month, two days ago I was saved— Glory be to God!' So he begins witness. 'Before I couldn't live without liquor. Since that time, so long ago, I haven't touched a drop.' This one is in Salvation Army uniform, paid for by his own honest toil—cash down.

All this is not flash-in-the-pan revivalism. The programme takes in the doctor, psychiatrist, probation service, practical and rel'gious teaching, all supervised by Leslie's skilled eye and warm heart. He knows that some of these men are just scroungers— waiting for their supper and anything else they can beg. He knows that many are cynical—laughing at him; ready to cheat their own mother for the price of a drink.

Even the singing of some is an act, put on because they think he is watching them. Some will go out from this place, from their pretended prayers, their charade of religion, to get drunk if they can, pick a pocket or sleep with a harlot. Yet others will kneel at the penitent-form or altar, as Leslie prefers to call it.

Just now a man and wife, through Leslie's ministry re-united after years of separation, are singing:

> Burdens are lifted at Calvary
> Jesus is very near . . .

Is it any wonder that many of the men with grey faces, deep hopeless eyes, bent and broken, poisoned by alcohol, cannot believe it? Yet some chance it—philosophically. After all, what have they to lose?

The penitent-form is soon lined with men kneeling. The quiet crooning of the prayer song goes on and on . . . Leslie prays, exhorts. Though he talks in the language of the King James' Bible, has a faith as austere as John Wesley, looks like a prosperous business executive, Leslie is a man who has been their way —the broad and wicked way to hell. He ran away from home at thirteen, and was often drunk before his fourteenth birthday.

Made callous after work in a foundry he was hot-tempered, travelling fast down the rip-roaring road to violence and crime. His twentieth-century salvation had a nineteenth-century *motif*, the theme music beloved of Sankey and Moody: 'Where is my wandering boy tonight?'

He could never forget his anxious mother, never get away from the knowledge that she would be praying for him. One night, tormented by the certainty of her agonized petitions, he went to a Salvation Army meeting and, he confidently asserts, was instantaneously converted. Within a short while three of his workmates at the foundry were also 'saved'. From the first Leslie was a soul-winner in the William Booth tradition.

As a young Salvationist he saw a banner in the Army hall: GOD-FEARING MEN AND WOMEN WANTED FOR OFFICERSHIP. He entered the training college. Those who had the task of moulding him found that they had a not readily malleable character on their hands. But such men get scope in the 'free enterprise' set-up of the American mainland. Leslie survived the discipline of being appointed to a slummy unit of Salvationist work in Toronto. There he made his first large-scale acquaintance with the dypsomaniac, the drug addicts, the fallen angels of Skid Row.

Later, he was sent to his first command, Haliburton. This was a logging community where the men were harder than the trunks of the great trees they felled, fiercer than the edge of their axes. He had to learn how to handle such men. There were mistakes and it took a long time—but he learned.

Then, when a move was in process, came a brush with official-dom. By now Captain William Leslie had a vocation for work among the 'down-and-outs'. He did not care to minister to quiet, progressive, respectable communities. His 'call' was elsewhere. He wrote to Headquarters giving his superiors the benefit of his opinion. They were neither grateful nor impressed. 'The Salvation Army is quite capable of appointing its own officers to the best advantage,' they retorted. He was expected to fall into line forthwith.

For a while he hovered on the brink of resignation, a step which, in the Salvation Army, can have dire and irreparable consequences. Then Captain Tom Crocker, *the* Captain Tom Crocker, heard of young Leslie's problem—'Come on down,' he wrote from Chicago. There Leslie's morale was restored, and his call to minister to the bums of Skid Row confirmed.

It was also a lesson in protocol. By holding his hand he gave the Army time to change its mind without countenancing in-discipline, and without official loss of face. Before long Leslie was appointed second-officer to the Sherbourne Street Social Service centre in Toronto. Here there were more than enough alcoholics, ex-convicts, drug addicts, thieves and gangsters of all varieties. His superior, on this first social service appointment, Leslie now insists, was a saint. As this title is not recognized in the Salvation Army we must simply call him Brigadier Bert McBain.

In the four-and-a-half years they served together at Sherbourne Street these two dedicated men, whose toil was a round-the-clock vigil, saw over a hundred converts, and by 'convert' is meant not the mass of seekers but the minority of genuine cases of religious conversion and reformation. Three of the men, with back-grounds as tough as any, are now Salvation Army officers. Many of the others are Salvationist lay workers or church workers of various denominations.

Seeking to transfer men from the gutter to Heaven was a grim task. Yet romance pierced the gloom. Leslie had time to fall in love with Nurse Mildred Williamson of the nearby Salvation Army Grace Hospital. The nurse was, of course, an officer. In one sense, therefore, this was a marriage of convenience. Leslie was acquiring a helpmate who would assist professionally in his ministry for men whose excesses had ruined their health. God, whom Leslie knew to be a millionaire, also operated a matrimonial bureau, where blessed, happy and durable marriages are arranged.

Captain and Nurse were sure that God had arranged theirs, yet there was no retreat into the idyllic delights of domestic bliss. Leslie began to make himself a nuisance to the Army at Headquarters by constant requests to be allowed to launch a Harbour Light Corps—in United States-Captain-Tom-Crocker style.

His superiors, who sympathized with Leslie's urge to emulate the Americans in rescue work for the bums, were busy men and harassed, as are most Salvation Army executives, by lack of funds.

Ten months went by, therefore, with young Leslie straining at the reins and foaming at the mouth. There were those who did not want the Harbour Light in Canada; they considered it a duplication of existing social services. Besides, it was new: some officers in the Salvation Army are very conservative. So Leslie acted, out of line. He began his own unofficial Harbour Light. Then a newspaper made a front-page story of one of his cases: THE BIG HEART OF THE SALVATION ARMY, with numerous column-inches of detail about a rescued family. Leslie not only helped the man, he provided food and clothing for the family, and found him a job.

There was a stir about this and the Army allowed itself to be convinced that it would be best to give young Leslie a slack rein. He was told, 'You can begin your Harbour Light at Vancouver. There we have a small centre for drunks and drifters. It is no great credit to us. Make it or break it.'

As he reconnoitred his new assignment his courage and determination were needed. Without them he might have taken the train back East where he had left his disconsolate young wife. The centre was an old cigar store, too small, dilapidated and with grossly inadequate equipment. But 'do it yourself' is also a

Boothian principle; Salvation Army officers are not expected to wait for equipment, premises, or money to be provided. Leslie pre-cooked the stew for the queue of workless drifters who came at nights. He used the back room of the old shop as a chapel.

From the first the Captain was the key; not money, bricks and mortar, or even public support. He went looking for a fitting centre for his operations. He had twenty-five men: he envisaged caring for hundreds. He told the Army about large, suitable premises he had found. 'Get the money, then you have permission to buy,' they said. Soon Leslie had his converted tramps praying that God would send the cash—he always had regarded Heaven as his inexhaustible bank. In the mail, one morning shortly afterwards, were 5,000 dollars worth of bonds. Other sums came too. He moved out of his cigar store into larger premises— the first move in a big property expansion, made necessary by ever-increasing need.

Soon the new premises were inadequate. Next door was a large garage. Leslie coveted it as a chapel. Headquarters in Toronto were sympathetic, but there were no cheques. They now say in Vancouver that as a result of Leslie's prayers the garage company went bankrupt. Leslie and his men did pray: the company did go bankrupt. Connection between the two might, of course, be coincidental. On the other hand, it might not. Certainly the premises were soon on the market—price 60,000 dollars.

He had 10,000 dollars in balance but no credit or collateral for the remainder. Leslie heard of a human bank manager, a man with a heart who went to church on Sundays. This worthy he telephoned; the man advanced 50,000 dollars. The conversion of the old garage, fitting it up as a chapel cost 50,000 dollars. That same Bible on which he placed such great emphasis, and which he made compulsory reading among his converts stated: 'Owe no man anything'—yet here he was 50,000 dollars in debt. He was, of course, well aware that the Salvation Army frowned on officers who contracted debts.

'We must pray,' he told his growing force of ex-drunks, thieves, wife-beaters, drug addicts.

The money came in: they bought their garage. But still, as with all Harbour Light leaders, he found himself embarrassed,

harassed by his very success. Every convert was a potentially
good citizen, but the after-care problem was a financial problem
to tax the resources of a Ford or Rockefeller.

When the convert must leave the protective environment of
the Salvation Army, the grim and lonely room which he rents
houses a legion of devils. Even the shaving lotion has an alcoholic
base. If the doctor prescribes liniment for neuralgia, to which
alcoholics are prone, there is alcohol in that which can be dis-
tilled. The stove polish, 'canned heat', which the landlady forget-
fully leaves about, can be rendered into a potent and poisonous
drink.

Major Leslie told the people about this problem. He and his
men were praying for a miracle to solve it.

The miracle was a farm. The cost, in hard currency, 85,000
dollars. The metaphysical element consisted of the acceptance of
such a fantastic idea as credible, and the well-nigh incredible
means by which the money was forthcoming.

Major Leslie's bunch of 'no-hopers' had already cost a small
fortune. The generous citizenry of Vancouver had many other
calls upon their philanthropy, and they had already dipped deep
into their pockets. They had given for the new premises for the
Harbour Light, for the new beautiful chapel next door. They
had provided trucks, cars, clinic, medical assistance, a generous
annual budget. What more could they do?

But if Leslie was greedy it was on behalf of those moved by a
divine urge to find a way out of the abyss into which they had
fallen. On TV, as a public relations specialist on the side of the
angels, he aimed again at the bank balances of the citizens of
Vancouver. In the columns of newspapers, edited by men who
refute the oft-encountered allegation that journalists are cynical
and callous, he was given space to make his plea. The people
responded. Vancouver agreed that work that had progressed so
far should not be spoiled at the last for lack of funds. The money
came in—or perhaps a calf, a cow, a chlorination plant for the
swimming pool. With the blessing and support of Headquarters
in Toronto, Major Leslie bought 'Miracle Valley' and the farm
upon it.

But one victory always leads on to the next battle. Leslie is a
fighter in an Army. 'The green pastures', 'the quiet waters' of

Biblical imagery, hardly seem appropriate. In his office are framed these words:

> Some wish to live within the sound
> Of church or chapel bell;
> I want to run a rescue shop
> Within a yard of hell.

13. WOMEN DRUG-ADDICTS

The lethal trade in narcotics provides the supplier with big easy money. In most cities, therefore, particularly those linked by sea with the Far East, traffic in dope flourishes despite all efforts of law-enforcement agencies. The Salvation Army finds addiction to drugs a tragic impediment in its attempt to save women and girls who are in moral danger. The compulsion of an addict to obtain a 'fix' is so intense that nothing can stand in its way: the girl will steal, lie, or sell herself. Obtaining money by false pretences is one of the more familiar items entered on the charge sheets of girls before the courts. The pimp or brothel keeper, even the bell-boy at an hotel, who may act as agent for a call-girl, wields tremendous power over the victim of this habit because he can obtain supplies of the drugs she must have at any price.

Marijuana is not physiologically habit-forming, but it can become psychologically necessary to its victim, and is often the preliminary to the deadlier forms of drug-addiction. It is a provider of dreams—wonderful escapist fantastic dreams, which release the unhappy nonentity from her drab world, substitute her sense of rejection, her poverty and frustration for rosy, marvellous illusions of grandeur.

The marijuana 'pot' is sometimes handed around at schools; it has an aphrodisiacal effect so that physical chastity can be an early casualty. In trouble with the law, in trouble at home, or finding herself to be pregnant, the 'pot' taker is ready prey for the pimp, gangster, blackmailer or brothel keeper and abortionist. She is outside the law: she must have protection. This she must pay for.

About fifteen dollars a day is the price of three 'fixes' of heroin in New York. When, as often happens, the one time schoolgirl smoker of reefers becomes addicted to heroin— eventually a 'junky'—then she will be a moral anarchist—anything goes. For a brief while, when young and pretty, the money for dope comes in readily. There's always a man, or men, or madams who arrange appointments with men.

But the drug-addict, more than most, is subject to the law of diminishing returns. Heroin plays havoc with health, for one reason particularly: the victim normally does not eat anything like sufficient food. Also, she forgets to groom herself and in her trade appearance is highly important. She may be a 'tramp', but she mustn't look like one. She often forgets to keep an appointment, not because of sudden moral scruple, but because she is in a doped stupor.

Then she is erased from the bell-boys' lists at the hotels and will be no longer *persona grata* with the agents in sex. The money runs out and she is likely to do something foolish: larceny, false pretences, soliciting. This will bring her before the courts, and often, to the initial disgust of some of the girls, into association with the Salvation Army.

Brigadier Dorothy Berry, of New York, who is well known and influential in this field, finds that the ravages of drug addiction have usually reached alarming proportions by the time the Army is called in. There may be a more or less acute mental condition, severe malnutrition, even venereal disease. There can be few more difficult tasks than trying to rescue such a girl.

The girl will, as a matter of course, be friendless, for her addiction makes her a beggar, always scrounging for loans which she does not repay. Sometimes she is so far lost to self-respect that she does not even keep herself or apartment clean. Landladies are reluctant to rent their poorest rooms to a known 'junky'. All this, and much besides, makes the assignment of rehabilitating a drug addict a long and laborious one. Victims come from various sources to the Army. Sometimes it is the friend or relation who can no longer tolerate the tantrums, the hysteria and unpredictable behaviour, and who has little or no understanding of drug addiction.

The Salvation Army's Publicity Department for New York is highly efficient, modelled on the American concept of letting all the world know what goes on, and no soft pedals. Everyone in New York, or in any other American city for that matter, knows what the Salvation Army does for the needy. Letters and phone calls descend upon the Salvationists at the various H.Q.'s in a non-stop avalanche.

Judges, or their probation officers, will ask the Army to assist in a particular case. A Roman Catholic priest, who has found long since that the Army is not in business to steal other people's sheep, will refer a girl to the Army. The girl may telephone, herself: reluctant, nervous, incoherent. She is often at the last ditch between herself and suicide. She has been told: 'Why don't you try the Sally Army? They help. I know because . . .'

When she arrives at the office of Brigadier Dorothy Berry, she is put in the charge of a professional caseworker. The girl is reticent and ready to run at the slightest provocation. The Salvationists tread warily. They are in a sense the secret service of the Army. The girl may give a false name, or refuse to give a name. Behind her in the shadows, deep in her mind and still a factor in her life is lawlessness: a pander, 'protector', a thousand nameless fears. She is more ashamed at having to ask the Salvation Army for help than she is of being a drug addict.

The Salvationists know and understand. They calmly put down the name they assume to be false, or insert a number if the girl refuses to give any name at all. Their first aim is to aid victims, not to get their filing system right. Though she be a cipher on paper, to the officers she is a soul to save, a challenge to accept in God's name.

Care is a round-the-clock assignment. From the time she becomes the concern of the Salvationists, there can be no let-up. Sometimes it is rather like protecting a witness on one of the notorious gangster trials—the girl has to be shielded from links with her past, from pimps and other undesirable contacts, from the importunities of peddlars of drugs who dislike losing a customer.

Sometimes the Army accepts responsibility for a girl who is leaving the Women's House of Detention to which she will have been sentenced for an offence connected with narcotics. The Salvation Army will have visited the girl regularly, and it also conducts frequent chapel services. Often the girls react favourably to this. Certainly health and mental condition improve greatly whilst in prison.

Upon her release the girl will be met by Salvationists. They will supply her rail ticket, find her lodgings, get her a job. The latter is no small task for, in many instances, parole requirements are that the would-be employer must be told of the girl's record, and that she is on parole. Even so the task is achieved, for the Salvation Army in New York has wide influence. The girl is able to start life afresh. The words 'rescue the perishing' are seldom sung now, even in the Salvation Army. But they enshrine a first principle which is still the motivation of the Salvation Army.

Take the case of Antonia Paressa. She was a dark-eyed, raven-haired girl of medium height, Italian extraction and in her early twenties. Her troubles began in an unhappy home, in the dark alleys of the slums of the Bronx, and at school where she made her first acquaintance with reefer cigarettes—marijuana. In her unhappy record there was sexual assault by an adult, who was sent to prison, plus such reckless indifference by her parents that the girl was taken away and placed with foster parents.

These well meaning people, clean and prosperous, were anxious to do the right by Antonia. But there was no real affection, rather a zealous 'do-goodism'. From the first, the girl's sophistication was too much for them; she could deceive them too easily. When she was supposed to be at classes designed to make her a refined young lady, she was, in fact, listening to juke boxes, consorting with the tough and promiscuous members of a teen-age street gang. Her descent was rapid. From reefers she graduated to heroin for which she had to pay—with prostitution.

When her foster parents heard even part of what had been happening, they were so horrified that they insisted on the girl being removed at once. Antonia solved their problem by decamping, living rough, working at times as a waitress but getting money also in less respectable ways. By now she was a 'junky'. She had to have heroin regularly.

When the Army first met Antonia she had been before the courts for soliciting and it was known that she was on dope. She was hostile for a number of weeks, and there were a number of backslidings before the Salvationists were able to win a degree of confidence and find her a job and an apartment. The physical change in the girl was astonishing, not only in her health which improved rapidly, but in her appearance. The girl who had been unkempt, pale, dirty, was quite pretty—transformed from the kitchen drab to beautiful Cinderella at the Prince's ball.

Most social work officers of the Salvation Army treasure letters from people they have tried to help. In Brigadier Berry's file, at the New York Headquarters, are a number of letters from Antonia. One reads as follows:

'I send you a snapshot of my daughter with my husband and myself. When I think of how it was in those dreadful bygone days, and how it is now, I can hardly believe it has really happened. We are so happy together, and Teresa is such a darling. We go to church as you told me. Best of all, my husband knows, yet loves me all the same! Thank you for your letter. We know you are our friend, and we are yours . . .'

But not all who come into the Army's New York orbit are saved from drugs, alcohol, or prostitution. The hardened prostitute is a particularly stubborn problem. When they are young, they are prosperous. Sometimes good work is done in prevention, but once the madams or men behind the scenes get the girl in their toils and she is launched on her 'career', then it is almost impossible to break their hold. The next stage is at the end, sometimes fewer than ten years, when she has lost her looks, her youth, her physical appeal which is her sole stock in trade. Many lonely, wretched women of this sort are to be found in the world's cities.

However, there are cases of a girl breaking out and away to become a good wife and respectable citizen in some country town or suburb where her past can never catch up with her:

'Oh, I'm all right. I don't intend to be in this business long. I'm saving fast. Soon I'll have enough to pay my part on a house. I have a steady boy-friend down in Alabama. We write regular.' The prostitute who spoke those words is by no means unique.

Many social work officers of the Salvation Army have heard the lady of easy virtue speak in that way and have later had her statement confirmed. There are always the exceptions and sometimes the astonishing 'break through' that makes everything worthwhile.

SHE CARRIED A GUN

We can call her Mollie. She had gone through the gamut of

folly when she drifted into New York, before her twenty-first birthday.

In her small town, up-state, she had shamed herself and her family by finding herself pregnant while still at school. Her main offence was that this dread secret became public property. Though the baby was adopted she found she couldn't stay at home to face her mother's reproachful eyes and undergo her father's incessant tirades. She fled. No tears were shed on either side.

The one thing the girl needed was a sense of belonging: this she had never known. On the city streets, in the cinemas, the cafés and clubs that made up the jungle of Broadway, she was soon a hustler, disillusioned and cynical. She was also a drug addict. Later Brigadier Berry met her in a State prison.

The girl had found love at last—a gangster's love. She carried a gun for him. Punishment for the criminal found with a weapon is particularly severe, so that the 'gunman's moll' has a precise function in the criminal's struggle with the police.

It seemed a price she could pay. A flat of her own, a man of her own; just for carrying his gun before and after the robbery.

One day, when the gangster held up a drug store, the man behind the pay desk resisted. He was shot. So was the gangster. Paralysed with fright, Mollie forgot to run. She was sentenced to thirty years in jail.

She had no one now. She withdrew into herself, making good use of the prison library, as lonely as if she were the only person on earth. Her parents stayed safely and respectably up-country. But the passing years in prison revealed that Mollie had a good mind, a capacity for life that no one had ever discovered, least of all Mollie herself. After ten years, still young and pretty, sensible and suitably chastened, she applied for parole. It was refused as first applications often are.

But she went on using the library. Brigadier Berry knew about her, for the Salvation Army is represented on the Parole Board and is a friend of the friendless. The Brigadier became convinced that the girl was worthy of another chance. When the second application came up she made proposals on behalf of the girl. The Army would help her. Parole was granted.

When Mollie came out through the big, high doors, into a world that had changed so much, she was not the same woman. In her case prison had been a place of moral and spiritual rehabilitation.

As she sat back in the cab she said to the Salvationist who had met her, 'I want to do something—something useful. It must be work for lepers.'

If she had stated a wish to be the first American woman astronaut the Salvationist could not have been more astonished. She began to tell the girl the practical difficulties, the distant geographical location of leprosy, the high cost of training . . .

It was all beside the point. The girl knew about leprosy. She felt she was an expert on it. She had read it up in prison. She had made her resolve. She was going to give the rest of her life to work for victims of leprosy.

After much hard, devoted and unselfish effort, during which the Salvation Army rendered every assistance possible, she became the Executive Chairman of a group in Washington D.C. which aids leper victims. She is also, incidentally, happily married. There are silver linings even in the dark sky of the underworld of women.

SALVATIONIST SECRET SERVICE

The Catherine Booth Home in Vancouver is a quiet house on a hill giving a breath-taking view of Pacific bays and islands, with the snow-capped mountains in the distance. But Brigadier Dorothy Barwick and Major Phebe Bolton, officers-in-charge, have little time for admiring the view. They operate a clinic for women in association with the Vancouver Narcotics Foundation.

Sometimes, when a mother is on drugs and there is no one suitable at home, the children must come too. The work is of the 'secret service' sort. Family relationships, 'skeletons in the cupboards', and the laws of libel make discretion highly necessary. Yet it is possible to gain an idea of what goes on in this rich-looking house, surrounded by flowers, trees and green lawns— a more fitting locale, one would think, for polite drawing-room meetings or church garden parties than the agonies of withdrawal from drugs, or the forlorn hope of rescuing a prostitute.

Simone, who is a patient here, though but twenty-four is

already divorced. She came after hospitalization for acute drug addiction, and the malnutrition which is a concomitant. She had lived with various men—the familiar pattern. With three 'fixes' a day, each costing about eight dollars, almost any man would do if he could provide the money.

The latest partner was a sailor, who knew not what Simone had been, and cared not, if she would be his woman. He was in funds, and in return Simone was a reasonably good housekeeper. All went well until she found she was going to have a child. This was not in the agreement, and her consort hied him away to sea again. Simone's arrest for soliciting followed.

It shocks one to find that Booth provided drugs *gratis* while Simone's withdrawal treatment was continued. In fact, the Salvationists who administer narcotics know that rehabilitation would not be possible without this policy of gradualism, which is carried out under medical supervision.

Even so it is a nightmare task. As the dosage is reduced the girl suffers mental and physical torments. When Simone could not have the dope she wanted drink—a transition from the frying pan to the fire that is not uncommon. The only concession Booth would make to the poor girl's torment was a cigarette. Only by such firmness could Simone be saved.

As the baby's entrance into the world became imminent he began to exercise a strong influence on his mother who uttered that phrase, the like of which is absolutely essential before a Salvationist can help the fallen in any worthwhile way:

'Brigadier, I know I'm a bad girl. What must I do . . . ?'

The officers began to show her. She was given sedatives to induce sleep and the good diet she needed to build up her damaged bodily resources, 'for the baby's sake', they said, and it was a potent argument. Phone calls from old cronies were refused. Simone was in a prison of salvation.

The unborn child was already affecting Simone in other ways than biological. She began to think of her fitness to be a mother. How could she rear him? (She was sure she would have a boy, and she did.) The girl was intelligent and, now that her health was somewhat restored, not unattractive in appearance.

Here was another of those buried personalities, one who needed only the right stimuli to awaken like the Sleeping Beauty to astonish everyone. One quiet Sunday evening, at Booth, listening to the music of a hymn, hearing the Bible read, Simone found herself responding to religion in a way that surprised her. She began to believe that she might begin again. The officers told her that God would forgive—and forget—what had happened.

She would never forget, she knew that. Her drunken father, her miserable home, her foolish, wanton teenage search for love among those who made a mockery of love . . . She was a Catholic. Odd though it may seem, she found nothing incongruous that her religious conversion was taking place here in this Salvation Army home. She went to the Army's nearby Grace Hospital for the baby to be born. There the Matron and others of the staff are officers. Most of the nurses are Christians. It came to pass that two great blessings were given to Simone—a new baby and a new faith.

Now she prays, something she ceased to do when she was thirteen. The Army found a job for her, an employer who had sympathy with the girl's problem. As always, at Salvation Army homes, there is an old members' association. Those who have been in are encouraged to maintain contact. Among the letters received gladly, an occasional visit, a phone call, those that give particular pleasure are from Simone. She is doing well.

Theoretically it should not matter if Salvation Army officers never succeed in winning souls. It is the seeking to which they are dedicated. They are not guaranteed a harvest for their toiling. Yet Salvationists are human beings. They pray for strength when some seeds fall by the wayside and are devoured and all their work is in vain. They thank God, and are encouraged when, as with Simone, one plant stands and grows, a proof of God's salvation.

Sometimes the woman caught in the toils of drugs or drink is a respectable matron, her dilemma hidden by her family. There are said to be about 200,000 of these on the American continent. Sarah's husband bore the burden of her alcoholism until, so people say, he died of grief. Her two daughters were distraught and shamed.

She had been to Booth before and was so intractable that, when the courts referred her there again, the Brigadier refused to admit her. However, the magistrate persisted. 'She says she will come only to you. You cannot fail her,' they said. Of course the Brigadier could not.

Sarah's body was a mass of bruises, inflicted by her latest paramour. Her daughters, ashamed, had left the city.

This one-time proud, well-educated woman was unwashed and clothed in rags. Nursing her back to health was a lengthy operation, and Sarah was told that another experience like this would kill her. It was her last. Not twenty per cent of the stories end this way, but Sarah's did—she was 'saved', as Salvationists say.

Afterwards, even after she left Booth, she attended one meeting a week. One day, while the Brigadier was speaking, Sarah interrupted:

'Please, please let me say something! I do feel that something wonderful has happened to me . . .'

Sarah is not now recognizable as the drab woman who broke up her home, ruined her family. Any week-end she can be found shopping among the prosperous housewives in Vancouver's super-markets. She is indistinguishable from any other of Canada's decent women.

About prostitutes the officers at Booth take a realistic view: 'They respond, they often make temporary improvement. But unless their basic problem is solved, a tremendously difficult task, then they do not experience religious conversion which is the only way we know for them to be reclaimed from the life they are living.'

Chief among the causes of prostitution, Brigadier Barwick puts emotional starvation.

'These poor girls sell "love" in a futile attempt to find love, something of which they have been deprived all their lives.'

Others of them are merely lazy women to whom prostitution is easy money. Some are silly teenage girls, seduced by lumber-jack or sailor with ample cash. When they are deserted by him they drift into one of the red light establishments round and about Vancouver's Skid Row.

14. THE SICK, O LORD . . .

There are two main groups of hospitals operated by the Salvation Army.

First the missionary hospitals.

They number about seventy-five, though a few are hardly more than clinics. Some specialize in one ailment, such as leprosy, tuberculosis, bone, skin or eye diseases.

They are to be found in Africa, India, Indonesia, Malaysia, Korea, Mexico, the Philippines, South America and the West Indies.

These cost about £500,000 a year to maintain, though much of the money is forthcoming from patients' fees and Government grants. More money must be found for them each year for the cost of healing rises alarmingly and they are a heavy drain upon Army finances.

As one might expect, the Salvationist hospital service of India makes up by far the largest item in this expenditure. Treatment of tuberculosis and leprosy, with aid for the victims of malnutrition, the high incidence of eye diseases and other maladies, call for more men, women and money than is available. Scurvy, rickets, beri-beri and pellagra are all endemic. These are, of course, deficiency diseases.

Secondly the community service hospitals. These accept private patients and are the kind of hospitals that can render traditional Salvation Army services yet finance themselves.

These 'commercial' hospitals sometimes make a Salvationist frown at what seems to be merely provision for the well-to-do. But the hospitals were founded in less affluent times, when poverty was widespread and efficient medical services in short supply. Apart from this the paying patient also 'has a soul' as old-timers would have put it. The very poor and the comfortably off should all come alike to the Salvationist.

By far the largest group of public service hospitals is located throughout the United States where they are usually named Booth Memorial Hospitals. The large unit at Flushing, New York, is a noteworthy example of this kind of Salvationist medical centre.

The Grace chain of hospitals in Canada are next in size. They are large, well-equipped and utilized by the average citizens of prosperous townships. The new hospital at Winnipeg rivals Flushing hospital for cost and modernity. It would be considered a tremendous asset in any community in any country.

There are numerous general, or general plus maternity hospitals in Australia, South Africa, Switzerland, France, Sweden, Japan and elsewhere. Many of these, as in the United States and Canada, have separate wings or annexes for maternal service to unwed mothers. In that case there will probably be, more or less adjacent, a home or hostel where the women or teenage girls will spend some four to five months in the Army's care before the child is born.

The Salvation Army's tradition of hospital service, to a great extent, owes its existence to this 'rescue' work, as such efforts for unwed women were termed years ago. From it, also, stemmed the Army's many homes for infants and older children, for it was often found that the baby born in the Army hospital became the Army's baby in a long-term sense, adoption being not then so conveniently arranged. To this day, in some countries, it is not uncommon for the mother to abscond leaving the Army to hold the baby.

Nursing is probably the woman Salvationist's first choice of profession; many Army women make it their life's vocation and it goes without saying that the common-sense variety of religion motivating such devotion usually makes for good nurses. A like disposition to medical missionary work for men is not so widespread, probably because a doctor's qualifications are much harder to achieve.

The famine of doctors, created by the lack of sufficient young and qualified men and women Salvationists, has in the past been aggravated by serious losses for, as one might expect, tension is apt to arise between rather strict Salvation Army discipline and the ethos of the medical profession.

As a rule doctors insist on managing their own affairs: the

Disciplinary Committee of the British Medical Council, for example, deals with erring doctors of the British Medical Association. Similar professional 'closed shops' exist in most countries. The Salvation Army Colonel or Commissioner is apt to look at things quite differently from the way the scientifically-trained doctor will look at it. The blind, unquestioning obedience of the zealous Salvationist, oft sung about in a phrase such as 'My all is on the altar', comes not so readily to the medical man, at least with regard to his profession. For him the operative word may be not with the General, the Chief-of-the-Staff, or the Territorial Commander, but in the learned journals of the British Medical Association, the American Medical Association, and other medical publications.

But the Army is always willing to learn. Anxious to help its officer doctors, the Army has now established a Medical Mission-ary Section at I.H.Q., in London. The Salvation Army officer-doctor in charge co-ordinates the world-wide work, concerns himself with the recruitment of medical reinforcements, tries to find essential new equipment and supplies.

In the past, the anxiety of a doctor not to become out-of-date has been given insufficient weight in the Army. Any doctor worth the name needs refresher courses, time for extended leave to work under a specialist or to study and work for a further qualification. The medical liaison man in London, highly-qualified himself, sees the validity of this wish of any good doctor to keep abreast with developments in surgery and medicine.

Lack of men is the great problem. New steps are being taken to counter it. The Army is now showing an increased disposition to allow non-officer doctors, even non-Salvationists, to serve for one, two, three or more years. In the past it has been assumed that officers alone could have the full sense of vocation and devotion required for such self-sacrificial toil. Already there is evidence that this is not so. The enlistment of specialist non-Salvationists is even more a startling idea in which the Salvation Army in Japan played a pioneer role. There is no doubt that the ecumenical movement, the thinner walls between various denominations, has made it less difficult for a non-Salvationist to work happily in a Salvationist team. So the idea is gaining ground that a Salvationist who is not an officer can be 'called' to special work for God. And that someone not a Salvationist can have Christian faith and zeal at least equal to the Salvationist. These are great victories indeed along the 'New Frontier' of the Salvation Army.

The Mothers' Hospital, Clapton, London, a Salvation Army service within a Welfare State, is considered in the following chapters, together with a missionary hospital in India and a general hospital in the United States.

Wherever it is, of whatever kind, if the hospital is operated by the Salvation Army then the motivation will be the same as that enshrined in the hymn:

> *At even, ere the sun was set,*
> *The sick, O Lord, around Thee lay;*
> *O in what divers pains they met!*
> *O with what joy they went away!*

15. LEPROSY PATIENTS ARE PEOPLE

My name is K. C. Joseph, a Lieut.-Colonel in the Salvation Army. I am Indian and Medical Superintendent at the Evangeline Booth Leprosy Hospital in Kerela State, India. I find the relevance of the Army abundantly demonstrated here in modern India.

We are solving many problems in this newly independent land, but we still have about two million victims of leprosy. This medical settlement of which I have charge is filled with them. We are also a farm and training centre, where weaving and various crafts are taught. Our hospital buildings and the farm embrace six hills, with seven fertile valleys between. All the workers are leper patients, for one of the worst things would be for such people to feel helpless, useless. We therefore encourage them to grow mango, corn, rice, tapioca, bananas, coconut and many other vegetables.

This fertility, this cycle of seed-time and harvest, illustrates what is happening here. In the old days Puthencruz used to be the place of doom. It was the accursed cemetery for the murdered, the suicides, the victims of smallpox, cholera, of any death by violence. People avoided it, for only the ghosts, the evil spirits, resided here. Now the victims of leprosy come, they clamour at our gates feeling that they are unclean, just as the lepers did in the time of Jesus.

And just as it was with Him, we can reprieve them from the imminence of death. About eighty per cent of them are cured by the new sulphone drugs.

Because we are the Salvation Army, we seek to cure their souls as well as their infected bodies, their afflicted minds. When they come they are distraught because of the belief many of them have that leprosy is a sign of the wrath of Heaven—*Karma*. They doubt whether there are effective remedies. Beneath their silent and stoical impassivity lies a deep sense of guilt. Many of them are Hindu and feel that the sins for which they are being punished were committed in another life. They have all lived by previous births.

We know the real culprit. His name is *lepra bacillus*, discovered by Hansen—hence the newer name for this curse, Hansen's Disease.

We say: 'You are not lepers, just hospital patients; you will get better. You have a bug, we can kill him like any other bug—like the TB bug.'

In the old days millions in India just lay down and died when they had tuberculosis. Now, because of a marvellous new treatment, they live. So it is with leprosy.

Many of my patients are young. Leprosy is a disease of youth, passed on in close and prolonged contact between mother and child, by family relationships. It is nowhere near as infectious as most people imagine it to be. It separates husband and wife, for leprosy is grounds for divorce. It sometimes estranges a mother from her children, for they cannot shake off the old superstition that it cannot be cured, that it is shameful. Now physiotherapy can prevent deformities of hands and feet after the sulphones have killed the disease. Plastic surgery can correct facial scars; delicate operations can restore movement to immobilized fingers or feet. This ancient enemy is being defeated. The Salvation Army takes care not to be left behind by the march of time.

We move. We began in India as part of the British 'establishment'. The pioneer here, former judge in the Indian Civil Service, Major Fredk. Tucker, who began Army work in 1882, would be astonished, yet pleased I think, to note that the leader in this vast Southern India Territory, a Commissioner, eminent man indeed, is Indian. His subordinate is British, a complete reversal of roles.

The staff of this hospital is 100 per cent Indian—medical, nursing, physiotherapist, dispenser; ward orderlies, dressers, supervisors and many other workers are all Indian. In my time we have treated thousands of patients, the vast majority successfully. There are 200 of them with us at the moment.

Most of my patients can read and write. We supply copies of half-a-dozen daily papers and the Government subsidizes our library of 1,500 books. Our patients are people. They matter to us, to God, to India.

Though money is in very short supply, and there are many items of equipment that we need, with additional staff to use them, much is done to give comfort to the leprosy patients. Some of them live in their own cosy cottages with roses round the door. There is little or no atmosphere of dread, the hopelessness and horror associated with leprosy in olden times. Instead there are optimistic discussions about adjusting to life outside when they walk out of the hospital, and how sad it was that the old people did not know about the vulnerable *lepra* bug, but just became frightened so that many of them simply lay down and died.

Our many child patients go to school. They smile happily on their way. In class we say to them:

'Leprosy does not exist because of the evil people do, but because they do not know about being clean and because they are afraid to tell the doctor quickly. They hide their malady. That is ignorant. This is because they think it brings shame upon them. But leprosy is not shameful: it is just a complaint that can be cured, especially if one gets at it in good time.

'We must all help to rid India of this malady, just as we are removing tuberculosis from India. Treatment, drugs, methods of prevention grow stronger every day. You must help.' They do help.

Not that I put forward this place as a one-way road to health and happiness. Some of the older people are permanently invalided upon us. They are the pre-sulphone patients, drastically damaged by the disease before they came to us, so crippled, or otherwise deformed, that they cannot be helped by modern treatment.

Even then we can do something worthwhile. Here at Puthencruz the *raison d'être* is God. We function on prayer and faith. We teach people to read the Bible. It is a real if somewhat sombre satisfaction to me as a Salvationist that when I tender the last consolations to a woman who lived too soon, before the benefits of Hansen's search could be given to her, I can commend her to that Heavenly Hospital where all are cured, where there shall be no more pain, as the Bible says.

I can hear her say: 'Thank you. I have no fear. They are coming soon to take me home.'

When our General William Booth sent Major Tucker to invade India, he was not thinking of the ancient malady that ravaged my country long before its invasion by that other General, Alexander the Great. Our Founder had one obsession, saving souls.

We have the best of both worlds, thanks to God. All this and Heaven too. They come to us for healing of their stricken bodies, shy and full of fear, their dark eyes imploring, just as the lepers came to Jesus long ago. What they seek, even when they are afraid, too inarticulate to give it words, is that same blessing: 'Lord, if Thou wilt Thou canst make me clean.'

Our reply is not with words. Action is needed now. Yet the end, for most of them, is the same as when He said:

'I will. Be thou clean.'

16. NEW FACES FOR OLD

At the gate the poor were waiting,
Looking through the iron grating,
With that terror in the eye
That is only seen in those
Who, amid their wants and woes
Hear the sound of doors that close
And feet that pass them by.
Grown familiar with disfavour,
Grown familiar with the savour
Of the bread by which men die.

HENRY WADSWORTH LONGFELLOW

It cost a great deal of money to make it possible for me to have a new nose.

When the young are scarred by Hansen's Disease it is worse for them than for the old folk. The doctors say that the infection is killed but what use is this if your lip or nose is eaten away? I am nineteen. I was pretty before the malady came to me. Afterwards my face horrified people and my prospect of marriage was gone for ever. In India a girl might as well be dead.

Then someone said to me, 'Go to the Catherine Booth Hospital of the Salvation Army at Nagercoil. The doctor there makes new faces . . .'

This missionary hospital is in Madras State, South India, and although I did not believe anything could be done for me, for my country teems with people who bear the marks left by this curse that eats away the flesh, I applied for admission. After some delay, because they are always crowded, I was accepted for plastic surgery.

The doctor who does this thing is one of a number of doctors at the place, which is as large as a town. His name is Williams, Harry Williams, and he is an officer in the Salvation Army, a Lieut.-Colonel. The letters after his name are many. These I do not understand.

When I went in I passed a horde of people waiting outside the gates. This happens in India. If one of the family must go to hospital then twenty relatives will accompany him, loitering about the place, worrying and chattering until the patient gets better or dies. In the old days they used to clutter up the wards and corridors and all the space inside the hospital compounds. Now that this is prohibited the families camp out in a large open *dharmsala* in one corner of the compound. They sleep there, cook little meals over wood fires, and wait impatiently until the nurses allow them into the wards to see their relatives.

Inside every bed is occupied. Babies are being born, although India already has more than she knows what to do with; hundreds of patients are receiving medicines and many surgery; nurses are being trained, doctors and staff kept busy in private and public wards. The children's wings, the annexe for tuberculosis patients, the operating theatre, eye wards, lecture rooms and much else is agog from dawn to dark and after. It must cost millions of rupees to maintain. Much of the money comes from America, Britain and other places abroad, but some comes from the Government of India. This must indicate, don't you think, that Congress approves of the work of the Salvation Army?

Before I tell you what this doctor did I must explain that during World War II many fliers were badly burned in crashes. Then great surgeons developed the art of skin-grafting and transplanting. Doctor Harry Williams, who gave me my new nose, went to England to a town called East Grinstead where Battle of Britain pilots received plastic surgery from Sir Archibald McIndoe and those working with him. In this art, and under this teacher, Doctor Williams became a specialist and what he did to me is this:

He lifted a flap of skin on my forehead, smooth skin not scarred by Hansen's Disease. This he twisted into a tube, grafting the end of it to the place where my nose had been. This was not very painful when I first came round from the anaesthetic, but you will readily understand that I now appeared even more revolting than before, for I had what looked rather like an elephant's trunk growing out of my forehead and stuck to my nose! I could not understand why my thigh was painful until the nurse told me that half the thickness of the skin there had been taken to repair my forehead! I shed many tears not only from the pain but also from the shame and fear I felt when I dared to look at myself in my little mirror.

Yet I endured it. Some of the people told me that Doctor Williams was a successful surgeon whose words were true. Two or three patients in the ward whose scars had also been treated by plastic surgery showed me how much better they looked since the plastic surgery operations had been performed upon them.

Doctor Williams watched very carefully to make sure that the graft took root and he explained to me what should happen:

'The tube which looks so unsightly is the pedicle. It is like a bridge, for it is carrying life-giving blood from your healthy forehead to the new tissues in the cavity where your nose used to be. You will have a new nose there if you are brave and if I watch it and mould it every day. Afterwards I will remove your "trunk" but leave your nose. All that will be left is a scar on your forehead and not a very obvious one if things go well.'

And so it was. Photographs have been published of this operation 'before and after'. No wonder that Doctor Williams has been asked to lecture in Britain and America.

As for me I can go home shortly and not be ashamed or afraid. I can look at people. The children will not cry after me and my people can accept me in their homes . . .

People talk so much in India that there are few secrets. Folk are afraid of those who had suffered from leprosy even though they are cured. Some of my friends had crippled hands and feet from this disease and they were as excited as I over hands that worked again and feet that were sound again. I used to go and see them in a most happy place called a rehabilitation department. One would be sitting next to the weaver learning to make cloth, another sat with the shoemaker—making shoes for damaged feet. Even those who could not help the carpenter (they still had plaster casts on their hands) would dust and sweep to make 'their department' the cleanest in the hospital.

Of course, whilst I was a patient at the Nagercoil hospital I learned many things about the people who work in it.

Just as cigarettes are said to make men ill in your country so the betel chew kills thousands in my country. They burn ocean shells into lime. Into this they mix the betel vine and areca nut which makes a bright red concoction which they chew incessantly and spit. Something in this addiction often causes cancer of the throat, jaw or lip and many of the afflicted come to Nagercoil where the deep X-ray therapy is often effective treatment if—a large if—they have not delayed too long. When the radiotherapy is successful the rebuilding of destroyed facial tissues by plastic surgery is available for these cancer patients also.

Some of the patients cannot wait—they must be admitted urgently. About 600 babies are born each year at this hospital, over 100 of them by caesarean section. Sometimes the mother is not married and it has happened that she will get out of bed after two or three days and vanish secretly leaving the Salvation Army responsible for the child.

Sometimes the children are premature. Indian mothers are often ill fed, or too young. One 30-weeks child weighed 1 lb. 13 ozs. It is now three years old and still in the care of the Salvation Army.

Sometimes a father will bring a child, ill, underweight, neglected. His wife has died and he pleads, 'Please take it, I will come for it when I have money. I will pay while it is here . . .'

He does not. Months go by and when he makes no appearance enquiries show that he has vanished. Again the Salvation Army must hold the baby. What a good thing that it has big wide arms.

The lady in charge of the Obstetric Department is Indian— Dr. Sara Daniel. She is a Lieut.-Colonel in the Salvation Army, which seems to show not only that Indians gain places of influence and authority in the Army but also that Indian women can. Dr. Sara has assisted at the delivery of thousands of babies at the Catherine Booth Hospital and she is known and loved far and wide.

There is one other thing I must tell you—you do not have to

be a Salvation Army person to get help at this hospital of the
Salvationists. Indeed, it is not required that you are even a
Christian. Most of the patients here are Hindus. Some of them
are Mohammedans. Many are Christians but not of any particular denomination, Protestant or Catholic are alike to them; sects
and creeds are details they do not bother about.

Some of the nurses in the school are not Christians but
so enjoy Christian truth and worship that they voluntarily
join in Bible study and other services. Whilst I was there one
Christian girl came for nursing but decided that she should
first become a Salvation Army officer and left for a year for
her training.

The Superintendent of Nurses is from New Zealand, Major
Vera Williamson. She is a happy lady and the more I knew of
her the more readily I understood how girls who came here with
neutral religious feeling often end up by being committed Christians. Men are trained as nurses here also, with emphasis on
orthopaedics (they love working with plaster and especially the
electric saw for cutting off plaster casts!). The chief teacher for
the nurses in this field is an American officer of high professional
qualifications, Captain Dorothy Finkbiner. The Government
has promised money to help her teach her special subject of
Public Health.

Perhaps you will understand that there is no need for anyone
here to disobey the laws of Congress that 'Christian missionaries
shall not seek to proselytize Indians from their native faiths . . .'
It is the way the missionaries live, not what they say, that has
force in this place.

Every day, in the morning, a bell tolls. Amid so much sickness
you might think it was the funeral bell. But no, it is the summons to prayers. The service is not at all solemn. Happy songs
are sung and there will be a short address—it must be brief
because everyone is busy. On Sundays there are longer happy
services, with the girls playing tambourines. There is a band,
with our own sort of gay and excited Indian music, and the
doctors are now dressed in their uniform as Salvation Army
officers.

The Hospital Pharmacist reads from the Bible. He is Captain
Ivan Hay, a New Zealander. As he reads I cannot help but

become conscious of my nose—my new nose. These are the words I hear:

'And the vessel that he made of clay was marred in the hand of the potter: so he made it again another vessel, as seemed good to the potter to make it.'

17. WHAT THE DOCTOR ORDERS

The flair for doing things in a big way, which characterizes Americans, has quite naturally shown itself in the Salvation Army in the United States. The Salvation Army Booth Memorial Hospital, Flushing, New York, already represents a capital investment of 11,000,000 dollars in buildings and equipment and further extension is probable.

In the 210-bed general hospital, approximately 11,500 patients are treated annually, and about 2,000 babies are delivered. New wings being constructed in conjunction with the existing hospital, contain single room living accommodation for sixty-four elderly women, and a forty-bed nursing care unit for the chronically ill.

The home for unmarried mothers, which is housed in another wing of the hospital, has living accommodation for sixty girls. This three-fold service—the sick, the aged, and the unmarried mother—in one tremendous unit, is unique, even in a movement which has a chain of hospitals girdling the globe.

At Booth Memorial Hospital the Army's genius for internationalism, and its disregard of race and colour barriers is demonstrated. Not only nationals of many lands, white, negro and oriental gravitate towards Booth Memorial Hospital, but Jews, Mohammedans, Roman Catholics, Protestants and unbelievers work side by side amicably. The unifying bond is the ministry of healing.

Writes a Jewish Rabbi, I. Usher Kirshblum:

'Confession is good for the soul. I must admit that on many occasions I paid no attention to the woman in the bonnet who stood on the street corner singing hymns . . .

'When I was confined to Booth Memorial, the Salvation Army Hospital, I got to know well the woman in the bonnet and respect her for her gentle hand and kindly heart and saintly soul. I had the occasion to learn at first hand what this Army stands for. I was able to observe how patients, regardless of race, colour or creed, are cared for. Every member of the staff, from the Superintendent to the porter, is motivated by the highest ideals of love and mercy for mankind. I have seen the chaplain performing the most menial tasks on behalf of the sick patients. I have become familiar with the financial aid extended so often by the hospital to those who are really in need of help . . . The Booth Memorial Hospital is a credit to our community, and deserves the support of all our residents.'

There are three kinds of American hospitals—governmental, tax-supported; privately-owned and operated for profit; and voluntary—non-profit. The Administrator has the difficult task of coping with labour relations, medical and nursing staff, and many conflicting needs. The Administrator at Flushing is Lieut.-Commissioner Llewellyn Cowan.

In a voluntary hospital, the average cost per day per patient is forty dollars for bed, board, routine and ancillary services. While most patients have hospital insurance which covers the bulk of hospital costs, and for most indigent patients welfare money is available, there still remains a deficit between earned income and cost of care. With an annual operating budget in excess of three-and-a-half million dollars, Booth Memorial Hospital has a deficit of about 200,000 dollars annually, which is met by the Salvation Army.

As with the Mothers' Hospital in London, and many Army hospitals all over the world, the Booth Memorial Hospital, Flushing, was begun as a refuge for unmarried mothers—in East 23rd Street, in 1892. Work for other members of the community began in 1919 when veterans returning from World War I increased the need for hospital accommodation in the metropolitan area. The new 210-bed hospital at Flushing dates from 1957.

In 1963 a new Home for Unmarried Mothers was opened as part of the group of buildings. It is a magnificent, modern affair but quite in the tradition of the first Salvation Army refuge, as regards its purpose, in Christian Street, London, where long ago a woman Salvationist 'spread a pair of clean sheets on her own bed for an unfortunate girl'.

This home gives resident care to 250-300 girls each year. They stay an average of a little over two months, and receive in addition to pre-natal medical care, case-work counselling, group psychiatric therapy, and the benefits of an occupational therapy programme. For the many who are still required by law, because of their age, to attend school, appropriate classroom schedules are provided, with the co-operation of the New York City Board of Education.

The home is connected with the general hospital by a corridor and a private elevator which brings the girls to the obstetrical floor, which they share briefly with the many happily married women who use these hospital facilities, although separate wards are reserved for them. Medical, nursing and hospital staff members co-operate in shielding the girls' identity from the general public.

As one would expect, a patient's life-history, for the Salvationist, is more than a physical matter to be left to the doctors. These can dictate their findings into a link-up of phones, which will automatically record and file the medical data. But no electronic device can record the sufferings of the soul. This is where the sure instinct of the hospital chaplain is needed.

Brigadier Ernest Newton, this Chaplain, serves in full-time capacity. He can observe the protocol of orthodox Jewry, or treat gently the religious sensitivities of a practising Roman Catholic. His complete non-sectarian impartiality has won for him the affectionate admiration of thousands of patients. In the synagogue he reads from the Old Testament in Hebrew headgear, as required! That he is in Salvation Army uniform otherwise strikes no one as being incongruous.

If he is not sufficiently a linguist to speak with those of many nations who need his prayers, he can co-opt the services of members of the staff, or even a patient. Greek, Russian, Hungarian, practically all languages are needed at some time at Booth Hospital. His language of love is universal.

Newton's mail reaches 250 letters a month, from Roman Catholic priests, ministers, patients young and old. His hours of work are quite inhuman—he is on call round the clock. Sometimes a doctor says, 'I have some bad news to give this patient, Padre. Will you come in with me?' Or a wife will say, 'Yes, I'll agree to your holding an autopsy on him—if you let the Brigadier in to see that everything is done right.'

'Dear Reverend Newton,' wrote a former patient, Irwin Schram,

'To me the Booth Hospital is a shining example of how America should be. It is democracy carried out with deeds, not words. There are Jews and Christians working side by side. There are whites and negroes working hand in hand. There is even a Chinese doctor. They are people not classified by religion or race, but *Americans* working together with one thought in mind, to help their fellow man. There are unwed mothers cared for by the Salvation Army. There are elderly people who will have a wing built specially for them, and there are people like my wife, heartbroken, disappointed, frightened by the future, being comforted physically and mentally by your staff and yourself. This hospital is a wonderful tribute to yourself and to your unselfish religious sect, not only for the things you stand for, but for the things you do, whether it's on the Bowery, at a plane crash on Sterling Place in Brooklyn, or a rummage sale in Freeport . . .

'With God's help, I hope my wife will again be in the maternity section in Booth Memorial next year. When this happens, I'm sure that with your prayers on our side, this time we'll have a healthy baby.'

His wife obliged. They've been back to Booth Memorial Hospital and this time a lovely baby was safely delivered.

'Dear Ernie,' a lawyer wrote,

'My wife and I expected the very worst when I entered the Booth Memorial Hospital, and now everything is so very different. We feel that we have just begun to live. I will always be very grateful. Thank you so very much for the cheer and encouragement you brought us . . .'

One father-to-be had a trying time:

'Dear Ernie,

'My sincere thanks for the wonderful support last Friday when my baby was born. Until I met you I had no idea of the character of the Salvation Army. They should be proud to have a man like you in their ranks. Once again thanks for the support you gave me when I really needed it . . .'

A doctor, who knew how near he had been to physical extinction, wrote:

'It's just a year since I was operated upon by such a wonderful

surgeon at the Booth Memorial Hospital. I went to his office a
few days ago. He found me in splendid health after a trip to
Europe, which I accomplished without any difficulty. I often
think of the way I was treated at the Booth. Such wonderful
souls! My constant prayer is for so noble a staff. "I was sick
and ye visited me." '

'It now seems that Lisa will soon be home with us,' a woman
wrote. 'We are mindful that many people, including you most
of all, shared in this miracle. Our thanks go to the dedicated
team, doctors, nurses and all at Booth Memorial Hospital who
played a part in answer to our prayers. It was my first acquaintance with the Salvation Army, but I am so impressed that I
would like to volunteer to do free voluntary work at the hospital
one or two days a week. I am trained in secretarial work, but
will be glad to serve in whatever capacity . . .'

One man seems to have enjoyed a vacation:

'It is very easy to recover from illness at your wonderful
institution! The nursing staff, the nurses' aids, the volunteers
and everybody connected with the hospital are doing a job above
and beyond what is expected of them. If one has to go to
hospital, then Booth Memorial is probably far and away the best
there is available in the country today.

'Fortunate to be assigned a bed on the eighth floor (room 818)
I hated to leave. The staff was so friendly and helpful that I
felt my recovery was made a lot sooner than it would have been
in another hospital. They didn't even object to me growing a
beard!

'Your personal visits every day were inspiring, and I will never
forget your morning prayers for everybody, even though I have
strayed far from religion. Your talk to the members of the
Hebrew faith, on the eve of High Holidays, was unexpected, but
greatly appreciated.

'The work of the Salvation Army is well known throughout
the world, but you really don't appreciate it until you have a
personal experience such as I had . . .'

One proud father writes:

'My wife and I want you to know how much we appreciated
your "blessing" on the birth of our second child at your wonderful hospital. It was another manifestation of the glowing spirit

that prevails there. It is reflected in the attitude of the entire staff.'

The link of physical with spiritual, the Chaplain's particular province, is indicated:

'I wish there were words to express the strength and peace of mind you and your words of faith brought to me. Take just last year, when I weakened spiritually and physically, and lost all desire to go on, and your endless hours of vigil and your soothing words of prayer brought me back into the fold once more, healing physically and spiritually. Whenever you came into our room we had a feeling of being surrounded by faith and love in God.'

A wife feared that her husband would be spoiled by the goodness heaped upon him at the hospital:

'This past week I've been visiting my husband in The Booth Memorial Hospital. He raves about the excellent food, and the patience and politeness of the nurses; in fact, all employees. He'll never be satisfied with me when he comes home! He says it's like living in a beautiful hotel . . . My husband enjoys the visits of the Brigadier. He says he is "so nice". What more can I say?'

To a woman seriously hurt in a car crash, the term in hospital was, obviously, more than medical treatment:

'What a joy to receive a letter from you! I can see your smiling face, your kindly eyes. Truly God is good. My broken, bruised body has been healed by the power of the almighty Father and the process of healing is taking place in my shattered ankle. I am hopping around on cast and crutch, and am able to rejoice with my family over my recovery.

'Thanks for your prayers, which reached the throne and returned to heal me as only the Great Physician can.'

18. IN THE HABITATION OF DRAGONS

All hospital matrons are martinets, so legend insists. They must enforce strict discipline, which lies heavily upon the tender young women who for months or even years are subject to their heavy yoke.

This has been given as a reason for the short supply of nursing staff. One would expect, therefore, that at the Mothers' Hospital, London, this lack would be acute indeed. There the Matron is also a Lieut.-Colonel in the Salvation Army, a military-style organization with a spartan system of discipline. As an officer, Lieut.-Colonel Smith must not smoke or drink and otherwise leads an austere life—'separate from the world', as Salvationists say. She is unmarried, hardworking, utterly dedicated to her faith and to the nursing profession—the signs, some would assume, of a veritable dragon!

In fact, her happiness, sense of humour, the cheerful common-sense Salvation-Army-lassie-look of her, helps to make nonsense of the legend of the dragonian matron. The Mothers' Hospital, the largest maternity unit in the Hackney and Queen Elizabeth Group of the North-East Metropolitan Regional Board, has an embarrassing wealth of applications for positions on the nursing staff—fifty a month, though the intake can only be about twenty every three months.

These applicants know what they are letting themselves in for. All of them are past their 21st birthday, having completed three years' general nursing for their State Registered Nurse qualification. When they apply to join the Mothers' Hospital for one year, it is to gain status as a State Certified Midwife. Not many of the applicants are Salvationists: some are not professedly Christian at all.

Yet they are unafraid of the reputation the hospital has: its Salvation Army attitude is known far and wide. This might suggest that newspaper stories about the heavy hand of hospital

authority generally, and the sternness of matrons in particular
is exaggerated. Or it might be that nurses are nowhere near as
interested in playing Juliet to Romeo as *Emergency Ward 10* or
Doctor Kildare make us believe.

Young women are told, when they apply to come to the
Mothers' Hospital, that morning prayers after breakfast are
obligatory. That is all the religious compulsion. Objection is
practically unknown and, as there is no shortage of alternative
jobs for nurses, the girl who signs on at the Mothers' Hospital
wishes to come. Some leave after their one-year course as un-
committed religiously as when they arrived. They are at the
hospital to get their midwifery certificate, not to be conscripted
into the Salvation Army.

As freedom of religion—and non-religion—is axiomatic in
Britain, there can be no objection when one or another of the
young women succumbs to the religious climate. This would not
help her if she failed her exams but when those things are satisfactory it pleases Matron very much indeed.

It is not surprising that conversions do take place. The woman
who wishes to be a midwife must be a thoughtful person, with
considerable sense of vocation. In wards, corridors, lounge and
dining-rooms she often encounters the bright face of Christianity. She makes friends, she listens in to ward services. She can be
quiet, and watch, and check the numerous Christians about her.

There are officer nurses in the Salvation Army, missionaries
far across the world, who date their religious crisis and victory
to their days at the Mothers' Hospital. Many who are not Salvationists, but committed Christians, know that for them the
hospital at Clapton was the starting point.

By agreement between the Ministry of Health and the General
of the Salvation Army when the National Health Service was
set up, all administrative posts within the hospital are filled by
officers of the Salvation Army. This means all the Ward Sisters
—but not one dragon amongst them!

Indeed, the idea of melancholic, repressive authority ought to
be unthinkable within the Salvation Army. Almost always it is.
Salvationists sing with heartful fervour,

'Joy! Joy! Joy! There's joy in the Salvation Army!'

Swinburne, of course, did not need the services of the Mothers' Hospital for any wife or child of his. Also, he seems not to have liked the Salvation Army, and was too much of a recluse to have learned much about it. This was unfortunate, for had he known the Army better he might not have written those foolish words of his:

> 'Thou hast conquered. O pale Galilean;
> The world has grown grey from Thy breath.'

Babies wot not of religion, so that the average of 2,750 safe arrivals a year at the Mothers' Hospital merely take their first deep breath and then devote their one-track minds to the task of drinking and sleeping, with occasional time off for yelling and the emission of other noises.

As the hospital is a training centre, medical standards have to be high. The percentages of neo-natal deaths, infant mortality within one month of birth, is eleven per thousand. This is much below the national average—proof, if any were needed, that religion does not necessarily hinder medical science. It seems to show, also, that it need not inhibit effective liaison with the machinery and bureaucracy of a Welfare State.

Though baby careth not, mother is keenly aware of what is going on. The hospital is fully booked seven months ahead, usually for first babies. If that first is brought into the world without untoward incident, the woman will probably be expected to have other progeny in her own home. The woman is not selected by the Salvation Army but through the National Health Service maternity service. In religion she is either Jewish, Catholic, Protestant, Hindu, Buddhist or nothing. It matters not. She will hear the ward services. There will be opportunity to ask what it is all about. Someone is almost bound to say 'God bless you,' which remark she can either receive, or reject as an impertinence, as she wishes. She will offend no one. The Army always keeps on trying.

There may be those among the young housewives who regard the Mothers' Hospital's religious emphasis as irrelevant, or even objectionable, but none such is known. A woman having her first baby is not normally in a critical mood—rather she feels like the Queen of Sheba after receiving the bounty of Solomon. Hundreds write to express their thanks.

'Thank you so much! I was as impressed by the spiritual vocation as by the professional competence of the nursing staff,' one woman declared.

'My first visit to the Mothers' Hospital led to my becoming a Christian. Now that I have been a second time, I am confirmed in my faith,' is a quote from another letter.

What the women respectably a-bed might not wish to be reminded of is that the ministry of the Mothers' Hospital sprang from that original impulse to help 'fallen women', in old Victorian days, when the Army's Women's Social Work began. Then the need was believed to be only among betrayed, seduced or merely wanton unmarried girls. For them the Army opened a rescue hostel in nearby Mare Street.

Slowly it dawned upon people that the poor housewife might suffer too—sickness, ignorance, malnutrition. Lassie officers of the Army found that these and other woes were endemic in countless homes where marriage lines, though they made the baby legitimate, did not make its birth less hazardous. In 1913, therefore, the Mothers' Hospital was opened with fifty beds, mainly for the respectable poor.

Now, as living standards have risen, even the word 'poor' is resented and may not fit the case. Poverty is deemed to have social stigma even among people whose income is only fifteen pounds a week. Many who use the Mothers' Hospital have an income of twice that. Under the National Health Scheme maternity service is free; the money is irrelevant.

Of course, the first love, the un-wed mother, is not cast out. To Army homes, particularly Crossways, at Stamford Hill, she is still welcome. Many other single women about to have a baby, who feel no need of being 'rescued', enter the Mothers' Hospital as does any other expectant mother.

Nowadays it is not considered necessary to isolate such a girl, either because of her moral solecism or because of fear that the majority of respectable matrons in the wards would feel affronted. Crossways girls usually occupy a ward together because they have grown to know each other, and wish it that way. Ordinarily, the woman who needs to have her child at the Mothers' Hospital goes into the wards. No special point is made of whether she is married or single.

Her National Health Service grant is not conditional upon her possession of a marriage certificate. Parents these days tend to accept their daughter's dilemma with much greater composure than used to be the case. The other women in the wards, if they learn of the girl's unmarried status, usually do so because she tells them; they do not flaunt their own propriety. Sometimes the girl does not tell, but the absence of a suitable father-type, at visiting time, lets the cat out of the bag. But this is not, in these days, anywhere near so savage an animal as used to be the case.

Lieut.-Colonel Smith agrees that society is modifying its censorious attitude towards the unmarried mother. At the Mothers' Hospital, of course, the feeling toward her is sympathetic. She needs it. She will undergo a considerable degree of emotional stress: family trouble, man trouble and, often, baby trouble. In about fifty per cent of cases the child is put to adoption. This is often a decision causing great grief to the girl.

To the Salvationist that is not all. Though they are having to modernize their tactics, William Booth's followers are not inclined to surrender their Christian principles. To them, Biblical injunctions against fornication are mandatory, let the New Morality say what it will. More than most, Salvationists know of the moral conflict involved in having a child out of wedlock — the misery that can follow upon a girl's loneliness and rejection; the death to love that is so often consequent upon illicit sex-relationships; the hurt to the innocent child, that suffers throughout life.

Yet nothing could be more wrong than to imagine Matron and her officer staff going from bed to bed seeking to induce a sense of guilt, morbid or otherwise. During the ten days or so that the woman is in their care — often more than ten days, for about seven per cent of births are by caesarean section — a gentle tact is exercised. There are no stocks where the wicked must sit in shamed penance, to be scolded by puritans.

There are mighty words written above the main entrance to the Mothers' Hospital. They make a theme for basic attitudes:

For the love of God is broader
Than the measure of man's mind;
And the heart of the Eternal,
Is most wonderfully kind.

Many a girl does find comfort and forgiveness—'the things which belong unto thy peace.' These are sometimes preceded by tears and penitence. A first baby makes you think. The mother, often hardly more than a child herself, usually the product of an unfavourable home environment, is a victim as well as a transgressor in a society that has jettisoned much of its old moral values.

Whenever the girl presents opportunity, Salvationists will seize it. Often when she looks at the new infant, the most wonderful child that ever was born, she feels simply that she is not good enough for it. *But she wants to be.* To the Salvationist, that is the moment of truth. With audacious naïvety, Army folk always have the answer to that one: *God will enable her.* Thousands of times a girl has said 'amen' to the bedside prayer, smiled, wiped the tears from her eyes, and begun a new life. This is the desired end of all Salvationist endeavour.

Matron, who worked for some years in South Africa, has no serious complaints regarding the National Health Service and the role of the Mothers' Hospital within it. A small grumble would be that sometimes a committee will choose to sit at the very same time as that chosen by the Salvation Army for one of its rallies, festivals or days of prayer at the Royal Albert Hall, the Central Hall, Westminster, or wherever. This is a deprivation that Matron and her staff bear stoically as a consequence of becoming enmeshed in the machinery of a Welfare State. There are many compensations.

The Secretary Superintendent of the Mothers' Hospital is a Salvation Army officer—Lieut.-Colonel Ernest Livermore, with a trainee Assistant, Major Lewis Johns. Both men hold official National Health Service status, and have to work on various committees. Also included in their responsibilities are relationships with the trade unions, the catering trade, and many other aspects of hospital work. The posts require considerable know-how in hospital administration. The Salvation Army, all over the world, is finding that more of its officers must take professional studies in this field.

As with the Matron and Ward Sisters, there is also a financial consideration of some interest. When the Salvation Army General signed the agreement with the National Health Service that administrative posts should be held by Salvation Army officers, he did not intend that the concomitant salaries should go to the men or women concerned: all officers in the Army must be treated alike. The National Health Service remunerates officers by the ordinary rate for Salvation Army officers' allowances.

Crisis within the anomaly of a religious hospital in a state controlled health service might be expected to manifest itself with regard to the medical staff. None of the doctors at the Mothers' Hospital is a Salvationist and the average medical man is as little inclined as was Lord Melbourne to allow religion to be mixed with everyday professional matters.

The Senior Consultant at the Mothers' Hospital, Miss 'X', FRCOG, is one of seven consultants who attend for obstetrics, gynaecology, and paediatrics. She was formerly Registrar, and says, 'There is a particularly friendly atmosphere, made possible, I think, because the nursing staff and administrative officers are committed Christians. Some things take place which seem to be irrelevant—such as the prayer always uttered by the bedside of the woman safely delivered of her child. Some of the women may be taken aback, at first, for many of them are not religious at all. However, I have never heard objections.

'On the contrary, women enjoy coming here. The standard of midwifery and general nursing is high. There is also that cheerful "Salvation Army" mood everywhere. You become used to it and look for it.'

As doctors usually apply for posts advertised by Regional Boards, and know the hospitals in the Groups concerned, they are aware beforehand of the Salvation Army connection of the Mothers' Hospital. This may mean that they are Christians themselves or, at least, that they have no particular objection to Christianity. But the Senior Consultant does not believe it would matter if this were not so:

'Religion is not rammed down the throats of anyone,' she says.

'It is rather the general attitude of the staff—something that gives special character. There is a sense of dedication, a willingness to work harder, to do the extra tasks without complaint.'

This would avail nothing, she is sure, if the medical standards were not maintained. Applications for beds in maternity hospitals always exceed supply. At Clapton the number of applications is much above average.

If a doctor gets professional competence from nursing staff and good medical facilities it seems that he is well content to work in a religious hospital. Many non-Catholic doctors, for example, work at Catholic hospitals. The reasons, Miss 'X' believes, are the same as apply at the Mothers' Hospital.

'Religion provides a plus-element. The staff, being Christian, seem to have something extra to give. It is noticeable, it is important, and patients appreciate it.'

As for the nurses, most of whom are non-Salvationist, their experience at the Mothers' Hospital is often similar to that of Miss 'Y', who gained her SRN at a big London teaching hospital. She applied to go to Clapton because it had a good reputation for training and because she'd heard it was 'a happy place'. She is a vivacious, pretty girl, who does not look quite the part as midwife, leave alone the thoughtful, religious sort of girl she is.

Her religion 'happened' after she arrived at the Mothers' Hospital. She had been to church as a child but all faded away as she grew up, especially when she was caught up in the busy three-years' training. The religion at Clapton made her suspicious, for she had been warned she would hear the siren songs of the Salvationists. In fact they simply expected her to work hard and study midwifery. Morning prayers were brief; there was no heavy-handed converting zeal. She could take it or leave it.

After some time watching, listening, thinking about the way this practical, common-sense sort of faith made such a difference throughout the hospital, Nurse 'Y' accepted an invitation to go to Army meetings. She had never been before and they enchanted her. She liked the music, the gaiety, the people she met. Doubts about herself began to assail her, for it is axiomatic in a Salvation Army service that if one has a conscience it should spring to life. Nurse 'Y' had one. She wasn't a bad girl: she wanted to be a good girl. Afterwards the young live-it-up dances and parties lost their zest. The idea of being a do-gooder nurse, that fulfilment of her idealistic girlhood dreams, faded away. After time spent in prayer, in reading the Bible, she felt willing to accept nursing as a religious vocation. A future as a Salvation Army officer became a real prospect. She has been 'sworn in' as a soldier in the Army.

Those who see a happy girl snuffed out by this, to be replaced by a solemn puritan, are quite wrong. The smiling cheerfulness is still there—only more so. At the staff Christmas celebrations the new convert was more vivacious and gleeful than ever. Her new religious faith rests as naturally, happily and beautifully upon her as a flower blooms in spring.

19. THE BABY IS THE ANOMALY

> One more Unfortunate
> Weary of breath,
> Rashly importunate,
> Gone to her death!
>
> Take her up tenderly,
> Lift her with care,
> Fashioned so slenderly,
> Young, and so fair!
>
> Owning her weakness,
> Her evil behaviour,
> And leaving, with meekness,
> Her sins to her Saviour!

Victorian sentimentality, expressed in Hood's *Bridge of Sighs*, also influenced the Salvation Army in its early rescue work for women.

William Booth had hardly formed his first battalions of shock troops before sorties were being made on dives, brothels and other habitat of erring women in London, Glasgow, Sydney and New York.

There was a naïve assumption behind such labour: one had only to get the unfortunate female away from her wicked environment, and then persuade her to kneel at the penitent-form. All would then be forgiven and forgotten.

Such simplicity has been modified by the hard facts and experiences of decades of service for seduced girls, unrepentant prostitutes, and betrayed children. A more scientific approach, though still based on Christian love, has replaced the readily shocked fervour with which early-day Salvationists set out to 'rescue the perishing'.

Many girls who have babies do not quickly acknowledge themselves as 'sinners'; the sense of sin is one of the casualties of modern life. This cramps the style of the woman Salvationist social worker. She sees the need for a tender conscience, for repentance and confession before spiritual rehabilitation can take place.

Such an attitude on the part of the erring girls is in short supply. Today's unmarried mothers do not generally feel disposed to suicide. Hood's pitiable magdalene went out with Queen Victoria, or soon afterwards. There are so many to keep one company these days, far less cause for humiliation and embarrassment, with about 250,000 illegitimate babies born each year in the United States, and over 50,000 in Great Britain, and a like rise in the illegitimacy ratio everywhere. The 'shocking' tends to become the norm.

Though the Salvationist must still consider sexual delinquency as sin, time has wrought changes here also. It is not, in the best Salvationist quarters, any more a sin than any other breach of the moral and divine laws. Perhaps few salvation soldiers know their D. H. Lawrence but they are coming to see that a horrified feeling about sex, because it is sex, is unenlightened. Sex is natural; it can be beautiful and sacramental.

Among the thousands of girls in the Army's care because of sexual misconduct are many who feel that their only social crime is in being 'caught'. Many of their girl friends in schools, colleges, factories and offices behave as they did. The baby is the anomaly.

The Salvationist social worker among women, though she often adds a college degree to her training in one of the William Booth's schools for officers, does not, however, forget William Booth's dictum : 'Go for souls!' The scientific attitude must not cancel out the need for salvation.

In the United States, the ratio for illegitimacy is about the same as in the United Kingdom, up to six per cent of all live births. The Salvation Army cares for many of these women, a third of them being in their teens and many under fifteen years.

One of the numerous Salvation Army homes and hospitals for unwed mothers in the United States is at San Antonio, Texas. To this home come girls of thirteen, fourteen, fifteen and older, for their babies to be born. Some are Catholics and members of other faiths, though the undenominationalism of the Salvation Army in America is so pronounced that such a detail is irrelevant. There is no 'sheep-stealing'. Often it is the priest who sends the girl to the Army.

Socially, although such considerations matter less in the United States than they might in Europe, the girls are not all or mainly from the 'wrong side of the track'. They come from good homes, and are of average education. Some of them are not hard to seduce.

A main topic of conversation with many of the girls at school is sex. They have the use of cars and all the modern stimuli: T.V., films, 'hot' music and dances, which conspire to titillate sexual awareness before they have the sense of responsibility to cope with it.

Elise is eighteen, dark, bright-eyed and vivacious. Anyone less suited to the role of a magdalene could hardly be imagined. The child of a British G.I. bride whose marriage did not work out, she fell an easy victim to the first man who offered her love, for she had always felt a sense of rejection in her miserable, rowdy home. She lived wretchedly with this man, much older than herself, until a horse kicked him to death. That solved a problem, for he was treating her abominably.

Up in Indiana Elise met a Mexican, the first man to show real affection and tenderness towards her. He would have married her but his mother did not approve—the girl was not of his faith. Now that Elise had given her love much too generously, the Mexican decided to preserve the family religious traditions. He began to walk out with a good, chaste, religiously acceptable girl. Elise was left with the baby.

Unlike most unwed mothers, Elise is holding the baby still. She seems to be able to cope with this addition to her responsibilities. Doubtless the change in her since she came to the Army home partly explains her ability to do this. Having a baby is a step towards maturity, but the all-pervading yet gently religious influence cannot fail to have a good effect on most of the girls.

Eighteen doctors rotate in a community service for the hospital. It costs about 55,000 dollars a year, for it is not a large one, but the town considers it a major asset.

Booth Memorial Hospital at Detroit is larger—sixty girls as compared with twenty-five at San Antonio. There is the usual high standard in accommodation—money is not the problem in the United States that it is in the United Kingdom and some other countries where the Salvation Army operates.

Except for parts of California, this is the area of highest illegitimacy. Large numbers of Negroes live in the city, and that these may have a more casual attitude to marriage and children born outside it, is sometimes given as an explanation. Whereas, formerly, the Negro girl used to keep her baby, the Army is now finding that more and more want to place the baby in adoption. However, there is a shortage of homes for Negro babies.

Detroit, like all Salvation Army homes in the United States, is integrated, so that whatever other serious problems there may be, white, yellow and Negro girls are seen in mutual need of friendship. Girls from all social strata are welcomed: the girl from the slum, the undergraduate from college.

Though in the United States most illegitimate children are put to adoption on the basis that mother minus father is unable to provide a proper home for the child, about fifteen per cent of all babies born in Salvation Army homes for unmarried mothers are kept by their mothers.

If the home background is suitable, and other circumstances are equal, then adoption is not encouraged. There are a minority of cases where, for strong emotional reasons, the girl needs the child. Yet for over 80 of every 100 infants, adoption is the answer —a decision fully agreed after consideration by all concerned.

Because many of the girls are below school-leaving age school teachers are employed at the home, a feature of many United States centres. Girls often go on with their high school and often university education with a 12-month hiatus. The Salvationists are not concerned with publicizing the girl's downfall, and the school or college may grant a year's leave of absence without any idea as to why.

Average length of stay is seventy-seven days, and up to 400 girls enter the Detroit centre annually. They are 'processed' before entering, and given after-care when they leave. Professional social service teams try to analyse the cause of a girl's moral revolt. Some are promiscuous, having been sexually experienced before reaching their teens. Some are victims of assault. The majority are conformists; the boy, the car, the knowledge that it is 'the done thing'. They believe their friends behave likewise, often they know they do. There is always the fearsome threat that if they do not, they will not get 'dates'. To many teenagers this is a fate not to be contemplated.

Like most United States social service centres, Detroit works like a clock. Characters who wind the clock include psychiatric social workers of one school or another. The psychiatrist is never far away when casework is being considered in America. But the Salvation Army officers take care that William Booth principles shall not be omitted because of the modern emphasis on psychological understanding.

It is not a matter of avoiding the penalties of sin, or making it easy for the wantons. No girl goes into a Salvation Army home without the spiritual and moral and social implications of her actions being brought home to her. But there is no wish to make the experience of illegitimate pregnancy a traumatic experience. Her offence is against God—and, possibly, the child. The Army tries to make that evident. Then, in God's name, and by the law He enunciates, it makes it possible for the girl to go and sin no more. In the Bible God promises to forget. The Salvation Army believes it should do what it can to allow the girl and others to forget also.

20. WHEN LOVE MUST DIE

Everything is huge in Los Angeles: the city sprawls outwards, so everyone must have a car—a big car. That calls for big roads, which create big traffic problems, and a serious health menace because of the smog. The people are big, business booms and the city grows prodigiously with California, into which migrants stream at the rate of 15,000 every day, every year. Of course, nearby Hollywood grows and changes too. And as it attempts to solve its own movie problem, it is still a magnet for the young and impressionable.

Here is a high birth-rate, with about five per cent born out of wedlock. Of the chain of Salvation Army homes for unmarried mothers in the west of the United States, the Booth Memorial Hospital at Los Angeles is a good example. It is managed by a highly efficient officer, a model of what a social worker should be, and it is large. The number of girls in residence is always more than a hundred. The annual budget is about 300,000 dollars, and the cost of expansion entails a further expenditure of 1,250,000 dollars on a project which is nearing completion. More and more girls must be admitted as the moral problems of the young become more acute. The cost of their care becomes ever more expensive.

However, Booth is calm: the Superintendent—professionally trained—is an officer who gets things done. She is given splendid help by Salvation Army administration, a good staff, a Hospital Advisory Council, Los Angeles citizens, a Women's Auxiliary, and the California State authorities. The Salvation Army in America can normally rely on excellent civic and public support for its good works.

Major Vivian Johnson, the Superintendent, has no illusions about most of the girls who spend their fifty or sixty days in her care:

'They are not innocent. Some of them are sophisticated

"petters" and "neckers". Others wanted the baby. They are aware of contraceptive methods; the birth was purposeful. Some girls think that the child will cause the boy-friend to marry them; to others the baby is an expression of rebellion or resentment against their parents or a hostile community; some want the child as something of their own. They have always felt deprived.

'When sixteen-year old Arabella came here—the girl by the window—she was violent and unco-operative. She had been adopted, and from the age of ten had been "acting up". Because of her great need she's been here for five months. At first she broke things, banged cans, screaming all the while. I have rarely known a more miserable, wretched girl. Though she has cause; the boy involved had intended to marry her, but because of a car accident was unable to.

'She refused to attend our chapel. Yet love and patience won her over. The day came when she could say to a new girl: "You ought to go to chapel Sunday. It's good. The organ is sweet and the singing's grand . . ."'

Major Johnson believes that pregnancy demoralizes the unmarried girl, not because of true guilt, but a consciousness of having violated a social code. The penalties inflicted on her by the community create bitter resentment. To get the girl to shift the emphasis inward to herself is one of the tasks at the Booth, and at any other Army hospital. Often there is a subtlety necessary that would bewilder the old-time Salvationist social worker.

Sexual freedom, for example, is so general among the young and their elders that it is not easy to arouse penitence on that score. One girl summed it up eloquently: 'Don't tell me I'm the wicked one! They all do it. You don't know married men like I do. Some of 'em go to church on Sundays—you'd think they were saints. But I could tell you! And I didn't fool about with half-a-dozen men, like some I know.'

Yet the unwanted baby is often the beginning of the mental and spiritual revolution. The girl comes to understand that the child may suffer because she cannot be a good mother to it. She cannot give it a proper home. She must surrender it to strangers . . . These thoughts, and the physical experiences before and after childbirth, prove to have a deeply spiritual effect upon the girl.

Often a high school girl must leave her school; even if not she cannot return for two months after her pregnancy. Employers do not readily accept unwed girls who have had babies. It is not unknown for the girl who has been to Booth, who is chastened by her experience, and given a clean bill of health by the doctors, to be told by a would-be employer that she will have to have another medical examination.

Loneliness is one of the greatest privations of the unmarried mother. Even if she has enlightened parents, in a more or less sympathetic community, things can never be quite the same. She is neither proper girl, nor true mother, and they know it.

The love affair is almost always irreparably destroyed. The boy-girl passion, sometimes of long duration, deep and real, young and lovely, does not survive the scarifying experience involved in bringing a child into the world in defiance of the conventional code.

The boy, or man, concerned with those unwed girls who need the services of the Salvation Army or other voluntary societies, usually drops the girl like the proverbial hot potato. The 'illegitimate father' has no rights over a child. Even if he admits paternity he can only be compelled to support. He cannot have a mandatory voice, cannot claim to be consulted on what the mother may decide to do about the child. Real love withers beneath the cold blast of family disapproval, religious puritanism and a community's often hypocritical social sanctions. Burns, popular in California, speaks for them both:

> Then gently scan your brother man,
> Still gentler sister woman;
> Though they may gang a kennin wrang,
> To step aside is human.
>
> Then at the balance let's be mute,
> We never can adjust it;
> What's done we partly may compute
> But know not what's resisted . . .

'Father', of course, is hard to nail down. For a dollar or two he may persuade one or more buddies to perjure themselves and own that they, too, had the girl. Any such admissions demolish her claims. Odd though it may seem, many girls have such pride that they will not tell—do not seek a partner in their plight.

Sarah, of Jewish faith, is aged 19:

'It happened because of my home. I did not get on with my father. He was a nobody. He could not even provide food enough for us to eat, and he made life hell for my mother.

'The back streets and the autos of the boys of the neighbour-hood were an escape for me. I knew sex soon after I was thirteen years old.

'When I was going to have a baby, they arrested one of the boys, the right one, I think, but they couldn't do anything about it because I had to admit he wasn't the only boy.

'It's funny me being here in the Salvation Army, and not a Christian. But I like to go to the chapel and listen. They don't try to make me join. Some of the things they say I do under-stand, and agree with. I hope to do better when I go out. The baby is being put to adoption. My mother has been to see the Major, and the Army will help me to get a job . . .'

Vanessa is about twenty-four and at college, where she is but one year from her master's degree. The father is a Ph.D. Lecturer at the college, so the child's I.Q. ought to be good. This does not help Vanessa, however, because he cannot be held responsible. She feels a loyalty towards him. He is married already, and the revelation of his part in the downfall of one of his students might ruin him.

With a good home, education and financial position, Vanessa is in less need of pity than most. She pays her way at Booth, something most girls cannot do. The child is to be adopted. Then she is going back to college, having been granted a year's recess by authorities who are quite ignorant of the true reason for it.

What she did find at Booth was a concern about herself. She admits that she was 'cheap', that she gave herself to a philan-derer without caring for him at all. In the quiet moments at the hospital she has time to think and even to begin to pray again, something she has ceased doing when she left Sunday School at the age of twelve. She did need Booth, not because she was poor, but because she had to find penitence and God.

Driving down the Los Angeles motorway at sixty-five miles an hour, with one hand off the wheel as she gesticulated eloquently, Major Vivian Johnson's blue eyes, set in a pale freckled face, were alight with pride:

'We go along with the psychologists, the caseworkers, the doctors and the welfare experts, but we make absolutely certain that we also go along with God.

'A woman wrote to me to say "thank you", not only for her daughter, but for herself and her husband. They had been drifting apart and the girl loved them both. This was a cause of their daughter's misbehaviour. It is a familiar pattern. The scandal stopped them, made them think, brought them to us for discussion about their daughter.

'You know what the mother said to me at the end? "Jim and I used to think only of ourselves. We felt self-pity because we did not love each other like we used to, and blamed the other for what had happened. Now we think as a family—wife, husband and daughter. We feel we failed her, but we thank God we found out in time . . ."'

It might well be assumed that the devoted Christian ministrations of the Salvation Army woman officer, her chaste and austere life, her absorption with religious matters in hostels, homes, chapel services, family prayers, would make her something of the nun-like creature of film and fancy.

But the popular image of the nun, as a withdrawn and inhibited woman, is probably faulty: the public idea of the Salvation Army woman officer is certainly so. In San Francisco, for example, drug addiction, prostitution, child-birth by girls of twelve—their babies delivered at the Salvation Army hospital by caesarean section—can be cited as a few of the everyday issues which keep a woman social service officer's feet firmly on the earth.

Across the bay from San Francisco, at Oakland, the Booth Home and Hospital for unmarried mothers, is another link in the Army chain of such services throughout the United States. Here are officers who have years of study of psychiatric social work, or the equivalent, added to their normal training and experience in the Salvation Army. Professional qualifications in branches of social science and hospital administration become more necessary every year as Governments and local authorities make the allocation of funds conditional upon the possession of a bachelor's or master's degree.

Californian laws on sex are strict, though not rigidly enforced. The age of consent is eighteen. Carnal knowledge of a girl below that age is technically illegal, though not always subject to legal process. The word 'rape' is often introduced into court proceedings, though there is little doubt that the under-age girl was a willing partner. Some of the girls at Oakland are between fourteen and seventeen years.

Strongly evident is the pattern in which the religious, well brought up girl seems to be the ready victim of the seducer. Very often, in the United States, it is the unsophisticated girl who is most likely to have the baby. Though the girl is well aware of the religious prohibition of illicit sexual relations she thinks she must agree for fear of losing her boy-friend. Few of the girls at Oakland are promiscuous. They are good, 'nice' girls. Parents or other interested parties can often find the 600 dollars cost per girl for her sixty-day term at the home. Others must be aided.

The stigma of unmarried motherhood seems to bear down much harder on the girl in the West than in other areas. The conception permitted as a trap into marriage, or a getaway from an unpleasant home-life, becomes an ordeal by which many girls are harmed deeply and permanently.

The mothers of pregnant unwed daughters are often the real delinquents :

Because of her mother's aggressive personality, Doreen had never been given a voice, or life, or soul of her own. If the woman had had twelve children, or a drunken husband, Doreen might have escaped. But she was the only child. Father, a timid, peace-loving man, took refuge in his business and his club. Doreen had always to live with mother.

The girl's old-style clothes were chosen for her; she developed no sense of dress, whereas her mother had a true flair, and the face and figure to model clothes attractively. Doreen felt she was the ugly duckling.

The girl's gesture of revolt was pregnancy. Even then Mum

enjoyed taking charge and tried to insist on having Doreen and the baby back home, where the child would have been used as a constant reminder of failure. But study of the girl had shown the Salvationists and case-workers where the real trouble lay. There was no future for Doreen unless she could escape from her mother.

In the end the baby's adoption was agreed upon. The Army found the girl a job at which she proved to be particularly competent. Truly adult, successful in business, she discovered resources in herself no one knew existed. She is now engaged to be married.

Sometimes the encounter that is to have such significant consequences is so casual and brief that the boy and girl are strangers even afterwards.

Aged fifteen, Felicity was forced by a sixteen year old boy. She was quite ignorant of what might transpire and, when pregnancy was diagnosed, found great difficulty in linking cause with effect. The girl's mother was furious, not so much at her daughter's near-rape, or on account of any moral transgression, but because the coming baby would make her a grandmother. She was a vain and vindictive woman who had kept her daughter in a state of delayed childhood, utterly ignorant of the most elementary sexual matters. The girl's father was a man of no status in her life.

While the parents of the boy-father encouraged him to 'stand by the girl', and would have financed his marriage to her, the mother vehemently opposed this. The Army arranged adoption for the baby and became 'father and mother' to the unhappy girl-mother. Back at school she remained within range of Salvationist after-care, and emerged much wider and more responsible from her shattering experience. Felicity has now graduated from college, and is engaged to be married.

Obviously, in the Land of the Free, a woman may exercise her right to refuse rescue if she so desires.

Janet, older than average at Oakland, did just that. For many of her thirty-five years she had been tied to a hypochondriacal mother, whose only response to her daughter's years of devoted care was criticism and abuse.

When the old lady died, and Janet inherited her bank balance and property, the prison doors opened on a bright escape avenue, fringed with new clothes, good hotels and gay friends. Janet was not pretty. She could not disguise her age, or her lack of sophistication. Amongst the young, beautiful, glamorous feminine competition of the West Coast she was a non-starter in the race to romance and home-making. Instead she found herself pregnant, and even her money was not enough to make the prospect of marriage tempting to the Don Juan.

The Salvationists at Oakland liked her from the first. This was one who knew her own mind. Though her flight to physical fulfilment had made such havoc, here was no woman of straw. In the atmosphere of the home, with the sound of the organ on Sunday mornings, Salvationist voices raised in prayer, the readings from the Bible, the sobriety and quietness of the long, sunny evenings, Janet rebelled—it was like being back home with mother!

Three weeks before the baby was born she exercised her right to walk out. To this day the Salvationists do not know what happened to her. Did she find happiness down the road? Or:

> My candle burns at both its ends,
> It will not last the night:
> But oh, my foes, and oh, my friends,
> It gives a lovely light!

as another American put it.

Liaison between psychiatrist and Salvationist is particularly valuable when abnormal mental conditions exist. William Booth's fundamental remedy for human ills, spiritual conversion, salvation, welds well with psychology, although the great Austrian, not religious, would probably not have felt complimented by any such suggestion.

Viola came from a poor white family, ruined in the Dust Bowl disaster decades earlier. Her mother seemed to be a nymphomaniac; her heedless father was an alcoholic. For the first steps in the thirteen-year-old girl's seduction, her mother played the part of pander.

When the child ran away, conditions were disclosed which constituted serious offences in law. The woman went to prison, the girl was put in a state institution for the feeble-minded. It was said that she had the mental development of a seven-year-old. Three years later she absconded. After spending some time as dish-washer and waitress in road-houses, she began hitch-hiking rides from all-night truck drivers. Soon she was arrested for vagrancy, found to be pregnant, and sent to Oakland.

Even the unshockable Salvationists found Viola hard to take. She had the table manners of an animal, was unwashed and verminous. Her hair was a collection of rat-tails, her finger nails filthy. Her language was a mixture of blasphemy and obscenity.

Practical, challenged, full of pity, the Salvationists gave Viola all they had. She emerged from hot showers transformed like Shaw's Eliza Doolittle. Folk were astonished to find there was a wild sort of beauty about her. More important, a professional check of her I.Q. rating indicated that she was not abnormal. Frightened, uneducated, rejected certainly, but not mentally below average.

The Army took the girl mother-to-be to itself in a special way. She accepted its religion with child-like simplicity; she became a Salvationist. Highly recommended by the Oakland administration she left to become maid-companion to a well-to-do widow.

Something of a beauty, she was also mentally and spiritually poised—well able to cope with life. She married in 1962. 'Case closed' they have written on the file at Oakland. Their hearts and minds are so engaged with the sad and the wicked that they must not ponder too long such a success story as Viola's.

Perhaps Donna epitomises most of what Oakland can give a girl waiting for her child to be born.

Farming family and horrified community sent her a 120 miles to the Salvation Army home across the bay above the Golden Gate. She came from a poor farm, a rural school, a backward area. When she arrived, she was as excited and astonished as *Alice Through the Looking Glass.*

The T.V., the happy music on the piano, the friendly people; the gadgets in the model kitchen; the chapel, the flowers, the stars and stripes and the yellow, red and blue of the Salvation Army flag, were all symbols made meaningful by lucid explanation. A real juke box, a class-room where one took lessons from a real typist-teacher; hair-do's by experts; help with the newly-discovered intricacies of beauty-treatment. Books on the shelves, barbecues and sing-songs under the trees in the evening. And no scolds!

Most important of all, for Donna, was the electric kiln where they taught her the magical art of ceramics, at which she displayed instinctive, quick aptitude: yet another unknown artist.

Filled with excited awareness, she took fire from her rich and happy environment. The view of the Golden Gate through the window, the colours, the friendship, and the feeling that she was safe, all added up to a new life for the girl to whom a woman's fate had come while still a child.

It was the preliminary to Donna's rehabilitation, or, as she had probably never been high enough to fall, her initial construction as a worthwhile personality.

She will have other problems to solve now that the baby has been adopted, and she is that much older, sadder, wiser. But the farmer's daughter, the small-town schoolgirl, has found herself, and a bit of heaven too. Life will not be able to push her about so easily in future.

21. THE PREVENTION OF PROSTITUTION

It is in the prevention of prostitution that the Salvation Army plays its greatest role. The Maywood Home at Vancouver illustrates this aptly. Brigadier May Taylor, Brigadier Lucy Ansell and their staff care for about forty women and girls who have been sexual delinquents. They notice, incidentally, that not only the consciences of the persons involved but the concern of the community is in process of being blunted in its reaction to this moral problem.

Many parents encourage their daughters to 'date' from the age of about twelve years. There is a scatter-brained idea of social prestige in this, even a vague belief that it is psychologically necessary for a girl-child not to feel 'isolated', unduly repressed or frustrated as she grows up. Many parents want their girls to mature early and, of course, 'normally'. So it happens that car rides or 'dates' with sundry boy friends are permissible long before some of the girls are mature enough to cope with the hazards involved.

If Salvation Army social officers were not too busy, and too sensible, their books and newspaper revelations on these highly scandalous subjects could be very lucrative. Captain Joyce Ellery, on the staff at Maywood, is a professionally trained social scientist whose casework material would make a Sunday newspaper feature-writer envious.

From her own association with the erring girls in her care she finds that at twelve years, or soon after, some of them become quite convinced that they are in love. When the girl has been to court, sometimes after being found pregnant, a maladjusted family relationship is usually revealed as the causative factor. There is no true child-parent relationship.

Sometimes the father is a withdrawn alcoholic, isolated by business commitments, or engaged in more or less permanent

214

acrimonious relationship with the wife. Teenage girls often confess that their moral breakout is to 'get even' with parents they feel have let them down.

Janice has light brown hair: she is fifteen. She has had two step-mothers since her own mother died in childbirth. Neither with the step-mothers nor her father has she had a happy relationship. She found affection with a boy who conspired with her to flout every wish of her parents. Her imagined love for the boy was really an expression of resentment against her father.

When she came to Maywood they not only had to arrange adoption for the baby but also to separate her from the boy whose influence upon her was wholly bad. Janice resisted for a long time, not so much because she loved the boy but because to give him up meant victory for her father.

After much patience and prayer the Salvationists succeeded. Janice responded to the influence of the staff, to the religion which motivated Maywood, and to the belated overtures of her family. The baby was adopted. Janice went back to school with a good chance of not beginning where she left off.

There are reasons for thinking that this sort of experience, which in times past was more usually permanently damaging, can now be forgiven and forgotten. A changed public outlook, greater skill among social workers, allow many of the girls to survive with varying degrees of composure and resiliance, the fate the Victorians regarded as 'worse than death'.

Clementine's father was a company director, though this did not make him react with greater enlightenment when he learned of his daughter's misconduct. His wife was a socialite; both had long neglected the girl. By providing her with generous pocket money, a good school, good clothes and a small car of her own, they considered they were free of further commitment. What they did not give was themselves. Neither were mature people.

What the girl needed, of course, was to share their lives, their love. They could not comprehend this, or interpret the various, obvious signals of imminent revolt. Mother had one formula for putting everything right: to take darling Clementine on a shopping spree. She equated love with bestowing the easily gained fruits of the acquisitive society. There was no real communication with the girl. She was alone in her own home.

When she was eighteen years old she left home, found a flat, and began a search for the affection she had been so long denied. She found it—after a fashion. Coming from such a background, she had a high potential for seduction. After a fleeting love affair, which left her pregnant, the putative father vanished. She went home where her parents just refused to talk about her plight. It was beyond their comprehension that what she had done was, in part, a result of their own shortcomings.

As money was available the girl was able to go to a private clinic. The baby was adopted. Everything was kept quiet. Then Clementine went back to school and everything continued as it was before. Mum and Dad did not change their ways but hoped that their erring daughter would change hers. She did not. After another year or so the girl was 'in trouble' again. This time she said, 'Send me to the Salvation Army. They have good homes. They can help me.' She was accepted for Maywood.

Two babies notwithstanding, the officers found that the girl's problem was not sex. For the men to whom she had given herself, for the experience which resulted in her conceiving, she was more or less indifferent. She was impelled towards her actions by a love-hate relationship with the parents who had failed her.

The officers at Maywood tried to make her see that she had cheapened herself, that the restoration of chastity would give her self-respect. She remembered with deep nostalgia the innocence and idealism of her childhood when she had been a Girl Guide. She exclaimed, 'If only I could be like that again!'

Salvation Army officers have great faith: 'You can,' they told her. She began to put her parents out of her life, and find herself. She must become a woman. God would help her. The Maywood officers witnessed a wonderful transformation in her, as they prayed and laughed and became good friends with Clementine.

The astonishing fact is that, after all, she went back home to those inadequate parents whose selfishness had contributed so much to her sufferings. Instead of wanting them, she was ready now to give herself to them.

Obviously, they get hardened cases at Maywood. Elaine was one. She had been a 'waitress', though a less polite name would be more exact for her.

Extravagant dress, cosmetics and off-beat conduct were her

escape from the unloved, unlovable person she had always been.
Placed in a foster home she had been 'dragged up', her foster
parents not even troubling to adopt her. At Maywood, they
found that her I.Q. was above average, yet she was hardly
literate.

Any man who looked at her was a prospect; again, not because
of love, or lust, but because she wanted to belong to someone.
She had a succession of affairs before the pregnancy which
brought her to Maywood. They tried to help her, but she was
too far away from them. The baby was adopted. She made
promises and uttered meaningless prayers. Then she went back
to the cafés. Because she was lonely, miserable, the first man who
made a proposition was the man for her. Elaine had to belong
to someone.

She came back to Maywood where another illegitimate child
was born, and again they failed with Elaine. All they had, all
the resources of earth and Heaven they offered to the wretched
girl. She did not accept either. What she wanted most was something she had never had, something everyone has a right to
expect—someone to love, and someone who would love her.

She will go on looking for this until she dies. As she is living
now, her expectation of life cannot be high.

22. BEAUTY TREATMENT AT KALIMNA

Teenage girls do not differ greatly in any part of the world.

Kalimna, in Brisbane, Queensland, is a modern excellently equipped Salvation Army home for delinquent girls. That fertile soil of Australia is attracting many immigrants from Europe, a mixed bag, some from warm-blooded countries, who bring problems with them. Often their young people cannot settle to the simple life on the land, but drift to the towns and cities with foreseeable consequences. Native Australians, and British immigrants also, have their quota of problem children.

Salvationist social service began in Australia as described elsewhere in this book. It is kept well to the fore receiving splendid public recognition. The State Governor opened Kalimna and the Queensland authorities found much of the £150,000 needed to build and equip it to present-day standards.

You might assume that girls sent from the courts, or by one of the welfare societies, mostly with very poor home backgrounds, would be pleased by the luxurious home with its swimming pool, modern design furnishings, colour schemes, good food and activities.

Yet their first reaction is usually loathing: many show their disgust in violence or studied insolence. Because of this some girls must be given a brief spell in a room where they can do little damage.

One girl wrote on arrival, '*There are three ways of committing suicide: 1. Drowning: 2. Hanging: 3. Coming to a dump like this.*' This she proudly displayed for the staff to see. She thought they'd be shocked. She was mistaken. They expect such reaction. They are prepared to wait.

Another girl plastered her room with the names of her adored boy friends, causes of her delinquency. 'Please God, let me out of this awful place,' she added.

Yet those who arrive in that mood of rebellion often come to hold Kalimna and its officers in high regard. Some make a spiritual discovery that changes their lives. Many do not again get into the moral and social dilemma which caused them to be 'sentenced' to Kalimna for their own protection for a term not less than one year.

Sermonizing is rarely encountered among social workers of the Salvation Army. The officers persuade, lead, demonstrate: they do not preach, leave alone hector or lecture. The softening-up process they pray for is gradual, sometimes long-delayed. But they have patience. The girl who weeps, refuses food, becomes hysterical, will subside in due course. She can be won to co-operation perhaps, by the offer of a perm, or a demonstration of sensible make-up by the home beautician. This is not such odd Salvationist emphasis as one might imagine. The correlation between good appearance and inner feeling has long been known to the soldiers in William Booth's Army. The Founder believed that soup and hot water were valuable preliminaries to prayers and the quest for spiritual salvation. It was a Salvation Army officer who wrote the song beginning 'Let the beauty of Jesus be seen *in* me'.

Numbers of the girls study for the State Examination in music. Other of the feminine arts taught at Kalimna are dressmaking, cookery, typing, deportment, ceramics . . .

All the time the atmosphere of the place has its effect. The family prayers, the short readings from the Bible, the private conversations with the staff, achieve dramatic results, although taking much longer than the old time, 'Kneel down, and you're saved!'

Girls who have alarming case-histories, being taken in charge by the state welfare authorities after suffering horrifying indignities, graduate into prim young misses at Kalimna.

As a girl settles down, she goes up in status until she is a sort of head-girl, with a charming room, flowers on her dressing-table, her own wardrobe and cupboards and even a framed picture of her favourite film star, or pop-singing idol. She has privacy: she is trusted.

She can abscond, and some do. But all are inevitably brought back. It is far better to accept it. Outings are allowed when a girl deserves them, and walks outside. Increased pocket-money allows her to buy face cream, lip-stick, to assert herself until after about twelve months she is deemed worthy of being allowed to attend school outside or accept employment.

23. BUT SOME GO TO BORSTAL

William Booth showed remarkable prescience in anticipating the development of social science. But the idea that it was sufficient of itself was anathema to him:

'To get a man soundly saved, it is not enough to put on him a new pair of breeches, find him regular work, or even give him a university education. These things are all outside the man: if the inside remains as before, you have wasted your labour.'

With that in mind, Welfare State notwithstanding, the Salvation Army in Britain still finds it has a part to play in Christian social service for the young; Redheugh Boys' Home, Ayrshire, is an example. The Chief Probation Officer for the county is Mr. A. H. Stevenson. It so happens that he is a Salvationist and his support for the home and its policy is not unconnected with its high standing and measure of success in rehabilitating delinquent or maladjusted boys. He finds that of hundreds sent there from the courts since 1952, when the place was opened, about eighty-five per cent have 're-established themselves in the community'. This is a higher ratio than average in homes for teenage boys. Salvationists believe that success is related to the Army's emphasis on the religious factor.

Not all the boys go to the penitent-form. Some are sent down to Borstal. Others go on to approved schools, where a tougher discipline takes the place of the Salvationist hope, love, prayer and Bibles. These are the minority of irreconcilables, who treat a compassionate and optimistic administration with the snigger reserved more frequently for obscene inscriptions on lavatory walls.

Most of the boys go out to work, play football, eat big dinners and, astonishingly, enjoy a visit to the Kilbirnie Corps of the Salvation Army. There the band plays gaily and the girls are pretty. Sometimes the girls go up to Redheugh for a party. They are, of course, well chaperoned by the members of the Home

League women's meeting, the Captains and the rest. One of many lessons the lads learn is that a Salvationist is a human being who can cease from preaching and have a good laugh like any other sensible body.

If the boy wants to run away, he does. Many do. It gets them nowhere. Inevitably the police bring them back. Better by far to be the boy Redheugh can trust. Most come to see that it is not a matter of doing what the Captain orders: it makes sense.

The long distance runners at Redheugh need not be lonely. A startling discovery a boy makes there is that someone cares about him as a person. Not a few have never had a chance to learn this. One boy, who is now married and in a good job, dates his acceptance of social responsibility from the occasion when the Captain had faith in him and was willing to allow him to go away for the week-end in trust that he would be back on Monday morning. He was.

Boys at Redheugh can take solace from the fact that while they sit through sermons and services for the good of their souls, the Captain and others of the staff often have to take courses and sit through series of lectures by sociologists of Glasgow University. These are arranged by the Scottish Home Department, which, with the Probation Service, tends to have a proprietary air as regards Redheugh. This is not only because the professionals pay some of the bills: they know they are on to a good thing.

Top boy at Kilbirnie Central School has more than once been a Redheugh lad, a model boy risen like a Phoenix from the ashes of his bad upbringing. This ought to mean something about religion and responsibility, one subject that the experts note, though they prefer not to comment on it—religion is as unmentionable as sex with many people. But Mr. C. Corner, Chief Inspector for Scotland of Child Care and Probation, is on record as saying that 'Redheugh is a home in the real sense to the boys.'

Let those be horrified who must—some of the boys who have been sent to Redheugh by magistrates are now Salvationists, uniformed, enlisted, if not conscripted, in William Booth's Army. 'I am not a volunteer,' the old man growled when refusing to call his growing Christian Mission 'The Volunteer Army'.

But none of his people are conscripts. If a boy anywhere, by the qualms of his conscience, the triumph of his near defunct better nature, or just by that flash of light that transforms devil into saint—if that boy wishes to be saved, then let him be saved. The name for it can be what you will. The Army agrees with Juliet. Call it 'conversion', call it 'committed', even 're-orientated', 'adjusted' or what have you. Being saved by any other name means all it must if it means, as it does, that many a lad sees the gleam and follows it into a happier, brighter country.

24. THE MAJOR COLLECTS COSHES

The House of Concord, near Toronto, in Canada, is a rather hazardous undertaking. Boys from sixteen to twenty years of age are cared for while on probation. They are adult offenders.

Major Archibald MacCorquodale, the officer in charge, had been a prison Chaplain, at Burwash, in North Ontario, and also Chaplain to the prison officer village community of 1,500 souls. There were 900 prisoners. He has, therefore, experience. He has also a highly modern approach. One wonders what William Booth would have thought of his tolerance, his use of the jargon of psychologists, his unshockable reaction to the horrifying catalogue of offences and perversions he encounters.

Though the forty or fifty boys in Concord are first offenders in the adult courts, many of them have a long record of previous offences in juvenile courts. Concord does not accept any boy: there is a method. Careful prior enquiry seeks to discover whether the lad would respond to this method.

On the Board of Admissions sits a magistrate, two psychiatrists, two probation officers, three Salvation Army officers. It can be taken as read that though the Salvation Army considers each point of view, it does not lightly surrender its own. The Salvation Army officer must not allow himself to be too easily pushed around by those with legal status or professional qualifications. The calm confidence of an officer with long experience in religious social service can easily be mistaken for arrogance. In fact it is a necessary defence mechanism: if a Salvationist's evangelical religion is left out of his calculations then his service becomes meaningless to him. Concord Home for Boys shows true Christian catholicity, true Boothian lack of discrimination in accord with the grand old man's oft quoted dictum, 'Go for souls and go for the worst.'

The Major does not ask whether a boy will be amenable to discipline, but whether, difficult case though he is, a way can be found to get at him, to find the key to the good that is in him. A boy has the option of coming or not; no one is compelled to go to Concord, although one must admit the alternative may be something objectionable.

Twenty-five per cent of all the lads are Roman Catholics, as is inevitable if the home is to cater for the needs of a community split between Rome and Luther. But then the court, and the priest, know all the facts. If a Roman Catholic boy goes, he goes because he wants to go and those interested in him want him to go. Concord has a very high rating as a centre for moral and spiritual rehabilitation.

Those who have obsolete ideas about the Salvation Army, that it deals only in soup, bread and jam, cups of tea and hell-fire, would find Concord something of an eye-opener. Not only are the degrees in sociology available, though never vaunted—there is an ultra-modern sociological set-up in which a team of scientists take part.

But it all has to do with MacCorquodale's knowledge of the Bible. Perhaps the most astonishing thing is that Freud and the Bible, in the catalysis which is this officer's enlightened Salvationism, make excellent bedfellows.

MacCorquodale thinks of each boy as an individual and encourages his staff to do so. The lad is taken on a 30-day trial and, if the preliminary report is favourable, the Courts commit him for a year or more. Sometimes acute emotional disturbance becomes evident.

Twenty-six offenders sent to Concord have been found to be seriously unstable and are now in mental hospitals.

The glib, too-easy explanation of delinquency as being caused by home background and psychological causes alone is not sufficient for MacCorquodale. He considers them, but the motif of sin runs through all his thinking and attempts at remedial action.

Yet, in part, he is ready to see the lad as a victim. Rejection is a word that frequently occurs. The feeling of inferiority, ultra-sensitivity, runs deep in many boys who have never known true love, that sense of being wanted that all mortals feel. The mothers of some of the inmates of Concord were drunkards or otherwise caricatures of true womanhood. It goes without saying

H

that many of the boys are born out of wedlock. The social dissonance created by this fact alone is an argument for marriage.

Many boys leave Concord with a sense of pride felt by a boy who leaves a good school. Graduates get Bibles! More astonishing still, some have learned to appreciate that oft-despised book. Some of the delinquents enter into an experience of religious conversion, though not necessarily Salvationism. The Salvation Army, in its social service, ought not to be and is not in fact interested in inducing apostasy, even when the membership of that other denomination is merely technical.

The Recreation Director at Concord is an old boy, a Roman Catholic, who entered into his experience of religion while at the home. One boy who was committed to the place hopes to be a Salvation Army officer and, other things being equal, the Salvation Army will be glad to have him.

The boys are taught farming, or trained for jobs as service station attendants or cooks. The courses are under expert supervision with the active assistance of the Department of Education.

100 DIMES ON A WIRE

Joe is taking one of these courses and is able to speak for himself:

The Major here is a real bright type and his nose is like a mine-detector. He can smell a knife, however well you hide it. His collection of bike chains, coshes, black-jacks and other killing machinery is always good for a column and a photo in the local paper when he goes about giving talks and lectures. You should see the old ladies open their eyes in alarm when they get a peep at his armoury.

Bing Crosby used to sing, 'Buddy, can you spare a dime?' Let me tell you that 100 dimes threaded on a wire rope make a felonious instrument that can knock 'em cold, all quiet like, before you can say 'knife'. The Major has some beauties.

I'm seventeen and I'd carried a knife for some time before I came here. Of course, I only came seeing it was that or jail. My time was one year and I thought that being the Sally Army I'd take them all for a ride, easy game. After all when you see them on the corner, singing about Jesus and praying like a lot of angels, you'd think it was a push-over.

Major MacCorquodale spotted my knife before I was hardly inside the front door! Before I had time to think I was looking after the chickens, collecting the eggs, filling the watercans like a big square fool.

Then Major found I was interested in cars. Very much, seeing I pinched more than one. He transferred me then to the training school for motor mechanics. 'You'll have all the cars you want to work on, Joe, and perhaps, in good time, one of your own.'

It has been a break for me to come here. I got to like the Major, having never had a proper father. My old man died of a heart attack; I saw him. But he never meant nothing to me.

My mother hanged herself. This is the truth I'm telling you. Not only was I wrong about the Salvation Army—they are really with it here—but I never met a man like the Major. He's a guy you can take to. He can tear a strip off you and still get you to like him. I don't go much for this religion stuff, but this place goes by it.

There's plenty of guys like me round Toronto. Two thousand get nabbed by the coppers every year. There's folk who think we're all a lot of no-goods. They put programmes on the TV about us. Of course, we always make a story for the newspapers when there's a shortage of murders or sex crimes.

It's in this place you learn that a bloke can cope with his private devil. Major reckons that about sixty-five of every 100 boys who come here make good and he's a good fellow for keeping the figures.

When you arrive you feel as mad as hell, but this Major just sits back and lets you work off your mood, black and full of hate for everybody, loathing the Salvation Army most of all.

Then into my thick head there comes a marvellous idea—the Salvation Army put it there! I need not be a rotter, liar, thief, a pestilent abortion! I might have been, but not now, if you know what I mean. Hardly before I could finish looking at the picture of old General Booth on the wall they had me listening to little sermons, singing hymns, an' saying prayers . . .

Very often a kid runs away. They always bring him back. In the end the greatest insult the Major can hand out to a guy is to decide that Concord won't keep him—he just ain't good enough. Most of us get to feel, before we've been many weeks, that we can go along with this place . . .

When I came here I thought I'd like to reform, and go into big business where there's lots of lolly to be had in oil, uranium and real estate—Canada's filthy with it; you can read about it in the papers every day.

But they made me fill in a lot of questions and got some guys from college to work it out so that I was only 88, whatever that means—something about me being not so hot on the top floor. Certainly it meant that I couldn't make a pile in business. So now they've learned me their Service Station Course. I'll go out there and get as much as I can out of the customers, honestly.

One thing I'm sure of: it's a mug's game getting involved with the coppers. You only get in deeper and deeper. The Major told us about men as spent nearly all their life in jail and he should know. He's been in clink many times, not for anything wrong, of course; he'd be praying with the blokes.

I can say with my hand on my own Bible that I'm going to give this religion business a proper trial and keep my nose clean.

SOME ARE ASKED TO LEAVE

My name is Meakings, Captain Bramwell Meakings and, with my wife, I am Assistant Officer at Concord.

One of my tasks is the mental rating and record of the boys here. We get them with ratings of 60-69, which allows committal to mental hospitals if necessary. Others are 70-79, borderline mental defectives, while most are 80-89 dull normal, and 90-109 average. Some are 110-119, bright.

This rating cannot be varied. Many people think of I.Q. as if it was mercury in the barometer, changing from day to day.

What we do find is that many a boy is not as good in performance as his rating allows. We are with the psychologists here: we dig deep to find the factors that cause the failure in character and behaviour. More often than not we discover causes related to a bad home, drunken parents, cruelty, school, job, sex or health problems to which the lad cannot adjust.

Though the Major has his eye on the target—to a Salvation Army officer this is always the religious solution—he takes the sociological factors into account. The case-worker, the probation officer, the psychiatrist, matter very much as far as we are concerned. We need them and we are happy to work with them.

A number of boys come here from middle-class background —ten sent here recently have fathers who are professional men —including a judge, lawyer, minister of religion and one university professor.

Some are from good working-class homes. But most, as pointed out earlier, are from 'bad' homes. Of a sample count over three years, I find that no fewer than sixty-five are illegitimate; while ninety-one have parents now separated or divorced.

We believe that the stress of life as immigrants is related to delinquency. Many of the boys who come here, or who ought to come, are of recent entry to Canada: Italians, Poles, Germans —almost all the countries of Europe. It should be admitted, however, that the largest group is English, 116 boys; indigenous French Canadian number forty-three.

But about the failures? We have moved a long way, since, in our early days, we somewhat naïvely imagined that all who knelt and prayed were 'saved'. Being converted is wonderful and it *is* essentially simple, but it is not as easy as that. We have lads with permanent infirmities that they must live with, be mocked by, for the rest of their lives.

These problems are not always solved even when the social scientists have done their best and the Major has called on God.

In a simple breakdown: of 349 boys we returned 158 to referal source with something accomplished. Often this is drastic; the lad is never the same afterwards. About sixty-five per cent of our cases are modern miracles of the grace of God mixed with the science of good men—God's men.

But forty-four just couldn't take it. We asked them to leave. They were obstructing the policy of the home, harmfully influencing other boys, showing no potential of progress.

Twenty-six went to Ontario Hospital, some with health problems that may not allow of their return to us. Others will come back. Thirty-four just ran away; one got himself killed.

We have forty boys with us at the moment. They are similar to previous samples. Some will fail: others will make the grade.

Any enlightened Christian can tell you that not all the called are chosen.

FORGOTTEN BY THEIR PARENTS

How do the 'graduates' fare?

Major MacCorquodale states:

Some leave us to walk, or more usually, run into the arms of a policeman. They are now in prison or gainfully engaged, *pro-tem*, in a life of crime. They came to us far down the slope after such offences as: robbery, uttering forged notes or passing counterfeit coins, fraud, illegal carrying of weapons, and so on. Eighty per cent of all offences are breaking and entering or theft of cars.

You have seen that more than half of these lads make good even if they do not accept that salvation which gives us our name.

Many of those who fall by the way need not, and probably would not, if there were better after care. There are boys in here for a year or longer who never get a line from a parent, never a visit from kith or kin. They are just forgotten.

We must do better. Our unit of operation is too large—fifty boys or more lumped together. The aim is cottages and the provision of that intimate good-home atmosphere some of these poor wretches have never known.

After the boys leave us there is need of a better reception by the community, which still works on the old and incompetent principle that a dog with a bad name must stay that way. Though there are some firms and individual employers who can believe that a boy is worth another chance, there are not enough. Too many treat the Concord old boy not as one who is making good—but as a 'ticket-of-leave' case to be viewed with suspicion.

Medling, who left us, is now in the Royal Navy and a skilled mechanic. When we first received him he seemed to be a highly suitable candidate for the gallows.

Reardon stayed here ten months in all. He left after the first month not understanding and unable to adjust. But he came back and made it. He is in a good job now and writes to me, I quote exactly: 'I'm proud! Going straight does work out. My sincere thanks to the Salvation Army for my progress.'

His final greeting is significant, for this was a lad who reacted strongly at first against the religious influence here: 'May God be with you,' are the words immediately preceding his signature. I have faith that God is with *him*. Perhaps his need is greater than mine.

One of my letters is from that minority with whom we come into contact who are good mothers:

'Thank you for your care of our son. This letter long delayed, for I have been waiting to see how things worked out. I have long and sad experience of the unreliability of my boy's promises and good intentions.

'This time it seems that he means it. He is doing well at his job at the garage and is happy, affectionate and co-operative. He has new friends, including a nice girl. It is the first period in years when his father and I have not had cause to be anxious lest he become belligerent and take off and get mixed with the wrong crowd.

'It was heart-breaking at the trial when the Judge asked, "Do you think this boy is worth helping?" The Army did think he was and so did I. My husband and I must ever be grateful that you had faith in our son.'

One other follow-up case, of which there are many: 'Major, I like this place very much. I now have a complete uniform and a room of my own. It takes me about fifteen minutes to get to work and I am getting on well with the boss and the others . . . My Probation Officer sees that I keep in touch. I have a tidy sum in the bank.

'What I miss most is the Sunday chapel at Concord, the singing, the talks and even the laughs! If you could hear me you'd find I still sing 'em at work and on the way down of a morning. I go to the United Church Sunday mornings and I like it. My regards to the Captain and everybody . . .'

As is inevitable our selection of the evidence tends to give a rosy picture of the situation at Concord. It is not intentional. We are often despairing, filled with grief at what we must see and be powerless to prevent. Here, more than most places, we know the truth of old John Donne's line: 'I am mine own executioner.'

It is like watching a Greek drama, where the characters enact their own destruction before the eyes of a silent, pitying audience which is powerless to intervene. It is as if the boys are puppets, the playthings of violent, terrible, depraved forces. Yet those who betray them love them. The community that consigns them here pays high taxes for education costs, hires the best welfare personnel, generously supports the Salvation Army and other agencies which seek to solve the problem of youth crime.

It is part of the universal dilemma. One who was never a juvenile delinquent lamented, 'When I would do good evil is present with me.' At Concord we still thank God for that salvation which is the motivation of our Army from the day in 1865 when it began its march. Hallelujah, some are saved!

25. THE COWS DON'T KNOW IT'S SUNDAY

Bayswater Boys' Home in Victoria, Australia, is about twenty-five miles outside Melbourne. It was acquired by Herbert Booth when he was Territorial Commander at the turn of the century. He paid £30,000 for its 500 acres, a tremendous sum for those days. The old General was cool towards the project, as being too ambitious, but time has justified Herbert Booth.

Australian welfare authorities of the time had called upon the voluntary agencies because of the failure of their prison reformatory system, excessive in cost and catastrophic in results. When Parliament made provision for grants to be made to suitable institutions, the Army qualified. Herbert Booth placed great store on the farm-plus-industrial centre so beloved of his father and advocated in the latter's *In Darkest England and the Way Out*. As such he founded Bayswater.

It remains sixty years after, but some of its buildings are ultra-modern, demonstrating the latest ideas in care and moral and social rehabilitation. Spiritual rehabilitation too, but that, of course, is a Salvation Army extra. The estate is beautifully situated and its potential as housing development area is tremendous. It would be worth many times what was paid for it, but the Army sacrifices development profits to continue its ministry for delinquent boys and needy children.

All the youths at Bayswater come from the courts and again their parents are the true problem. It is not unknown for the mother to be a prostitute and the father an alcoholic: one problem creating the other.

Standing on the hill, looking across the green slopes below, made fertile and rich by a modern irrigation system, it is difficult to believe that such dilemmas exist as do exist in the tall red building erected by Herbert Booth all those years ago. Let Number 44 on the Admission Sheet speak for himself. He is eighteen years old and has been ten months at Bays-water:

'My old man stabbed my mother. He had good cause. She got better, but he went to jail and I, who had to go on living with her, started missing school, getting into trouble with the police who were always calling for one reason or another.

'Once I set fire to a place just because I had a grudge against the guy who owned it. I started breaking and entering houses, factories too.

'Why not? Everybody kicked me around. Do you know what it feels like to walk up to a crowd of kids your own age, your own language, like yourself, human and Australian, and then notice how quiet they get, frozen? Their mums and dads have said to 'em, "You mustn't mix with the likes of him."

'So I got twelve months' "sentence" to this dump. Don't think I welcomed it. It could have been the Belsen gas chambers—it would be all the same to me.

'There's over fifty guys here like me, hard and rotten types and some fairly good ones. You can take your pick. But the man in charge, a brass hat named Lieut.-Colonel Stevenson, and others who work with him, have a good idea who's who and what's what.

'A number of us run away at least once. The Army people seem to expect it. But you have to settle down; the coppers always bring you back. After that it doesn't seem to be worth it any more.

'There's a first-class dairy herd here, pigs, poultry, orchards and market gardening. I didn't know any of it, but it was fun learning.

'Maybe they'll make a farmer out of me. Did you know that you can cut up maize and pickle it sort of, make silage out of it? We have a machine that does it. The stuff comes carted from the fields in big loads, pulled by tractors. Then it gets minced into little bits as big as your finger. You sprinkle treacle on it and it keeps for ages. The cows like it. It smells nice. I could eat it myself.

'But you get decent grub here, and the chance to relax after a long day in the hot sun. They show films, some of 'em exciting, real films from Hollywood. Now and then they send some professor johnny from Melbourne, from the college, and he talks to us about sex and psychology and human behaviour and all that junk. You give him a horse laugh at first, but as a rule it gets interesting and he makes you listen and even understand the stuff.

'What my old man would think of me, falling for that, and him in prison, is anyone's guess.

'There's athletic coaches here and we play football. We cannot play like the League, but we are good as teams go in Australia. We have won games against hard competition.

'Those who can't take the farming learn to make things in the factory. We do good trade with schools and clubs and other joints making chairs, easels, ladders, toys, building blocks, shelves, trestle-tables and lots of stuff. Some of the fellows here get to be so good at woodwork that they go into the trade and don't have to go stealing when released. They actually stay on the level. But I'm going to be a farmer.

'Did you know that one of the big black-and-white cows can have a fifteen-pound calf—money pounds I mean—every year or so for ten years? If you look after her properly she'll give three or four gallons of milk a day every day, which you can sell to the highest bidder. There's more money in it than in the Broken Hill silver mines! I'm beginning to get this: a bloke can do better being honest than being a crook. My old man never told me that!

'It must cost a million to run this place: electric machinery, qualified instructors, mechanics for the latest farm gadgets. The Salvation Army wallahs here also have training; some of 'em have been to college, which shook me at first. I thought that all Army people were converted burglars, low types like me. They get students here too. These come on three-month field work courses from a Government training school. When you get to know them, they're all right. When they first come they're very green and high hat.

'You can earn a quid a week here and be allowed to spend up to five shillings of it at the canteen: such extravagance! But no drinks: the Salvation Army does not encourage riotous living.

After a while, if you toe the line, they let you have week-ends off, that's if you have anywhere decent to go. If, like me, you have nowhere, nobody, you stay around and they try to make your life tolerable over the week-end. Of course, the cows never know when it is Sunday; that milk comes from the milking machines whether the Army's going to have a meeting or otherwise.

'Believe it or not, my old man would reckon it disgraceful I've been to the Army meetings. It grows on you; seven of the lads here have become Salvationists and I am told that hundreds of the lads have done so in times gone by. Not that they make you. There's pressure to behave: if your reports are bad you lose privileges. If they are very bad, you could get transferred to a real gaol where there are no cows or snack bars—only 'bulls' and iron bars.

'If you fail here you might go to Turana, that's a Government centre. There you get no remission at all, nobody to fill in a form and say you've been a good boy, which is what can happen at Bayswater. If the worst happens you'll find yourself in Pentridge. There it is so bleak that some of the toughest guys in Australia go white as a lily at the thought of it.

'Funny thing is, and I'm not the only one who says this, the religion of these Sally Army people gets you. Mind you, we are all right innocents at religion, when we come. Maybe that helps. I didn't know nothing about it. My old man taught me lots about coppers, and other people's property, but nothing about saying my prayers or reading the Bible. He didn't go in for that stuff.

'When I came here I had three particular enemies:

1. A copper, any copper.
2. Anybody who locked me up or kept me from doing what I liked.
3. Those big-headed johnnies who try to tell me things that are good for me, when I don't want to learn.

'It took a long time and more than a bit of patience to change my mind about most of that. Now I'm happier here than I was at my real "home". I dunno whether I'll join General Booth's

Army, but I reckon as how they put me on to something good. Likely I'll be able to get a job when I leave here and I reckon to keep it and stay away from the law. The Salvation Army have made me believe in religion: but they haven't succeeded in making me love coppers any more than before.'

26. 'THEY HATE IT WHEN THEY COME'

Down the hill, in the valley below the farm, are the Bayswater Cottage Homes, where we accept lads aged from eight to fourteen years. All are housed in modern-style cottages, where there must be House Parents in the approved modern manner.

My wife and I (Major and Mrs. Griffin) are House Parents for the Salvation Army in this self-contained group of cottages in which the Education Department of the State of Victoria displays keen interest, providing financial assistance.

They also 'interfere', in the sense that they make suggestions and expect us to move with the times. Though Herbert Booth was farseeing, he could not visualize the changes that lie between the Victorian era and the twentieth century.

You might wonder why the powers-that-be do not run the homes themselves. There are sociologists, welfare experts, humanists, altruists galore in Australia these days. The truth, in my opinion, is that there's always something left out when the mere secularist does the job. Herbert Booth would not have approved of Freud on that count. Something extra is needed—the religious element.

The children here take to religion like ducks to water. Just as they play and laugh in the fields about here, grow quick and strong in the Australian sun, as naturally and happily as they do, they take to family prayers, a story from the Bible, a simple meeting for worship on Sunday mornings. It is my belief that this is missing, to their tragic loss, in the lives of many children today because their parents cannot provide it. When put on superficially, not coming from experience, from within, it is false, embarrassing and incompetent.

This is where so many parents of these tragic young people have fallen down. They could not help the children to apprehend what they had not apprehended themselves.

A beautiful thing about the Bayswater Cottage Home is that here we can see the younger lad saved before he can become delinquent. When he comes at the age of ten, say, he is simply a lad with a problem father, a delinquent mother, a domestic tragedy, a mild neurosis. Then he is so near to us, so closely woven into the intimate atmosphere of the small units that we soon get to know him and he gets to love us. Of course, we love him from the first.

One lad left to go home because of his real parents' assurance, 'Things will be better in future.' Yet he ran away from his own home to come back here! This was the first, the only real home he'd ever known.

Obviously we arrange school for our boys, some go to the State high school. Many of them become scholars and do well in after life.

They come to us as rebels. Remember many are taken away from their homes because they are in need of care, or protection from social or moral danger. During the first few weeks we might have a few runaways. But the lad who hates the place usually learns to love it.

The Manager here, Major Alfred Francis, with Mrs. Francis, does a good job. The University or Education Department often send experts to study the work here. One woman, with good qualifications and experience in this field, said, 'We may know more of what is in the books, but when it comes to doing the job, the Army can still lead us.'

Of course, it should not be assumed, these days, that the Army officer doesn't know what is in the books. There are some important matters, however, that you cannot learn from books.

Herbert Booth, in the 1890's, had little or no knowledge of social science in the professional mode of our time. But that did not disqualify Herbert Booth from doing wonderful work in the psychological field now important to all social workers. There are two ways to learn, don't you agree, the scientific, academic way, and by heart and ear, intuitively.

If you wish for proof that the authorities think highly of us and sometimes turn to us when others have failed, we can offer it. One boy who came here, stayed here and made good here, had been in eighteen institutions previously. Sometimes the cause of this is so obvious, so preventable, that it makes one weep for the prodigality of pain, the avoidability of tragedy.

One boy was deaf in one ear, had poor hearing in the other. Everyone complained that he 'wouldn't take any notice'. He was stamped as a rebel. His own mother had rejected him, 'because he won't listen'. She did not ask herself why he did not listen. We found out why and saw that he had the skilled treatment he needed. It was like the 'open sesame' to the cave of Ali Baba.

Yet we too have our failures. When the best has been done we see some who remain as closed doors, their minds, their hearts obdurate against us. One boy left here to die. He felt like a caged bird, a trapped animal. When we gave him the option —we must—he ran. They found him by a railway bridge stabbed to death.

That is exceptional, but some will not be saved: they exercise their right to be damned. At such a time it is possible to doubt if the Bayswater labour is worthwhile. Then the car arrives at the gate with another group of lads. They are neutral as a sheet of white paper. We know by carefully checked records that we can make good with more than half of them.

Pioneer Salvationist Herbert Booth would accept that, even if he were not satisfied with it.

27. THE CLUBS IN THE BASEMENTS

If Salvationist service for delinquent boys has high repute among probation officers, help with their emotional and spiritual problems before they get into trouble of any serious sort, is also important. Two examples of Boys' Club of America work conducted by Salvation Army officers show that Salvationists allow considerable variety in method. Only the South in the United States could produce Brigadier Julius Mack Satterfield, proud wearer of the Order of the Founder, highest Salvationist honour, conferred not only for his Boys' Club service, but for all the other services rendered by him.

William Booth's firm rule that corps commands should be changed at intervals not longer than one to three years went by the board because of this man's unique qualities. He served ten years at Lakeland, in Florida, ten at Spartanburg, South Carolina, and twenty-five at his latest command, Winston-Salem.

Born in Charlotte, North Carolina, in the Bible-belt, Satterfield had no marked youth problems of his own, unless one counts poverty a problem. Home, school, social environment, were all favourable for the robust, evangelical kind of religion he saw in a Salvation Army open-air meeting.

Early warning of his 'eccentricities' was that he did not enter to be an officer as he went along in charge of a corps. He learned quickly.

It was soon evident that in Satterfield the Salvation Army had a man on its hands. In the highly individualistic climate of the South, he flourished as the green bay tree. He must be one of the few Salvation Army officers who have ever commanded the corps in their own home town. When he was appointed to his first command, New Bern, N.C., it was a post of considerable difficulty and challenge.

'Send Satterfield,' someone said. This vote of confidence was more than justified.

It was not long before the most striking of his idiosyncracies showed itself: he took deep root wherever he went. It was not always possible to transplant him.

No other corps officer has a record approaching Satterfield's: fifty-one years, and but seven corps appointments. To a degree unusual, even in the United States, where undenominational, socio-religious work for the whole community is the norm, Satterfield's services became part of the life of the whole town. It was mainly with the young people.

Married, with growing sons of his own, he was provided with a fireside information service. He compared the lot of his carefully reared children with that of many others: reckless, Godless, and sometimes violently anti-social. Even the very good boys and girls were bored, frustrated, restless.

In Florida he sat out the last night with a boy in the death cell. In the morning he walked with him down the corridor to the electric chair. He learned how many little things, how many avoidable things had destroyed the boy. In prisons, reformatories, police courts and slums, he encountered young people hurt in their own homes, or degraded by gang life.

Always able to improvise, he began his first Boys' Club in a basement. There was room for eighteen lads: he gathered the loneliest, the toughest he could find. He began to sound the tocsin from his platform in the Salvation Army hall, at clubs, citizens' groups, in the press, on the radio, and later, T.V.

The burden of his alarm signal: We are all to blame for the condition of our young people. We must ask God's forgiveness, and beg Him to help us. We must spend money, and give our time and services to save our children before they are in trouble. Afterwards it is often too late.

By 'our children', Mack Satterfield meant everyone's children. Not only those in the better schools and going up to college: the young in the poor quarters; the Negro children, too. The first Chairman of his Boys' Club at Winston-Salem was the head of the State Bureau of Investigation. Many other prominent and able people assisted.

The eighteen boys in the basement became hundreds, thousands of boys, and all within the splendid Boys' Clubs of America system—to which Satterfield adds his Salvationism. Herbert Hoover, one-time President of the United States, prominent in Boys' Clubs of America, pointed out:

'Even the taxpayer can understand that the cure of gangsterism is a thousand times more expensive than the diversion of a boy away from a gang. We can do the latter for forty dollars apiece, while the former costs 10,000 dollars, and often does not succeed at that.'

Judge Crews, of Winston-Salem, said of Satterfield's work: 'It is one of Winston-Salem's big factors in crime prevention.'

Paeans have been sounded on radio and T.V. 'In Satterfield you see the Salvation Army on the march,' wrote one newspaper columnist, Chester Davis.

The Sheriff of Forsyth County shook the Brigadier's hand. 'Brigadier, I reckon your work saves the county hundreds of thousands a year.'

But much of the money has not been saved: it has been diverted. Kilns for the glazing of ceramics may be highly efficient in keeping a boy usefully occupied, but they cost a lot of money, as will the salary of the instructor. Electric tools are costly, as are the buses for the baseball teams, and the large, fully equipped gymnasium, and the swimming pool that cost 118,000 dollars.

The student now at North Carolina University, majoring in photography, and the number of former club members who are professional photographers needed expensive cameras and dark room equipment that their own homes and schools could not provide. They also had to have a highly paid professional teacher.

One rich reward of his long term work is that Satterfield sees the boy as father to the man; when that man leaves the club he sends his son. These succeeding generations respond readily to club programmes, for co-operation at home is essential. The policy is gradualism: through all the wide range of activity— arts, crafts, athletics, sports, library, camping, indoor games— the idea of religion as a basis for character filters through.

About drink, on which Salvationists have no option, Satterfield must use persuasion on the non-sectarian Boys' Clubs of

America lines. But no boys can be long in the Satterfield orbit and remain unaffected. In a recent check among 1,000 of his boys, who were of age to drink if they wished, eight took beer, and five liquor occasionally. The rest were abstainers, not because they had to, but because they wished to. Success indeed.

The immense sums of money, well above half-a-million dollars, required for work on the Satterfield scale, could only be found by touching the hearts as well as the pockets of the citizens of Winston-Salem and the round-about Forsyth County. One member of the famed Reynolds tobacco company is on Satterfield's Advisory Board, and many other influential people have been generous supporters.

Satterfield has become a town 'property'. People say, 'He is a good man, he looked after my son.'

On the plane to Atlanta, the co-pilot, about to enter his cabin, asked a Salvationist, 'Do you know Brigadier Satterfield?' When the passenger replied that he was on his way to see him, the airman added proudly, 'I'm one of his boys.' There are thousands of such boys.

Of course, he has skilled help and strong financial backing, a field, alas, that makes comparisons highly unfavourable for Britain. Men's Clubs sponsor various projects, and parents' committees render powerful and generous assistance. The library is modern, expensive, much used, attractive; ranging from comics to the books the maths student may want for university study.

Executive Director David Rickard, B.A., a dedicated professional social worker, and a key man in Winston-Salem work for youth, gets over 6,350 dollars a year; the Programme Director 5,150; the Physical Training Director, 4,485; the Swimming Director, a like sum. There are other full-time staff, and other high costs, and also many able people who give their services free.

The range of activity of the club includes model planes, radio construction and repair, leather craft, wood shop, art, baseball (the coach for this is from the police department). Boy Scouts and choir are also active.

While time marches on in the South, as elsewhere, and girls are not always the well behaved and sheltered creatures they were, or were assumed to be, in former times, Satterfield has already opened a Salvation Army Red Shield Girls' Club for them, and an extension is being considered.

It is found that girls respond well to club life. Though administration differs in detail, the policy is the same: to provide a place where they can get together in busy happiness while they learn practical matters of home, community and conduct. The Girls' Club supplements what is done by home, school and church, and provides, where necessary, that omitted by them.

Hard-headed citizens who have to provide money to build and maintain quarter-million dollar projects do not just agree that a Girls' Club is needed without careful enquiry. Schools in the area of Winston-Salem, where the club was to be built, agreed to distribute questionnaires. Principals and teachers were first given details of the plan.

Obviously, there could have been no co-operation of this sort had the scheme been for the recruitment of Salvationists. This was service for the community without regard of creed—an idea that is always a main platform in Satterfield's youth work.

It was noticeable that the percentage of forms returned from the parents of pupils was lowest at the junior high school—fifty-four per cent. At four elementary schools, where girls from first to sixth grade attended, returns were just short of eighty per cent: 630 girls with the approval of their parents wanted the club, agreeing that there was need for it. Fifty of these girls indicated an interest in timbrel playing, traditional Salvationist activity, but swimming, cooking, sewing, baton-twirling and the girls' chorus headed the list, with hundreds of applicants apiece.

Adjusting the popular conception of American youth, gathered from films and comics, is the fact that 288 expressed a wish to join Bible classes.

Though Satterfield is an 'old-timer' and a Bible-belt man, these results and many other highly complicated tabulations were processed on General Electric electronic computers. Young Director David Rickard was responsible. This mixture of age with youth, traditional with modern, is one of the constant surprises and joys of American Salvationism.

Brigadier Julius Mack Satterfield, O.F. has now retired in fact —officially he had to retire at sixty-five. That was in 1952. With him it was a mere technicality; he went on with the job until August 1963, and it is true to say he is still doing it. While he has strength he could not cease from caring or working if he tried.

When they are 'promoted to Glory', the Satterfields are to be laid beside Julius Satterfield, Jnr., lost during World War II in air combat over the Himalayan Hump in Burma. He was a good boy who helped his father with the Boys' Club work.

Brigadier Satterfield has a uniform ready in which he must be attired to go on his last journey. There will be a memorial stone. But the greatest memorials are the men and boys who have passed through the club. Many a lad whose life began in a dark basement, where opportunity and decency were denied him has, through the Boys' Club work of Mack Satterfield, come up to the light: he lives clean and walks proudly now. Satterfield, the Boys' Club and God all had something to do with it.

28. THE BOYS WERE COLOUR-BLIND

While Brigadier Julius Mack Satterfield, O.F. might be termed an old-time Salvationist, Douglas Eldredge, in charge of Salvation Army Boys' Clubs at Baltimore, Maryland, is new-style. In his office hang numerous certificates. One is:

BRIGADIER DOUGLAS ELDREDGE, having met the requirements set by the National Association of Social Workers, is a member of the Academy and certified as a professional social worker . . .

It began long ago, and there are years of study and practical experience behind it. Yet Eldredge does not omit the old-time religion. He could not be a Salvationist if he did.

Older generations of Salvationists used to say, 'All that is required to help people and win them for God is hard work and the salvation of the Lord Jesus Christ.' Many made a good case for this, without degrees or diplomas, which of themselves prove little.

Yet county, state and federal authorities in America and all over the world are more than ever insisting on professional qualifications as a preliminary to financial aid. With many other Salvationists, Eldredge's task has been to reconcile professional social service attitudes with Salvationism.

The mixture might seem odd to many: Indian lore, 'cowboys', a ranch, forest, snakes, even a small zoo. About 3,000 boys of the Baltimore area are in the scope of the work at any one time: three clubs in the town, Puh'tok Camp and Top Bar Ranch in the country. To Eldredge, Indian lore is no escapist gimmick. He knows it expertly, and uses it for religious purposes, having acquired his first knowledge of it from Ernest Thompson Seton, a world authority.

Full Indian regalia, camp fires, 'war dances', tepees, are part of the programme the boys enjoy immensely on their own 400-acre camp. As they absorb some of the Brigadier's Indian lore they learn that scalping was a white man's invention, and that the Indian was a deeply religious person. 'Hiawatha invented the League of Nations,' says Eldredge, creating a basis for brotherhood between the Maryland boy and the vanished Indian.

He considers that this helped him to integrate the clubs, a matter of considerable delicacy in his part of the United States. The boys' link with the 'redskin' has helped to break down white insularity. There are boys on the boards of government, a majority of them, and they had to agree to the decision to integrate the clubs. It was not easy or instant. But they did accept integration. There are now many Negro members of the Salvation Army Baltimore Boys' Club.

Governing Boards, boys and executives, knew there would be adverse reaction. They advanced cautiously, but they advanced. One angry white parent took his boy away in protest. But in time the change was accepted. One of the mainly white clubs has a Negro programme director.

A mother was nonplussed when she called along to thank 'our Don Faulkner', whom her boy had praised as 'the greatest' club leader. Don Faulkner was a Negro. But after the initial surprise the boy's assessment was accepted.

'The Indian is not red,' Eldredge tells his youngsters. 'He is bronze, rather like the Chinese. Indeed, he probably was Asiatic, coming to America over the Bering Strait.' The boys' respect for Indians is increased by this, though why is not easy to understand.

As a boy encounters colour he also must face the problems of mixed religions. One common ground is the forest, the pool—nature, which Eldredge and his staff know so well. The boys will all gladly join in an Indian prayer.

One of the proudest moments in Eldredge's life was when in the pow-wow by a campfire, a boy wept. 'He was overcome by emotion. He felt something,' Eldredge declares. 'From then on, instead of being just a passenger, he was one of us. He had found God, Who is in many places.'

'American life began in the open-air,' says Eldredge to the boys. 'It is still the best of America.' Looking at the tanned and fit boys who hunt, run, swim, chop trees, and walk twenty miles at a stretch, one can see his point. Whether he is talking about Indians or the Pilgrim Fathers, he is a master of his theme, with that rare gift of not being a bore about a specialized subject. He dramatises everything, talking about the death of 'witches' at Salem, New England, where he lived; or the fact that it was his hero, Seton, who really launched the Boy Scouts.

'If Baden-Powell had not listened to him when Seton visited Britain,' says Eldredge, 'the Scouts would have been a semi-military organization based on Baden-Powell's experiences at Ladysmith or Mafeking.' Awful thought!

As a young man, Eldredge was content to be involved in Boys' Club and Boy Scout work. But he wanted to give it a stronger religious drive. When he enquired how this might be done, he was told, 'Try the Salvation Army.'

When he called at the local Army headquarters he was disappointed to find that the only person on hand was a pretty blue-eyed typist.

'May I help you?' she asked.

'No thanks,' he said. But he was wrong. She has been his life-long helper.

When her father, the Commanding Officer arrived, Douglas Eldredge, who had been making better acquaintance with the typist, was asking himself how this man would do as a father-in-law.

He married the typist shortly afterwards, and she, being an officer's daughter, helped him with inside know-how in the Salvation Army. He was soon busily engaged in organizing Boy Scout troops for the Salvation Army in the Southern New England Division. His success was considerable; his fame spread.

The renowned Commissioner William McIntyre, stationed in territorial headquarters down in Atlanta, asked him to organize Boy Scouts around Washington and in Virginia, and arrange a display by 300 boys in honour of George Washington's birthday. He was quite specific:

'Eldredge, I need a man who will wear out the soles of his shoes, not the seat of his pants.' The boys did parade, and Eldredge became first a Salvationist and then an officer.

Near Atlanta, in a typical mill village, the great depression of the thirties lay like a blight on the people. Forty per cent were illiterate, so Eldredge and his wife sought to relieve the boredom of unemployment by commencing night classes at the Army citadel. He has always sought to give Christianity its full implications. But neither the mill officers nor the manager approved of this. It was the time of labour trouble, and literate workers are always more difficult than the other kind. At least, that is what the mill manager said.

Yet Eldredge had the pleasure of seeing the city imitate him, starting its own night classes. He organized a Boys' Club and found that some of the lads came to his Sunday night meetings. They were rough and noisy. One or two of them joined the Salvation Army. When he visited their homes it hurt to see how poor they were. Some of the house walls were covered with newspapers in pathetic attempt to keep out the cold. Pneumonia was endemic among them. Everyone consumed an enormous quantity of snuff.

When the Eldredges left the suburb of Atlanta, the highest compliment was paid to them by an old lady well known for her dexterity in spitting. She could hit a dime at ten feet. Chewing her tobacco wad she said regretfully, just before she spat: 'We're sorry you're going, Captain. You got to be like one of us.'

Baltimore was his next appointment, where there was a serious youth problem, aggravated by unemployment and hardships created by the depression. Like Satterfield, Eldredge began in a basement; the ceiling was five-and-a-half feet from the floor. His first Boys' Club was really a dungeon.

Kiwanis, Rotary and other citizen groups did help but they knew so little that most of the work fell upon the Captain. Of course, there was no question of only looking after little Salvationists. With any other American officer—Eldredge thought in terms of helping the community. There were thousands of needy lads, many of them getting into trouble and acquiring vicious habits. He wanted to help them all.

Boys were flocking to his clubs: he now had ten clubs, all in cellars. But he needed a suitable building. Next door to one of the corps buildings was the Young Women's Christian Association, a spacious, wonderful place. If he could get that he might stage a demonstration that would convince Boys' Clubs of America that his work should be sponsored.

He got the building on loan. Some out-of-work lads painted the place, while others rehearsed for the coming show. The news spread quickly. Soon he had 1,000 applications for membership and a regular attendance of 250. Everything went with a bang, and the owners of the building felt that the work should be supported. They offered to sell for 20,000 dollars.

It was a bargain. The place is now worth 400,000 dollars. It was the first big development of Baltimore Boys' Club, continued with dramatic results over many years. Eldredge, like Satterfield, has been long enough in his job to see some sons follow fathers into the club movement. The years of toil have been made worthwhile as lads have lost their recklessness, found their better selves, and made headway in the world. A noted physicist, authors, professional men, all pillars in Baltimore life, have been through one or another of the group of clubs.

Proof of the contribution the Boys' Clubs make to Baltimore is seen in the contributions Baltimore makes to the Boys' Clubs. The Community Chest, a citizens' united fund-raising effort on behalf of non-denominational good causes, contributes well over 150,000 dollars yearly to Eldredge's work.

When the Glen Martin Aeronautics Company found that it had a youth delinquency problem on its housing area, nothing would meet the need other than another Boys' Club, so the Middle River Club was opened. The Community Chest gave an extra 20,000 dollars, while Kiwanis, Optimist Club, the American Legion and many other groups assisted.

The United Services Organization, a sort of United States Armed Forces NAAFI, vacated splendid premises. Just the thing if they could get it . . .

Of course, there was the small matter of money. The Salvationists went to see Glen L. Martin.

Boldly they asked, 'Mr. Martin, we suggest you buy the place and rent to us for one dollar a year . . .'

Martin smiled. He knew about Salvationists and had just read what a Baltimore judge had said: 'Since the Salvation Army has opened a Boys' Club in the Middle River area, delinquency has about ceased to exist.'

Martin replied. 'No, I'm not disposed to acquire more properties. I have too many now. You go up to Washington and ask what the United States Army will take for the place.'

Eldredge and his Divisional Commander did that, and found that the price was 90,000 dollars. They went back to Mr. Martin who found the money. Today the property and equipment are worth more than a quarter-of-a-million dollars.

Even bigger problems were solved in the Franklin Square quarter where Negro boys predominated, and where the Council of Social Agencies had reported delinquency and the acute need for a Boys' Club. This was before integration in Baltimore.

But Eldredge and his staff were not interested in extension working on a segregation basis. It was contrary to the whole philosophy behind their work. The boys did not want it. All the educational drive behind the clubs, behind the Indian lore, behind Scouting had been towards the brotherhood of man.

There were difficulties. It was hard to find a building, so they started in a little store front. Soon they had a fine property, a good staff, including a Negro Director. Best of all, the boys were 'colour blind'.

Eldredge is proud that he has been a friend of Father Flanagan, the one and only founder of the true Boys' Town. He has been in Eldredge's home, taken off his shoes which always seem to trouble him, put his feet up, reached for the tea-cup. Talk was often about that one great theme of both men—the wonderful boy of America. Two items about the priest linger in Eldredge's memory. He is a Roman Catholic with a deep admiration for the Salvation Army. The other fact is that it was a Jew who gave him the money to begin Boys' Town.

As one might expect from the children of a single-minded couple, both the Eldredge boys have been infected with a similar zeal for Boys' Club work. Robert and Gordon have qualified at Springfield College, Mass., one of the two institutions in the United States where the art of youth leadership is taught.

Here basket-ball was first played, and George Williams, founder of the Young Men's Christian Association, worked. Recreation, at Springfield, is a sacred subject. In its lecture theatres and on its campus the Eldredge boys understood better what their father had been trying to teach by camp and field and forest to thousands of boys in Salvation Army clubs.

Years afterwards, Eldredge's friends are legion: boys become men, but remember. Every Christmas, to cite one of many examples, he receives greetings from a lad who once lay and shivered in a sleeping bag in camp. Eldredge threw his own thick coat over him.

'That was the first time anyone had ever done anything like that for me,' said the boy. He never forgot it.

Eldredge is shy of saying it, for he seems to have something of the reserve and caution of the Indians he so much admires, but everyone who knows him is fully aware that behind the skill, the expert knowledge, the long years of labour for the young, is profound religion. Like any other Salvationist, though in a different way, Eldredge fights for God.

29. THE MASTER

The reason why a good officer in the Salvation Army does all possible for his own children to have a good education is that those children shall be better equipped than he is to 'work for God', as the parent would put it. There may be a sort of snobbery involved with some of them but, generally, like Abram, Salvationists have the habit of putting their children upon the altar, and with the purest motives. Some of the children grow up to resent this vicarious offering, and often refuse to confirm it.

Living with the Army Captain can be difficult for the child. The son of the Commanding Officer is expected to be the paragon: many people take it for granted that he will, everywhere, all the time, exemplify the goodness and high principles preached by his father at the Army citadel. Inevitably a normal boy cannot attain such standards, so that the 'O.K'—officer's kid—may become something of a problem child. Perhaps this same tension is a reason why one reads in the newspapers of parsons' sons in trouble in the police courts.

But our man gained an open scholarship to Oxford, taking a first in English, and later, at London, a B.D.—Greek, Hebrew, the Bible. I did hear that Oxford might have elected him to a fellowship, for he had that sort of mind, but he entered the Army college for training as an officer, married an Army lassie, and hied him away to Africa, master of a Salvation Army Grammar School in Nigeria.

The curriculum is approximately that of an English grammar school and what the young African finds there may be the key to riches—an office job, a post as a teacher, a civil servant.

There are about a hundred boys and girls, from twelve to twenty years of age. The cost of their schooling and board is about £60 per annum, and parents have to make tremendous sacrifices to find their quota. Some may pawn their precious land to pay school fees.

Some of the cost is provided by the Government. The itch, as it was in nineteenth-century Britain, is to get away from the land. 'Farmers are fools,' the boys say, as they reach out for a slicker way of life that presupposes the rat race and the baser elements of the affluent society of the white man's world. Subsistence farmers are wretchedly poor. A lad, wanting a salaried job, may hope to support the rest of the family.

Our man wishes to transmute this by the catalyst of Christian faith and sacrifice, to something bigger and better. Already some of the boys are Christians—on the dotted line. It is a mere technicality. The trouble is to make it stick. Many of the boys are not Christian.

'If I am not a Christian, then I would be a villager, and they are nothing,' a lad will say, expressing with poignant and naïve over-simplification the dilemma of Africans who give up one culture before they have found another. As the Salvationist is always emotionally involved in his religion, the master, with those other Salvationists working with him, and thousands of other Christians throughout Africa, regard their mission as the vitalization of this pseudo-Christianity. It is slow and hard, but they do not fail entirely.

'Rice Christianity,' in Africa, is the same phenomenon as 'taking a nose-dive' in Chicago or Birmingham, England, where men will pretend religion to gain bed and breakfast. Many find that they bite off more than they can chew. The man who comes to scrounge, remains to pray. Some African boys and girls who come to acquire learning discover, also, a faith.

Many of them do not know their own age, because their parents could not register their births, being illiterate, but the young Nigerians have a great hunger for book knowledge. The worst punishment that the master can inflict upon a young African is to suspend him from school, or send him out of class. One of the books they read, with associated text-books that prevent Marx and his school of authors having a clear field, is the Bible.

Adjacent to the school is a training college, also Salvationist, where another officer university graduate from New Zealand is Principal, and whence young Africans go far and wide with fit qualifications as school teachers.

Though not all become Salvationists, many do absorb the deeper ideology, the secret faith of the African and other Christians. The heat of the noonday sun, the hazard to health, the deprivations, the separations from home, are all supportable because of the knowledge that this is not just putting maths, English and some science into youthful heads, excellent though that is. One hundred years after the Salvation Army was born, the dynamic of the Salvationist is still as William Booth commanded, 'Go for souls . . .' This is being achieved in Africa.

But not as a recruiting drive for the Salvation Army as such: one adjustment time has brought about. A fervent believer in the ecumenical movement, the master does not see himself a recruiting officer for William Booth or any other General. The new frontier of missionary service in Africa is undenominational. Christ alone is the Common Denominator.

At night, when the heat becomes tolerable, and the baby is asleep, he may have a moment to spare to take up a book or talk to his wife, a school-teacher and officer like himself, and without whom his task would not be supportable.

Perhaps he will take up *Encounter, The New Statesman, The Spectator, The Times Literary Supplement,* sent to him by well-wishers in England, for he is a poor man, as is proper in a Salvation Army officer.

He will think briefly, perhaps, of Auden, or Eliot, or the Snow-Leavis controversy. How irrelevant that seems now. Even the tutorials, the Common Room, those green, rich years, years of learning. It seems a life-time since . . .

He puts the book down, for he has to go out again. The carpenter needs instructions, and there are other tasks to do before the long day closes.

Any Salvation Army quarters is open house for those in need. A villager calls to plead: 'My wife's baby is coming much sooner than we thought. She cannot deliver: I need help to get her to hospital. Can you . . .'

Through the night the weary Salvationist will drive, trying to be unresentful. He is familiar with his availability. He knows that all over Africa, all over the world, he is one of thousands who are likewise servants for Christ's sake.

Now, as he puts the car away, he feels drained of energy and longs for sleep. But he notices a glimmer of light in one of the dormitories. It is a tiny paraffin lamp, and he knows what it signifies. How many times, examinations almost upon him, he has done likewise in the comfort of his rooms at Oxford. But here, at this hour, it is forbidden. The narrow margin of health and eyesight does not permit over-indulgence in the luxury of study.

So he goes to the student who had hoped to be undetected in his 'crime'. It is such a little light, and he makes no noise at all. So much depends upon his success at this school. He suffers from anxiety neurosis concerning possible failure, and is pathetically grateful if the master can assure him that it is best for him to sleep, and that his prospects in the examination are good. Sometimes the lad will be annoyed because the master will confiscate the light.

As he locks the door and his day ends, the master remembers that he will soon be sailing for England, to furlough. His eyes are giving him trouble, something to do with the climate, the blaze of the sun, or perhaps it is psychological. He doesn't know.

It would give him an excuse if he didn't want to come back here. Then the child could have real milk, and there would be a change from palm-oil stew.

But as he falls into sleep, he knows that he will come back. Having hitched his wagon to this Bright Star, he is not jumping off now.

Part III

THE SOLDIERS

Pauline Tees emigrated from Glasgow with her family which settled at Parramatta, in New South Wales. She was a steady girl with a Presbyterian background. Though her pretty face brought her many invitations she thought more of 'doing good' than she did of party-going and 'dating'.

She could not help noticing six-footer policeman Hugh Mackintosh, though he was not exactly her type. He had a fiery temper, played football on Sundays and went drinking on Sunday nights. Though this, of itself, did not offend too deeply her Presbyterian sensibilities she was influenced by her brother's warning: 'Don't you have anything to do with that big policeman. He's a trouble-maker.'

Hugh thought her a 'square' of the first order. Her bright eyes and charm were wasted on him.

Meanwhile, he was making a name for himself, and not the sort a policeman thrives upon. He was sent off the football field for bad-tempered play. Mackintosh had the red hair, the genes and the temperament of a wild one. His police bosses, though they had no objection to a reasonable amount of toughness, warned him to watch his step.

As a strong-arm cop Hugh had made enemies and one day he gave them their opportunity. Outside a youth club, where there had been complaints of vandalism, a man twenty-four (Mackintosh's own age), a convicted thief with many bookings for traffic offences was showing off to a crowd of teenagers by revving his sports car to peak. He was truculent when spoken to and Hugh forgot his own strength . . .

The young man's parents reported him on a charge of assault. Hugh was suspended and, when the police hearing went against him, was dismissed from the force. The Superintendent said, 'I am sorry I have to do this, son. Lodge an appeal and you will be back in a couple of weeks.' He did appeal, and meanwhile went to work in the railway sheds.

To a Salvationist workmate at the railway sheds he said:

'Religion? What's it all about?' The Salvationist produced a New Testament and suggested places where Hugh could read. He tried, but the book was unfamiliar and incoherent. He had no interpreter. A tune kept ringing in his ears, with snatches of the words he had heard Salvationists sing as he passed their open-air meeting—*He lives! He lives! Christ Jesus lives today!*

'How is it that you are always happy and singing, and nothing ever seems to worry you?' he asked the man at work. 'What is it that you have and I have not?' It was not long after that. The people in the town, the young man, the bullies and toughs who had feared the big burly cop, would have been astonished to see him like a child, on his knees by his bed, uttering simple prayers, reading his way slowly through the stories of the Bible.

Two weeks after his conversion Hugh went to a Presbyterian Fellowship meeting and heard Pauline Tees pray. 'God told me this was the girl I should marry,' he says. For the first time he really looked at Pauline, and what he saw was good. Hugh was in love. He suggested to her that night that they go out together the following Saturday night. 'Let's skip the Fellowship dance, and go to the Harvest Festival in the Salvation Army.' She agreed, and that night he proposed. Four months later they were engaged.

Being converted solved many problems for Hugh, but it threatened to upset his appeal against his dismissal from the police force. Though there had been some lying by the other side, as he looked at his case again, as a Christian now, Hugh knew that his side of the story was not wholly correct. He asked his new-found Christian friends what he should do. 'You'll have to tell the truth—the whole truth,' they said.

This, because of that *esprit de corps* which obtains within the police force in any land, and which existed to protect Hugh, would involve other policemen.

Poor Hugh—the wages of sin might be death, as the Bible says, but the wages of righteousness were nothing to write home about if present experiences were any criteria.

'We'll get engaged when I get back in the force,' he had said to Pauline, and that was what he wanted with all his heart. But if he told the truth according to his new-found religion, he'd never get back and he'd compromise one or two of his policemen friends who, out of loyalty, had backed up his story about the young man incident.

'Can I refuse to give evidence?' he asked his solicitor.

'Not a chance,' that worthy replied. 'It would be tantamount to a confession.'

Yet now, with Pauline praying for him—and loving him—Hugh found strength. He insisted on changing his plea to guilty, but guilty only to what he had done. This was nothing like the degree of violence of which he had been accused. Pauline and he prayed and placed the responsibility for the outcome on God, as well as upon their lawyer.

In cross-examination the young man was made to admit that after being knocked down, 'brutally assaulted', he had not gone to the police station to report it, nor even to the hospital, but straightway to a coffee bar to drink, eat and amuse his friends. Other parts of the story were demolished also. Hugh, though his plea of guilty was accepted, got off with a fine of £10 for a technical assault, and £10 for not telling the truth. Later he was reinstated into the police force, poorer as well as less ready with his fists.

But in another town, far away, at Adaminaby, where the Snowy Mountain waters were being tamed, thousands of workers from Italy, Yugoslavia, Britain and other lands were harnessing the Murray River, some getting drunk on Saturday nights, making merry in the streets, and needing police control. But Hugh had it all taped now. He still used a strong arm, but it was the strong arm of the law—he'd be a Christian cop, of which, newspaper stories to the contrary, there are legion. Also, as a surety for his good behaviour, he married Pauline, his personal 'Guardian Angel'. It should have been a very Eden.

Alas, Adam had established a precedent in the Garden of Eden, and it didn't work out. True, there were no more strong-arm tactics, but people do not really expect a policeman to pray. They are capable of resenting it when he mixes religion with the law, and so, it must be admitted, do the police.

When Hugh dared to pray with a man, drunken and obstreperous, instead of charging him, the man felt insulted: he was a Catholic and objected to heretics taking over the work of the true priesthood. The calm, patient cop, who went into the bars to break up the party at 6.30 p.m., as required by law and by Australian housewives, often found that what he really needed was something far more obvious and dynamic than kind words. Yet how could he, after all that had happened, and knowing that Pauline had confidence in him, how could he do a Jack Dempsey on the revellers? He agreed with W. S. Gilbert that 'a policeman's lot is not a happy one'.

Then Mackintosh met two officers of the Salvation Army named Kinder and Greentree. The latter made even Hugh's large-scale tough Christianity seem insipid. He had been a wool-shearer in his unregenerate days—he estimated that his first weekly allowance as a Salvation Army officer was just £100 below his pay for a good week with the shears. To see Green-tree with the mobile van, music-making, tea-making, going about the camps and townships in the Snowy Mountains, opened up a vista to Hugh Mackintosh that made the police force seem a dead-end. Here was a man doing a man's job! Greentree had the right idea—Mackintosh now wanted, more than anything else, to be a Salvation Army officer. The quieter, less obtrusive Kinder also had a good influence on Hugh and helped him greatly. Both men became his heroes.

It was a call from God. So with Greentree and Kinder in mind, Pauline and Hugh went to the Methodist Chapel where they heard the preacher say, 'If Christ needs you, don't count the cost'. To the young wife this was a grave issue. There were hopes of a new police station and residence worth £20,000 at only 17/6 a week rent, and better prospects for Hugh. Should they throw it all away? But Hugh was sure and, in a little chapel at Eagle Hawk, used by all denominations ministering to the variety of races and creeds engaged on the gigantic hydro-electric scheme, Captain Wesley Kinder publicly enrolled Hugh and Pauline as Salvation Army soldiers. Exactly four weeks afterwards they were both at Sydney, in training for officership.

There, his greenness being extraordinary, even in an Army that welcomes all, Mackintosh caused shock waves to reverber-ate throughout the venerable training college, by confessing that he did not even know the name of 'The Army Mother'. This was about the same as for a Catholic not to know of Mary.

Indeed, though the Army prides itself on tactical fluidity, Mackintosh was something of a trial in the training college; orthodoxy is firmly entrenched in these Army centres. He played a guitar and the bagpipes, tapping his foot vigorously over the offices of the Principal. That worthy was distracted, to put it mildly.

Hugh wrote doggerel verses to well-known hit-tunes. William Booth allowed this, but squarely on the beat—Hugh Mackintosh gave them a swing and a pop. It was rather trying for 'the establishment'; yet he survived the spit and polish and got through the examinations.

With morale and spirit heightened, and after a year's training, he went to Cremorne as officer-in-charge. Here he began a series of Bible studies, and confesses they taught the Commanding Officer more than they did the soldiery. In the open-air meetings a number of drunks and wild teenagers were attracted by the 'hot' music of Hugh's guitar. They risked much by lingering, for behind the modern beat was a blazing passion to win them for God.

At Uralla, Hugh advertised a 'Hill-Billy Show' in the local paper, shocking the sedate; yet converts were won who are steadfast up to now. One day he would be a 'negro minstrel', another, a 'highland piper'. There were many critics of these 'stunts', but they stopped the crowds, and again there were converts.

Some who thought 'Tea and Sing-song' gatherings undignified, were reminded by Hugh, who was catching up on his reading of Salvation Army history, that old William Booth often held 'Jam and Glory meetings'. In an outback area, with 17,000 square miles as his 'beat', ex-constable Mackintosh wore out tyres and cars on the dirt-roads as he called at farms, hotels and aboriginal reserves—all men coming alike to the Captain and to his God.

When the General of the Salvation Army visited Brisbane, Hugh took along a contingent of converts, star amongst whom was Albert Dennison, a fully uniformed aborigine who could, incidentally, make music on a gum tree leaf. This art made headlines in the newspapers, as did the modern style 'singalong' of the party of converts led by Hugh Mackintosh's guitar.

The one-time cop and Pauline, his wife, are very happy now. The trouble with being a policeman, as Hugh sees it, is that you have to arrest a man, and that is all. Now, though he still tries to 'arrest' people, by God's grace he can see them change their ways.

31. THE ANGEL OF THE BRONX

Thelma Gundersen, Captain at the Bronx[1] Corps of the Salvation Army in New York, looked romantically attractive on television, and in the *New York Times* magazine feature, which did a five-page story about her.

A modern *Angel Adjutant*, in fact, from the Harold Begbie story of a devoted woman officer in Britain more than fifty years ago—a prototype for *Major Barbara*, a heroine for *Guys and Dolls*.

But the poor apartments down the mean streets of the Bronx have little that is dramatic or glamorous about them: they are solid and drab, 'prisons' in which the Puerto Ricans are concentrated. There are more of them in New York than there are in San Juan, the capital of Puerto Rico. There are also poor whites, Negroes, Spaniards and Chinese and all that melting pot of races lives out its struggle to get a firm foothold in the country of the free.

But love can make a cloister of a back alley, a sanctuary in a small back room. And love motivates Captain Thelma Gundersen. To the Puerto Ricans and all the others who come within the all-embracing orbit of her ministry, the Captain is as much an angel as any mortal female can be. The women, the teenagers, the children, flock to her services. She teaches them to sing the theme of her life, in a gay, lilting melody:

> *I am a C- -*
> *I am a C-h- -*
> *I am a C-h-r-i-s-t-i-a-n!*

Boys and girls, men and women, who live in small rooms in

---

[1] At time of writing. By now she may be posted to a distant frontier of Salvationist service, India, Africa, anywhere. All Salvation Army officers are expected to be expendable and mobile.

crowded tenements, who suffer from a sense of rejection, find in the Captain and her team of Salvationists the acceptance and practical assistance they need so much. So good are youth groups formed among the young people that one of them was a hit in a T.V. feature, while the other two were rated best Salvationist youth sections in Metropolitan New York.

Ask the Captain if she intends to marry and she quickly answers 'No'. This reduces the potential of good wives by one, but it is great for the Puerto Ricans.

'Come quickly, Captain!' they cry, or shout through the door, 'Mamma is going to jump out of the window. Pappy has been beating her . . .'

Though she laments her lack of academic social science qualifications, she has an experience of human relationships that many lecturers in universities would envy.

'You must speak to me in English,' she tells her people, 'though you may pray in Spanish.' She knows that in New York English is essential to their economic efficiency—if they ever get any. But when they make petitions to Heaven, their own flowing, fluent Spanish is better. It enables them to be natural and peaceful as they pray. 'God is your Father. He loves you. He is listening,' she tells the teenage girls, the burdened house-wives, the gangs of small boys and youths.

Many of the husbands of the women are fickle, some are promiscuous. It is easier for a Salvationist to supply soup, blankets, or a ten-day holiday up country than it is to comfort a deserted weeping wife, whose only offence is that she is tired, and a little bedraggled, perhaps, from overwork, poverty and anxiety. Yet Captain Thelma has acquired the art of such divine consolation.

Dish-washing, office-cleaning, all the more menial jobs, added to a sense of not-belonging inevitable after the transfer from the island to the city, are apt to demoralize Captain Thelma's people. Many seek strength in drink: there are quarrels, assaults. Very often, the decision has to be taken, 'Shall we send for the Captain, or should we call the police?'

But the young ones, helped by a benevolent civic administra-tion and Board of Education, are climbing from the illiteracy that has handicapped their parents. Many of them are sent by the Captain to holiday schools and camps—a vision of paradise to most of them, who normally have no holiday.

The girls in the Bronx mature early, marry soon. Some have babies out of wedlock while yet schoolgirls, which is a not uncommon phenomenon nowadays, even in colder climates. However, those within the Captain's orbit are saved from a hundred moral dangers, become corps cadets, girl guards, timbrelists, singers. They learn domestic hygiene, eat at a table covered with Captain Thelma's spotless white cloth. They are allowed to use the washing-machine, are taught the blessings of soap, hot water and a bathroom. These unimagined delights are a few of the proofs of the Captain's ministry.

Some of the gaiety, the warm friendliness, left behind on the sugar-cane plantations of Puerto Rico, is conjured up at the Captain's happy meetings: pumpkin pie for Thanksgiving; rice and beans for Lincoln's Birthday, all free, or for a song, with music and laughter and a few words about God from 'The Angel Captain'.

Sometimes a girl goes astray amid the many temptations of the Bronx streets, alleys and avenues. The lure of the juke-boxes, the fearsome pleasure of a joy-ride in a car, are not easily refused when your home is a jungle of imprecations and profanities.

When she strays so far that the fall cannot be hidden—and so readily forgiven—the Captain gains admittance for her to one of the Salvation Army hospitals for unmarried mothers. Obviously, Captain Thelma does not stand with those who would throw stones at magdalenes. If it is possible, and often it is, for the girl to be taught her lesson and make a fresh start at the good life where she left off, then the Captain is there to be the shepherdess of that restored lamb.

Goodness shines through, so bright, so awe-inspiring, that the Puerto Ricans put the Captain on the pedestals normally reserved for their saints and angels.

'What would you like to be when you grow up?' asked a not startlingly original T.V. interviewer of one of the Bronx string band and timbrel girls.

There was no hesitation: 'I'd like to be a Salvation Army officer, like Captain Gundersen.'

The Bronx corps officer is always cooking up new ideas. She arranged for Spanish-speaking women who attend the corps to teach the English-speaking ones and vice versa. This was aimed at fostering that Christian sense of neighbourliness too hard to nourish in the teeming, screaming old apartment houses.

European immigrants and native American Salvationists cook delightful Puerto Rican West-Indian dishes, for the Captain asks good cooks to bring along a dish so good that the ladies of the women's meeting demand to be taught how to prepare it.

Sometimes the warm feeling felt for Captain Thelma can have embarrassing results. When the children are daily released from school for their religious instruction at the 'church of their faith', many strays from the Roman Catholic Church put in an appearance. This is not encouraged, although some children stubbornly persist in following the dictates of their affection rather than their family traditions.

Naturally, as with any Salvation Army officer, Captain Thelma is not toiling so hard and so long just to provide fun and games, or for any other merely social purpose. Like St. Joan of old, the Captain is a woman with a vision—a call to attack the foe that has seized upon the land. In her case the foe is not the English, but the devil.

'God will help you to overcome the craving for drink,' she tells the men who are entering the crowded saloons. The unfaithful husband finds that her tongue can be barbed indeed; more than one threatened marriage has been saved by her efforts at conciliation.

Salvationists do not include the halo among their accoutrements, perhaps because they practise such a practical brand of Christianity that their earth-bound eyes cannot see such celestial symbols. But the girls nonetheless insist on clothing their Captain with all the glory and purity of a Teresa, or Catherine of Siena. It becomes her, although she would be astonished to be told that anyone considered her to be a saint of any sort.

One day soon, there's to be a pilgrimage to the Bronx, not comparable with the great pilgrimage to the grotto at Lourdes, where Saint Bernadette saw her vision. No Salvationist would dare to suggest it. But the Army gathering is to involve many good people. It is a new citadel which will cost 200,000 dollars, and will enshrine the vision of Captain Thelma as a place of blessing and healing for the young and old, whose need calls out to God from all about the southern area of the Bronx.

32. THE PADRE OF THE COMMUTERS

The eminent Victorian, William Booth, might not at first approve of Captain Martin Lingard, officer in New South Wales, Australia. He is one of many who belong to the new frontier of the Salvation Army and at time of writing is in charge of a corps in a western suburb of Sydney, Australia.

Like any Australian, Lingard can accept challenge. When he led a very small corps with nine soldiers, and the winds blew cold and no one seemed interested by the old routine, he shocked some of the old faithfuls by making adventurous experiments. The Sunday evening open-air meeting he changed to early afternoon, so that he could get at the football crowds. He begged whole pages in the local newspapers, sub-letting some of it to advertisers and making a profit for the funds of his poor corps. The number of his soldiers increased.

Explaining the Army, he finds, pays off. Many people have ludicrous ideas about it, and far too many Salvationists assume that the public understands when it does not. Lingard, on radio and in the press, tells the public about the Army, not only that he is asking for money, but why it is needed. He finds that this information changes pennies into shillings, shillings into pounds: indifference into positive goodwill.

In best Booth tradition he resists 'separatism', narrow sectarianism with which no Salvationist should be infected, though many are. Ex-Navy himself, he got himself appointed chaplain to the local Naval Association. He could then mix with the men who would not go to Sunday meetings.

He joined a business men's club. He allowed himself to be appointed adjudicator in a choral society. An accountant by profession before his call to officership, he angled for and obtained permision to address the Society of Accountants. All this made him known and increased his influence.

Such aggressive pushfulness, which in another would be brash egotism, is in Lingard simply the justification of his ministry. He is by nature quiet—a typical accountant type. But he has to be in the world of men if he is to save some of them. Any Salvation Army officer who did not seek to save souls would not be true to his vocation.

Lingard plays down the money-begging image of the Army. The gag 'another elevenpence ha'penny makes a bob' is, to his mind, an injurious joke overdue for interment.

'I don't look on new contacts, even people of status and means, as likely prospects to ring the bell on the cash register,' he says. 'I want to rope them into a circle of Salvationists, firm friends, or even casual acquaintances, who will make up part of that Christian community that is the proper Salvation Army corps.' He makes no bones about using the social round for his God-ordained purposes. Psalms and madrigals are not, in any case, much suited to the Australian scene. Barbecues or motor scrambles can serve the same purpose.

His 'parish', which includes those many non-Salvationists who are happy to be associated, gives the Army about sixty pounds a week. He encourages his people to send gifts far and wide: contributing to an ambulance for a newly independent country; cheques, consignments of tinned foods, clothing, medicine—New Guinea, Nigeria, Brazil, Rhodesia. Twice weekly this former Chartered Secretary and Associate Accountant from six to eight in the morning stands a beggar, box in hand, at the railway station. He regards it as good public relations, and is in no way perturbed about it. He finds that the people want to see him there, and appreciate the opportunity to give to the good work. It is more than a beggar-giver relationship. They ask about his affairs; he enquires about theirs. He is the padre of the commuters.

He runs his own 'protection racket'. Once fortnightly up and down the High Street and hotels, he and his people solicit aid. He is welcomed. It is as if he affords protection. They know what he is doing for their own town; the vagrants he houses; the drunks he tries to save; the shamefaced un-wed girls, who are sent away quietly to have their babies at the Salvation Army maternity hospital; the children who are cared for in the Army homes. All that and more. They dare not refuse to be involved.

The proof of the good is there: they know it. Though Australia is a rich land, with its own State welfare, there are many yet in need. Lingard pays for grocery parcels for those who are feckless, knowing not the way to get the State aid, or whose need is upon them before the rules of officialdom can allow of charity. He intercedes in domestic problems, seeking to reconcile husbands with wives, helping deserted children, watching over the newly-released from prison.

Among Rotarians and other business groups, he practises and preaches the acute implications of Christianity in industry and business. He sits on the Inter-Church Industries Committee. And always modestly, with care not to flaunt the Salvation Army flag as if it were the only good banner aloft in the sky. 'The penitent-form is a wonderful spot, but we must not be so arrogant as to assume that only those who have knelt there are God's people,' he says. 'Salvationists are not the only pebbles on the beach. We ought to develop in our people a greater involvement in "that wicked world" which is often not so wicked as we consider it to be. We must break down the barrier between the so-called sacred and secular. It is an artificial distinction. All of life, all the people, all the time, were the concern of Christ. We have too many Sunday-go-to-meeting Salvationists—Sunday soldiers. I try to break that idea though I find it is the younger people who respond best to it.'

33. SAND IN HIS SHOES

Eric and Joyce Fox tell a story that some would regard with scepticism; Salvationists would regard it as matter-of-fact. He was with the R.A.F. in Algiers, during World War II; she was about Ipswich driving an ambulance. They were man and wife. He attended a meeting at a Red Shield servicemen's club out there, while she attended a youth rally at Ipswich. It was the same week-end and both, without knowing the other's mind and heart was being committed, offered to become Salvation Army officers. They were 'called' as Salvationists say.

But there were too many official delays and, in the rosy dawn of demobilization, their dual offering seemed far-off and unreal. They decided to forget about it. They had money. They bought a house. He found a good job. Then God seems to have punished Eric Fox, infected him with wanderlust, so that a new home and a good salary became ashes, not consolations. The first child ought to have been a firm anchor, but it did not take hold. He sold his home, and bought a better, making a profit withal. But still he itched from the sand in his shoes. Ipswich, it was certain, could not be his final abode. He felt he had to run.

He wrote to Australia House, but another baby was imminent, and the emigration officials would not book a passage. A revivalist visited the Salvation Army at Ipswich and both Eric and Joyce felt qualms of conscience about that earlier 'call'. They went to the penitent-form and offered to make amends. But now the Army officials made further difficulties: there were two children—in those days a troublesome complication. But while the Army tarried, Australia House hastened to inform them that there were now good prospects for a passage to Australia.

With free passage and the promise of a home when they landed, they set out. It proved to be a voyage like Jonah's. There were severe storms, and the ship's engines broke down. There were food troubles. Measles and enteritis broke out among the immigrants, two children died and one of the Fox infants became very ill. Mrs. Fox, a trained nurse, felt revolted at steerage conditions aboard. The young couple were most miserable and inwardly echoed the lament from the Bible: 'I remember my faults this day.' They were running away from God.

And if the passage to Australia was as Jonah's voyage to Nineveh then Tasmania was the belly of the whale. That was where the couple found themselves. They had been promised a house: there was no house. Promise after promise, so persuasive and warm back home in England, were now seen as fairy-tales. The reality was cold and bitter. One of the children contracted impetigo, a dirt disease. This was unspeakable humiliation for Mrs. Fox, a proud and careful mother.

With Jonah the young man prayed: 'I cried by reason of my affliction unto the Lord. Out of hell cried I . . . and Thou heardest my voice . . .' The 'contract' they had broken, their call to officership became critical now. They made their way to the nearest Salvation Army officer and told their story. All Salvationists know about Jonah, and Eric Fox had sympathetic hearing in Tasmania. Within a month the couple were training to be officers.

After preliminary appointments in Victoria they went far west to Geraldton, on the Indian Ocean, a remote coastal town, whose 10,000 population was based on cray-fishing. Eric's range of activity reached for hundreds of miles into the bush. His little band of twelve players was a welcome sensation on the sheep stations.

If he missed calling they asked, 'Where did you get to last year?' At many a farm he would stay the night, talk over supper, justify that call to furthering the gospel that had brought him by such a long walkabout to God's appointed place. He visited remote and tiny schools, he conducted little services in chapels, huts, the open-air meetings. He followed lonely dirt tracks where, as time had shown, to run out of petrol was to die in the desert. He saw the incredibly beautiful carpetry of flowers in the arid bush appear from birth to full bloom magically after a tropic rain. He'd stop by the coast at Shark's Bay and see the fins offshore. He knew that for miles, far over this almost deserted wilderness, he *was* the Salvation Army. It made him proud and yet it humbled him. Sometimes when the bright stars seemed so low he might have touched them he spoke softly to God, a mere whisper, for he knew that there was no need to shout. The Hound of Heaven had caught up with him.

34. THE PROUD MAN

Major William Cairns, also of Australia, comes of dour Presbyterian stock, though softened by the influence of his mother. That Will was not a typical modern may be deduced from the fact that his reading during Navy days with the Royal Australian Navy took in Fosdick's *Twelve Tests of Character*.

His best friend was killed on war service. Cairn's disposition to seriousness increased. After being demobbed he entered fully into the faith and works of the Brisbane West End Corps, his Scottish ancestry, perhaps, being responsible for his argumentative interest in theology of the Knoxian sort.

But he fell in love, and was caught in the toils of a 'call' to officership, each crisis enough to cause him great concern.

It was just as well that he was a strong man, for when she was the religious as well as the bonnie lassie he could properly wed, and when they both might go to be trained for that apostolate of poverty which is Salvation Army officership, the prospect of advancement in business was offered him. Now the fleshpots of Egypt were a lure from that holy land where the manna becomes tedious, even though Heaven sends it.

But the lovers did not join the rat race. They departed, first the male, then the female, to the training college in Sydney. After which, as is sometimes the way in the Army, they were separated, as if to test whether they were fickle. Their first appointments put 200 miles between them, the second, 600. It is a way the Army has of testing character. But it was true love: the cords held.

William quickly found that the successful business man can be a sad failure as a revivalist. There were about 600 people in the town to which he was sent from college. These were shared between five strong places of worship not counting his corps, which was poor and dilapidated. 'What are you doing here?' one of the ministers asked him. It was a question hard to answer.

Yet it came, the realisation that in that religion-saturated town there were those who needed the ministry of the Salvation Army.

A woman asked Cairns to help her boy, ex-sailor like himself, whose marriage was foundering. When Cairns left the town with 600 population, he left 600 friends, many of whom had cause to thank God that they had ever met him. The corps closed down. He is not too sad about this: he does not consider that the scope for Army work consists only of making soldiers. It is work for God, and that was done, and that remains. Besides, the little town has the Army in its heart even to this day.

After time as a training officer, Cairns went to a coal-mining area. The men worked and lived hard, ignoring churches, chapels and preachers. So Cairns went to them, taking in the hotels, football grounds and race courses as his field of ministry. His lines were stretched far: 100 miles or more out among the farms, cattle stations, sugar plantations. They'd see his car, put the kettle on and when he stopped at the door, welcome him as one of their own. In a way he was. They might give a pound to the Salvation Army: Cairns gave something beyond price.

At Cairns, far north, 2,600 miles from base at Sydney, he might have expected a special welcome. Was not the city named after the Cairns clan? In fact the reception was lacking enthusiasm, for the corps was going through a difficult phase. Tourism was flourishing: the Great Barrier Reef, the volcanic craters and spectacular hinterland being the magnet. Cairns encouraged the Army to open a People's Palace, the sort of affluent working man's hotel that is beloved of the rugged, outback Australians who fear the prices and the sophistication of the ordinary hostelries.

So the appointments followed each other, the nomadic moves from town to town; living in quarters, never quite having a home of one's own, always uncertain of the future, for it is part of the officer's life that he is considered a sacrificial pawn on the chessboard of Salvationist activity. Forced to be versatile he wanted to be sedate—a parson rather than an officer. He passed through a phase of doubt about the Army doctrines, particularly the omission of the sacraments from its worship.

He became infected with the intellectual bug; becoming

interested in scholarship and theology while developing a distaste for the collecting box, sometimes, not always, a necessary weapon in the Salvationists' war. It grated on his pride. During a whole precious holiday period, when he should have been relaxing, enjoying life with Bernice and the children, he was deep in a brown study of doctrine and his own inward unease. It looked as if the Army was going to lose a good officer.

But at Wagga Wagga, 'the place of many crows' where he never saw a crow, he was so busy seeing people converted, helping destitute immigrants, and men on the track that he lost his doubts. Action on behalf of others is excellent remedy for theological indigestion.

After a year at a desk job at Headquarters, Cairns was appointed to East Australia's number one field command, Sydney Congress Hall. Some eyebrows were raised at this, for he was 'only a Captain', a relatively youthful officer. There were many with senior claims to the post.

Sydney is an exciting city—brash, rip-roaring, a frontier metropolis, full of challenge and stimuli to unorthodoxy. He sought, with considerable success to get the Army up-to-date on radio, TV and more often in the news. He was for streamlining method to meet new situations.

Any air of domesticity, which is profoundly non-Salvationist, he sought to banish from the Congress Hall, shaking up some in-the-rut faithfuls by importing scientists, an archbishop, bishops, civil-servants, radio recordists and television cameras to special meetings designed to attract the non church-going Sydneyites. He agitated about hunger to people who ate three cooked meals a day: found himself involved with vagrants, social misfits, people with problems of many kinds. The question whether William Booth had been right in dispensing with the sacraments in Salvation Army services became a vague academic matter.

So many of his meetings were broadcast that a few of his people complained. Such gatherings were stiffer, ran on tight schedules. He stood firm. 'Outsiders' were brought into their orbit, for the Salvation Army must always thrust outwards. It must never be a cosy institution.

Though the Salvation Army in Sydney, and in other Australian cities, has a large social service department, Cairns added his own to his corps work. The drunks and homeless receive supper on Sunday evenings; worthy cases are given accommodation in one of the Army's hostels or at an hotel. The man who chafed under the weight of a collecting box, now leads his people in generous giving, thereby minimising the occasions to 'cadge' in the legendary Army manner. From this giving, not from begging, the Congress Hall spends hundreds every year on school children in New Guinea, and on other good causes.

Cairns is an attacking sort of officer, and his people hammer away at the city. There are something like a hundred broadcasts or TV transmissions annually, some of which show the Captain in 'man to man' attitude always harping on that one theme—salvation from sin through Christ. Sydney has its full quota of sins. In city and suburbs the band, singers, young people shout out the good news of the Bible to the people, accompanied by gay music, the skilful jingle of timbrels, and impressive marches in which the pretty teenage lassies make a brave showing.

Privately he is a very happy man. Bernice is a good officer-wife, a tremendous help with his arduous tasks. He finds time to play a game of cricket or go swimming with the boys. A friend said, 'Religion has urgent family obligations. In trying to save Sydney, don't lose your own family.' Cairns heeded the warning.

35. BETWEEN THE FIRST AND THE EIGHTEENTH HOLE

In the United States the Salvation Army officer is a larger breed, taking shape from his immense country. In line with its social and economic pattern, he is more a free and diversified agent. His European officer colleague is constantly surprised by the wide variety and originality of his manoeuvres, all the more so because in Biblical and doctrinal matters, the American Salvation Army officer will most probably be a simple 'Bible from cover-to-cover' believer.

Tom Cisar is a Captain in California. Just past thirty-two, he has been an officer for twelve years. He illustrates aptly many of the differences between himself and his fellow-officers in other parts of the world, most of whom would regard him as better off financially if not superior socially. Indian or African national officers would regard him as a rich man. Yet as poverty and riches are relative terms, these assessments are misleading.

In real terms, Cisar's status is about the same as an officer in any other country. His stipend would be regarded as 'peanuts' by the average businessman or United States skilled worker; it is below that of many church ministers in America. Cisar can occasionally use a beach-hut, a holiday-trailer, or a mountain cabin, but they are loans from well-to-do admirers of the Army's good works.

If Tom Cisar thought much about his social position he might wish for a second car; the Army car is driven to pieces by the excessive demands made upon it by the Army's good works. For his wife a better sewing machine would be delightful. It would be wonderful to have his own little vacation cabin in the hills, and not just loaned to him. Yet, as he has little time for mountain life, or his wife for needlework, they lose no sleep because of anxious thoughts for tomorrow. When he came into the Salvation Army he knew that it was not a road to riches.

Those heroic figures who are converted sportsmen are made

much of on the West Coast. Tom Cisar is one such—a 'muscular Christian' in the Charles Kingsley tradition. He gained a college scholarship as basketball champion and later took a course in youth leadership with the Salvation Army, becoming a soldier and brass bandsman in the Los Angeles Congress Hall.

Doing well in his job, he was settling into the groove when he was suddenly seized by the conviction that officership was a man's job, the job for him. His first appointment was Spokane, as second officer, where the tutelage and personal influence of Brigadier and Mrs. Goldthwaite, the officers in charge, did much to help. In his one year at this place he worked hard and showed good promise in his probation period of officership. He also 'dated' various girls, a phenomenon unique to America as far as officers are concerned. From the many, he chose Doreen Goldthwaite, the daughter of the Brigadier, and presently married her—celibacy not being a Salvationist mode.

But for his second year's officership, still unmarried, he went to Havre, in charge, where he must show how he could battle without close supervision. Here the people were mostly farm workers, and there were tremendous economic stresses which created great problems for Tom Cisar. Many poor Indians on the Reservation, and large numbers of jobless transients needed food, money for hostel charges, the cost of transportation . . . in a land where the Welfare State does not fuss in exclusive monopoly of medical care, child care, or pauper care. All this, remember, in addition to the task of maintaining the everyday corps life.

Cisar found that as the Salvation Army Captain he was the one to whom the stream of need was directed. He begged 7,000 dollars, and kept the deep freeze full of meat. The hungry were fed and many kinds of wants were supplied.

When the Milk River overflowed, the young Captain, a mere boy, found that he had to do that quick up-growing which is a part of the American way of life, for there was a man-sized emergency on his hands. Getting money was the least of it. Ensuring that the supplies reached the genuinely needy was more; striving to add spiritual ministration to material aid was most important of all.

After marrying Doreen, who had completed her training at San Francisco, Tom moved to Helena, the State capital of

Montana. He now found himself disturbed by adult thoughts on the unsatisfactory public image of the Salvation Army. Too many people thought of it as a social service: a give-them-bread, give-them-clothes agency for the under-privileged. 'It is not for the likes of us,' the solid and prosperous citizens would tell themselves.

Deliberately he began to avoid conforming to that faulty image, and even to change it where he could. While preserving the traditional activities, youth sections, services, open-air meetings, he tried to fraternize on a man-to-man equality basis with the business life of the town, and with the local church ministers. In the press, at clubs, women's meetings, and wherever he had the opportunity, he explained the Army's mission as being for the townspeople, regardless of social status. 'God,' Tom informed the rather startled townsfolk, 'is as heedless of the size of a bank balance as He is of colour or country.'

At Bremerton, Washington, a naval base, he was appointed Chaplain in the Civil Air Patrol, an upper bracket position, but he also took many poor children to holiday camps, and otherwise preserved the Army's 'help-the-down-and-out' image. He kept on trying to merge both images to one. The Mayor and the Chief of Police, with other prominent citizens, were co-opted for places on the Advisory Board; influential housewives were enlisted in the Women's Auxiliary. He nominated various citizens for awards for public service as Christians. He found that the Army was becoming involved in the life of the town, and not just the poorer sections.

Most of all, Tom Cisar re-thought his own tactics, and here he was singularly fortunate in the sort of tolerant oversight he was receiving from his superiors in the Army. Only imaginative and sympathetic supervision could have gone along. Now Cisar determined to carry the war right into 'enemy' country. How else could he be a fighting officer?

His traditional stance was the platform, where he expounded and explained the Bible: preaching to the converted, carrying coal to Pittsburg. His hearers were often already saturated by the message he proclaimed. In the open-air meetings it was not much better. Many of those who passed by in their Buicks, Fords and Chevs, and who nodded in friendliness, could not hear and had no time to spare. Those not in cars, ever a diminishing number, were going somewhere quickly, as Americans will.

Yet some of these excellent, friendly men hunted or fished, for the doctor enjoined rest while the ulcer or blood pressure subsided. So Tom bought a gun and got himself a rod. There was, let it be admitted, a certain ambiguity about his quest. He had in mind those Galilean fishermen to whom Jesus said, 'Follow me, and I will make you fishers of men.' Tom was a fisher of men, and a hunter of men, if it came to that. He was human enough to enjoy the shoot, although he did not become much of a shot. Always, though the gun was plain to see, the Bible was there, reachable in his pocket. The true Salvationist objective; 'Go for souls', was in his heart. There is, of course, more than one way to cook a goose.

Up in the hills one businessman, a hunter, sought Tom out. 'You are the Salvation Army Captain? I've heard of you. I wonder could you do something for my boy?' The Captain visited the son's home, where there was serious domestic upset. The real hunt! As a result of his intervention, the son and his wife attended the Army meetings and the pattern of their lives was radically altered for the better. It was an opportunity to give proof of his ministry that could not have presented itself if he had not taken off his uniform, if he had not abandoned, for a time, the pulpit and the preaching corner on Main Street.

If the gun of the hunter is a strange Salvation Army weapon, then the golf club is hardly less so. Tom knew that some Salvationists do play golf, a sober, restful game which many of them find to be free from the concomitants of other sports—gambling and bad language. Though he finds this opinion rather naïve, Tom is not put off by the occasional hazards to religious susceptibilities. Even basket-ball players, he found, could swear under their breath, and betting is not unknown on the campus. Cisar regards 'unshockability' as essential to the new approach of the Salvationist to his century-old objective.

So Tom got himself a set of clubs and angled for invitations to go round on the Country Club course. As a guest this was not hard to achieve. He soon found that a man who will not attend church to be preached at from the pulpit will talk about religion, his own religion, or lack of it, on the fairway. Somewhere between the first and the eighteenth hole one country club golfer did accept Christ, as Tom puts it. There were men whose tension, whose personal problems could be assuaged, but not cured, by golf. 'You need the good news of Christ,' said Tom. It is the same when the Captain goes to the various clubs and societies with which a United States man's life abounds. All conditions of men, a wide field where, even as the other man sips his whisky and Tom his coca-cola, a word can be spoken, more potent than a sermon.

More and more people are coming to the meetings, and the general public have revised their opinion about the corps as they watch it and take part in its activities. The Salvation Army, they know, is not only a social service agency which will give lodgement for the transient, care for the children, find a hospital for the teenage un-married mother. Need exists, also, in many of the homes of the well-to-do. The respectable can be lost. Some among the virtuous need to be saved from the vacuum that is a meaningless existence.

The word 'sin' has been pushed out of common usage, even among many preachers. The readily admitted wickedness, over which the extroverted Victorians wept at William Booth's penitent-form nearly a century since, has been replaced by a multi-patterned, many-named system of 'isms', alibis and rationalizations which, at best, have made the wrong someone else's fault, and at worst, made it merely a neurosis.

Captain Tom Cisar can also spell out the word p-s-y-c-h-o-l-o-g-y. He has read some of those new books. If that's the way they want it, that's the way they'll have it. There is no essential difference: it is merely a matter of method.

Tom's conversion, his faith, his call to serve mankind is at one with those who made the Salvation Army a hundred years ago. But like Galileo, who risked his life to assert that the earth orbited around the sun, and tilted on its axis, Tom Cisar knows that the winds of change blow variously year by year. Even the Salvationist must not ignore that fact.

36. ALAN HAD IT ALL WORKED OUT

Most people would think that Alan Gowlett made a poor bargain in exchanging Antarctic exploration for officership in the Salvation Army. They might not understand that he is an officer because he was an explorer.

He served his apprenticeship in exploration in Macquarie Island, down in the roaring forties, about 800 miles south of Tasmania. With winds up to 120 miles an hour, with twelve sunny days in fourteen gruelling months, with tensions and depressions existing in the party, Gowlett's Salvationism was put to severe test.

His parents, as parents are wont to do, had anticipated God in allocating their son to the ministry, but Alan decided that he would have none of it. His sojourn on the desolate island was merely a means of making money. No trumpets were summoning him to paths of glory.

He had acquired a considerable knowledge of electronics while in the Armed Forces and on Macquarie he was responsible for all electrical equipment and the deisel engines. Back home his young wife was working as a telephonist. They were saving money fast. When his ordeal ended they put a large down payment on their first essay in gracious living, a comfortable home of their own. He had not even incurred the expenses of drink, cigarettes, or gambling. Salvationism is financially economical.

Among the scientists he had seen tension relax after men had consumed alcohol: but one or two just went on drinking and drinking. Alan did none of these things. He had it all worked out: he would be careful. They might go to the devil. Religion, of course, was not on the scientific programme.

Back home he found a job, furnished the new home in luxury, and resumed his happy married life. Week-ends and other occasions were devoted to Salvationist activities—most of it pleasant and rewarding—a sop to his conscience, a mute on the insistent inner voice which kept telling him that God needed him as an officer.

When applications were invited for another expedition, on the mainland of Antarctica this time, he was favourably considered. In January '55 it sailed for MacRobertson Land. He was away fifteen months. Again the cash accumulated. He looked after the snow weasels, other types of vehicles and the power station. He was kept busy. Low temperatures crystallised metal so that crankshafts snapped like matchsticks. Fuel froze, drivers petrified by cold, drove engines so hard that breakdowns were normal procedure.

Yet he had time to think. The explorer glow was wearing thin; money-making had lost its glamour. He had rediscovered a book he had neglected: the Bible.

Once, with the expedition doctor, he talked about men who drank too much, who broke down under the stresses of life in the frozen South. 'Men who drink or become violent are often showing symptoms of an inward lack, a kind of spiritual starvation,' the doctor said. Alan felt suddenly conscious of his own low efficiency ratio as a Christian. He began to pull his religious socks up. Now when the sound of his Salvation Army trombone echoed over the Polar ice, he put his heart into it; men began to take notice that Gowlett was laying on 'the Sally Army' with a thicker spread. He was not so prone to hide his light under a bushel.

Home from MacRobertson Land he went to the commissioning of Salvation Army cadets at Sydney and Melbourne. Elizabeth made no bones about it: 'I want to be an officer,' she insisted, and wept because he would not consider the idea. Alan wondered whether her idea was merely psychological compensation: she was childless after nine years of marriage, and he knew that she wanted a baby very much.

She prayed: time effected changes, and the call to be an officer came to him. In January '59 they were commissioned to corps work—a far, far harder task, Alan found, than looking after the snowcats on the glaciers in the frozen South.

Three days after their commissioning, three weeks in advance of due time, Jennifer was born. Both dreams of Elizabeth had come true: officership was good for the birthrate! Round and

about Adelaide, in South Australia, the young couple explored
the land for God. At Port Lincoln, among tunny fishermen;
Millicent, up country; Peterborough among the railway folk;
Kadina, where the copper mines had closed—the young couple
gave proof of their ministry. They are now at Darwin, Northern
Territory, 2,000 miles from Headquarters.

Though Gowlett's name is on the map in the Far South,
where a peak is named after him, 68° E; 70° S., and though he
proudly owns the Polar medal, he takes a greater joy from the
fact that so many people know him as the Army Captain, and
that some acknowledge him as the preacher, the pastor, the
evangelist who led them to prayer and to new faith in God.

K

37. THE AFFLUENT PILGRIMS

One of the harder fields for a Salvation Army officer's battles is the rich one: in history and in a real sense today the Army is a reaction to poverty. Then consider Captain and Mrs. Frank Linsell of Perth, Australia, who were given permission to sell the old Salvation Army hall for £15,000, a bargain indeed, for the congregation had all moved out to the suburbs. The ancient 'glory shop' had become obsolete.

When the Leederville hall was opened many years ago, the people walked or came by tram; nowadays the prospering Salvation soldiers and the rest of the congregation drive in by car.

Industries have grabbed the space where the hall had been, and a motorway is to run where the officers lived. The city paid £3,000 for the old house so that it could be pulled down. So the Salvationists, and the mass of the people they want to influence, are now out on the rich perimeter of Perth. Like Moses, Captain Frank Linsell must lead his flock into that land of milk and honey.

But the gracious life, even on Salvationist scale, is expensive and the general public, used to supporting the Salvation Army's good works do not expect to support Salvationists themselves, those sober, thrifty, hard-working people who, obviously, have 'gone up in the world'. These must pay for their own religious exercises.

For a hall built in a splendid area by the Commonwealth Games Stadium: £30,000 including land. For a home for the officers, quite a modest one: £5,000. To confront his people with their financial obligations, Linsell invited them all to a magnificent dinner at the Town Hall—an American idea for fundraising which seems to owe something to the notion that an army marches on its stomach.

The difference, of course, between expenditure of this sort and the money Salvationists beg for victims of leprosy, children, the aged, unmarried mothers and others, is that, being domestic, the Salvationist must give it, not get it.

Captain Linsell regards money as a holy word, and the contract to give regularly as a sacrament. He bids his people look from their lovely new homes in Perth, down on to the shining Perry Lake, and reminds them they are walking on pleasant places, one of the glamour spots of the world. For such a green pasture they should be thankful. He asks them to ponder on their faith, their happy way of life, their many blessings far above price: and then dip into their purses.

'We have £20,000 and we can borrow £10,000 which we will have to repay at £36 a week,' the Captain said.

'Our income from regular weekly gifts, from Salvationists at this corps, is £20. Measured by what God has done for us, and by the economic prosperity we enjoy, this is not enough. I want you to think about the obligations of Christian stewardship . . .'

When he had finished, his people promised him £70 a week— really promised, after prayer and thought. They even signed on the dotted line, by light of day, for Captain and Treasurer and Secretary to witness . . . It hurt, but they were brave and fully conscious.

This 'contract' to support the citadel of salvation in prosperous Perth suburbia produces remarkably generous giving. One woman Salvationist gives £5 weekly of hard-earned office pay. But she is not married and earns £40 so that the amount seems fitting. The thirty-shillings weekly by a man with four indigent teenage daughters, is perhaps more generous. A soldier who keeps a small shop gives £3 a week. Young bandsmen, with the expense of courtship to sustain, give £1 a week. This is perhaps less in the eyes of the heavenly accountants than the two shillings per week given by teenage school children out of their meagre pocket money.

At Floreat Park, Captain Linsell's corps, the average of giving is high. When they go to their rows of smart villas and detached houses on occasional canvass for 'the Army of the helping hand', the people are buoyed by the knowledge that they are not asking others to do what they do not do themselves.

Much more important than money is their adaptation of

Salvationist activity to its new environment. William Booth could hardly have foreseen that his Army would fight on such terrain. Both Captain and Mrs. Linsell teach at the new day schools, using the Government Agreed Syllabus of Religious Instruction.

As new houses and good salaries do not of themselves solve moral and social problems, the need for the Army in the affluent community exists as it did in London's nineteenth-century East-End slums.

The Captain, having received training, takes part in Marriage Guidance Council work. He can speak of social, economic, psychological problems, even the pros and cons of contraception, with a scientific detachment that marks him as a New Frontier Salvationist. The programme of meetings goes on all day Sunday and every week-day, taking in young and old. The need is not for soup, as in the far-off days: it is for the bread of Heaven.

There are signs that the move to a new field will not prove to be a setback. Congregations are now larger, and converts have been welcomed into the corps. Linsell, in the new and rich land, knows that what has changed is merely superficial. Bad men still need to be made good men—souls still need to be saved. The Captain agrees with T. S. Eliot:

> We build in vain unless the Lord builds with us.
> Can you keep the City that the Lord keeps not with you?
> A thousand policemen directing the traffic
> Cannot tell you why you come or where you go.
> A colony of cavies or a horde of active marmots
> Build better than they that build without the Lord.

38. 'ONE OF THE BEST PAPER-HANGERS IN LOS ANGELES'

In California, at the Los Angeles Tabernacle, is the paper-hanging Salvationist, Band-Librarian Ralph Powell, who has a distinction to which few Salvationists could lay claim: he comes from Mormon ancestry. He is a tall, dark, happy-looking man, born in Utah where, despite that State's deserved repute for sobriety, his father was drunken.

But his mother was an uncomplaining Christian and Ralph was brought up as a Methodist—until what she considered to be 'modernism' drove her away from that Church. Ralph married Venice Burt, who had been a Mormon. At that time of youth and love, when old ideas are readily jettisoned, they met at a dance. Both were cool about religion.

They moved to Los Angeles where Ralph began drinking heavily. Venice followed him to the bottle. As there were two infant children they could not go out for their drinking but instead invited friends to their apartment, requiring three-fifths of a gallon to see them through an evening. It cost more money than they could afford, but both had passed the stage where they merely wanted alcohol: they needed it: they could not get along without it.

Venice smoked heavily too. Their indulgences kept them so poor that she cried in rage at what was happening to their love, marriage and home.

'Don't bring it tonight,' she would say to Ralph in the morning. But by evening her nerves would be so ragged that she would greet her husband, returning home from work, with the command: 'Go back and get something to drink, Ralph. I'll have to have it.'

Passing the Tabernacle Hall of the Salvation Army, Ralph saw the notice: DAILY VACATION BIBLE SCHOOL inviting school children to attend every day. Like many other parents, Ralph

293

believed in religion for his offspring, although he had discarded it for himself and, as often happens, the children were the bridgehead by which the Army won these parents to conversion.

At first Ralph just left the kiddies at the Army Sunday School and then went about his work or hurried home to drink and read the Sunday papers. But the school was followed by a service for adults and the Salvationists exerted patient but persistent pressure on Ralph and Venice until they agreed to stay with the children for the family meeting.

From the start the band, singing, brief 'sermons' and lively meetings attracted them. The Salvationists had the good sense to leave them alone to the influence of the meetings and not go 'fishing' for them — 'fishing' being a method by which personal pressure is used to induce people to go forward to kneel at the penitent-form. Without this, in time, Ralph and Venice came to see that they must go forward. They wanted to do better for the children: they knew that they could not solve their own drinking problem.

The Captain talked to them, leading them gently to the point of decision. They held out stubbornly, bawling at the children, quarrelling themselves, drinking more than ever as if to balance the new feeling of guilt which possessed them. Yet one Sunday they 'surrendered', to the great joy of all the people.

Both stopped drinking at once. 'Suddenly, life became wonderful,' Ralph says. His clients noticed the difference in his work, while the neighbours commented that the noisy apartment where the bawling took place had quietened down. Ralph prospered, too. A sober paper-hanger is much better at his job than a drinking one. Even in the morning, when hangovers had previously made him dizzy, Ralph could hang a roll of paper without a wrinkle or crook.

Venice agreed that they should make their home a place of prayer and Bible reading. In two years, under the guidance of the Tabernacle's woman prison visitor, they went through the Bible by that route beloved on the West Coast of the United States — 'from cover to cover'.

Ralph now visits the prisons regularly; he leads meetings in the Harbour Light Corps where his victory over drink gives him particularly strong authority with the alcoholics; he is the

Secretary to the League of Mercy, that corps organization to assist the aged, the sick, the victims of domestic emergencies and much else. But perhaps the best tribute to the one-time bleary-eyed boozer, Ralph Powell, is given by a friend who knows him very well—'He's one of the best paper-hangers in Los Angeles.'

39. THE PERILS OF PROSPERITY

Hollis Reed was born in Hamilton, New Zealand, son of a piano tutor. He was sent to the Salvation Army in boyhood but made no youthful commitment with the Salvationists. The country was in a state of rapid development, the new frontier mood that induces restlessness, and at seventeen the lad left home to make his way at Wellington.

He found employment in the confectionery trade, becoming in time, the accountant. He was getting £4 15s. a week when he married.

By now he had become a Salvationist, and he began courting seventeen-year-old Edna Trout when he was nineteen: poverty made them wait six years before they could be wed. Their romance was wholly within Salvation Army orbit—meetings on week-days and Sundays. He had to get Edna home each night by ten at the latest. They were very happy, and went to live in a wooden house that cost £1,000 for which he borrowed the money.

Their home was frugal; there were no theatres, dances, drinking or other expensive social life. He began to prosper.

Religion in business seemed to have disadvantages. You couldn't, if you were a Salvationist, meet a client over a drink. It took him some time to learn that there were men who could understand Salvationist scruples, allow him to order ginger ale and still do business with him.

When Accountant Reed was sent to Auckland as manager, his material success seemed the antithesis of Salvationism and people prophesied that prosperity would sabotage his faith. But Hollis proved them wrong.

He was sure that he could not find a true spiritual home outside the Salvation Army. He got to work, therefore, causing the branch to flourish but not neglecting his Salvation Army duties.

Six days he laboured in the office, and on Sundays he led the boys' band and the Bible class of forty members.

Promotions came regularly as if both God and the boss approved. Certainly his Salvation Army leaders did. It was clear to the owner of the firm that Hollis Reed had a head on his shoulders. He was presently made general manager of the whole combine with headquarters at Wellington. His big chance to hit the business jackpot came with the opportunity to buy out the owner, now living in Canada. This man could doubtless have obtained a better price on the open market, but he knew Hollis Reed and liked him. A partner, the manager up at Auckland, was available. Hollis visited Canada and was told that if he could raise £70,000 in two weeks the company was his. He was well known in the city as a Salvationist: he had no great difficulty in raising the capital.

He and his partner had a bargain. The £70,000 business is now a fifty-shop, five-factory, 500-employee concern, undervalued at £250,000.

Reed has never been distressed by the anomaly of being a well-to-do Salvationist; though it is, on the surface, as inconsistent as being a rich socialist. But though William Booth recruited his first legions from the poor districts of East-End London, and the large industrial towns, this was fortuitous: Hollis Reed does not admit that there is any such thing as a 'working-class' religion.

Certainly in the conventional sense there is no working-class in New Zealand—the country is one rich, mammoth farm, run on egalitarian lines, where Jack may be as good as his master and very often is.

The wealthy confectioner has proved that success and religion of the Salvation Army brand go well together. It is what a man is, not how much he has, that determines whether he is good or not. Hollis Reed has made the integration of business and religion work well. He is currently President of the Wellington Manufacturers' Association; he is on the council of the New Zealand Manufacturing Association; he is a member of the Joint Steering Committee of the City Council. He is also on the Council of Christian Education and, inevitably, in Rotary and similar groups.

But he gives due time to his home and religion; if anything had to go it would not be his Salvationism. He has long been active in the Wellington City corps, in the Sunday School, and, for many years Treasurer and Corps Sergeant-Major, the latter being the top 'NCO' job in the Army. He goes about leading meetings and preaching, taking Edna with him. The fact that they travel in the Jaguar hardly calls for comment in rich New Zealand.

Hollis admits that active Christianity is extra weight to carry in the hurly-burly of business competition. There are six major companies to share the trade of two-and-a-half-million New Zealanders. Not all business men wholly and always subscribe to the principle that there must be truth in advertising, and ethics in method; Christian relationships with customers, wholesalers, and employees. A cocktail party or a business lunch the Reeds can negotiate, for everyone knows that Hollis and Edna will require soft drinks. But there are other traps for conscience that are less readily avoided in the cut and thrust of modern business. Hollis remembers the words in the Bible: 'What shall it profit a man if he gain the whole world and lose his own soul?'

The perils of riches intrude also into the home. Hollis has another place by the sea; he has a boat; he goes on round-the-world trips. Yet his hearth must be kept as a family altar. His children must have not only Christian precept, but parental example.

'They are not only listening,' says Reed, 'they are watching. If my life doesn't back it up they will not accept it for themselves.' The sirens of gracious living do not ensnare him. True, the Jaguar can take them quickly to the beach paradise and inland scenic beauties the like of which are hard to find anywhere else in the world. But it doesn't. The children grew up to know that when Dad takes the wheel the car makes for the Salvation Army, three times on Sunday, and week-days too. They were happy that it should be so: they have accepted it for themselves.

Despite St. Paul's warning that the love of money is the root of evil, Hollis makes the daring admission that having money gives him great pleasure. He has provided for the children; bought a £20,000 home; takes delight in allowing Edna to spend money. She is a thoughtful spender, who loved him and helped him all those hard years when there was no money available. Perhaps his conscience is clear about all this because he gives generously to good works, not only in the Salvation Army.

Like other self-made men in the movement he wishes that non-officer expertise and talent were utilized more freely in the Army. He considers that more heed should be given to the opinions of the Army's non-officers. Yet he is highly appreciative of the labours of the good Salvation Army officer and he finds that by far the most are good—he's known a black sheep or two.

When the corps officer comes to the house to pray with Hollis, as every commanding officer must in due course, to admonish him if he needs it, and talk about the good fight, then Reed is not the rich man relieving the poor. He listens with humility, not at all affected by the fact that he has a thousand for every pound sterling the officer may have. To Hollis Reed and Edna the Major is in spiritual authority over them: he is the Lord's appointed.

Hollis has found a way to breathe in the stifling jungle of success that suffocates so many 'success story' Christians whose money rushes to their heads. When he had to make way for a younger man at Wellington City corps some were dismayed at the thought that Hollis might retire to his riches and the memories of his good life.

Not at all: Hollis and Edna accepted the part of Envoys for youth work throughout New Zealand—carrying on the good work, and at their own expense. When not away on Sunday duty, Hollis is the door-keeper, the commissionaire, so to speak. When the General of the Salvation Army, campaigning from London, visited the city, a screaming baby was disturbing the huge congregation in the City Hall. It was most unseemly and embarrassing, yet no one, neither mother nor anyone nearby in the gallery knew what to do about it. From his place by the door downstairs the door-keeper went up, took the child and carried it down and out into the porch where its screams subsided. All was well. Apart from the voice of the General, silence reigned; the mother sat back to enjoy her respite. Hollis, outside, as he went on nursing the baby, might have recalled the words of the Psalmist:

For a day in thy courts is better than a thousand. I had rather be a door keeper in the house of my God, than dwell in the tents of wickedness.

40. CO-OPERATIVE CHRISTIANITY

Alas, that so many times for so long Christianity has been divided against itself. Now, and perhaps it is not too late, it is closing its ranks. The denominational barriers are coming down.

Douglas Collin, M.A., Cantab., is a lay tutor on the staff of the David Livingstone Teacher Training College in Northern Rhodesia (Zambia). Though he is a Salvationist missionary he finds it an advantage not to be an officer—in this he is a rare bird indeed. As a schoolmaster he does not bear that conventional missionary image that is not always an asset in modern Africa.

The Livingstone College is a co-operative effort, made necessary, perhaps, because of the inability of the separate denominations to find the funds for such a large training establishment. Possibly it is also a response to the African desire for non-sectarian expression of the Christian faith. This co-operative church effort is taking place all over the world.

The idea has some of the advantages of a business take-over. Staff problems are eased, but the acid test is the morale of the differing groups, the inter-action of tension, often felt rather than 'tell't'. Some members, to mention one instance, feel that all the Bible is literal truth, historic and scientific, while others seek to interpret it to a modern world with myth and a twentieth-century cosmology.

There is also tension, obviously, when a student from one religious background finds one of another doing openly, and with the consent of his denomination, that which members of his own church would pronounce as un-Christian.

Collin is responsible for training teachers to teach English in primary schools, though his background in the United Kingdom was that of a grammar school master. He taught English and history. If there is monotony in his present task, any academic devaluation, he makes the sacrifice gladly as part of his commitment as a Christian.

He works among 200 African students whose highest level before training was post form II. They have a great hunger to learn English. Indeed, the language is of great functional necessity in Africa. Douglas Collin considers that English will become *the* language of the erstwhile British colonies and that the African dialects will become as Welsh is in Britain. From this distance it is perhaps safe for him to make such a statement.

At first glance the sacrifice Collin makes is not obvious. For him there are reasonably good living standards. He does not, as a Salvation Army officer would, have to give up that part of his salary above his official allowance rate. He lives in a plus £6,000 house and receives more than £20 a week. His real salary is, therefore, considerably above this.

But he has to have a car and a fridge, and has paid over £400 for superannuation and fare home for his leave. He must also find fees for his child at what used to be a European school.

His sacrifice is certainly not apparent on the score of isolation. Livingstone is a tourist centre for people coming to see the Victoria Falls. Visitors call, to whom the couple play good music from their Pye 'black box'. Husband and wife, both children of Salvation Army officers, are, perhaps naturally, music devotees. They hear occasional celebrities on tour, and Collin's wife, June, a gifted pianist, has made contributions to the musical life of the town as a soloist and accompanist.

The rub comes in being away from home—they are not in Africa to make a new home, a regular life, a fortune in the copper mines, like the average Northern Rhodesian. Whether they admit it or not, they are part of a mission in the Livingstonian and Mary Slessor tradition. They are doing what they do for God.

Collin was well known for his work with the Salvation Army Students' Fellowship. As a leader of its choral group and as a keen Salvationist musician at Barking, London, he lived a crowded, happy life. He led the students in a number of B.B.C. broadcasts and made one or two commercial recordings.

The 'extremist', 'eccentric' or even 'crazy' quality that some people see in the Salvation Army makes it hard for those who love it to accept any alternative to it. The Army favours the ecumenical spirit but gets great fun out of being the Salvation Army.

The Collins, husband and wife, languished, therefore, when completely deprived of free-and-easy Salvation Army style meetings for worship. They had been accustomed to this from their infancy. Both were 'dedicated' at the age of about twenty-one days. This was in public, when their parents stood beneath the flag, the band played, the songsters sang, and they were expected not to bawl even though they knew nothing of what it was all about.

Now both went to church, June becoming church organist. It was all very well, and everyone was kind, but it wasn't Army.

Time has shown that the soldiers in this movement often act rather like an outbreak of influenza, a volcanic eruption, or a manifestation of the disproved theory of spontaneous generation. There was another European woman Salvationist in Livingstone, as well as a number of African Salvationists, whose uniforms were packed away because of lack of opportunity to wear them. Encouraged by the college students who urged that something should be done for Africans on location, they got together and decided that they'd make a Salvation Army of their own. Meetings began on the African location at Maramba.

Douglas Collin, although he enjoyed it greatly, had some misgivings. Another sectarian expression? Were there not too many already? The Africans had no doubts. They relished the Army's singing, hand-clapping, timbrel-playing, the exhortations to repentance and conversion.

The open-air services were near a beer hall, and the Army always reckons that to be a good venue. From such a hot spot inside the beer hall have come thousands of its best soldiers and officers.

Two other Salvationists have now joined Douglas Collin on the college staff at Livingstone. Inevitably, a brass band is in the making. Africans and Europeans are working together in a new Salvation Army unit the like of which might become generally established in newly emergent Africa—so thinks the lay-missionary schoolmaster.

41. THE SECRET ARMY

The first General of the Salvation Army had to wait a long time for his first large-scale successes on the field of battle. By life expectancy of his day, he was, at 49, an old man before his small force became the Salvation Army, and that only in Britain.

He may have felt that time was on his heels, and abhorred conferences—'talking shops' he termed them. He always believed that it was the Liverpool Annual Conference of the Methodists that forced him out into the wilderness, a destitute preacher without a church. When, after resignation and years of disappointment and privation, his own Christian Mission began to forge ahead, it was in turn endangered by the garrulous and hesitant proceedings of its governing committee.

In 1878, therefore, he made himself the soldier-dictator-*supremo*, though always a benevolent one. The dramatic advances which followed this action he saw as a consequence of it.

Naturally, this made him all the more in favour of one man rule. Offers of aid tended to be suspect with him if they did not emanate from beneath the fold of the flag. Outsiders were permitted to tender money and advice: he used the money.

In Booth's mind the reason this had to be was because the work of the Salvationist is made possible by the power of personal salvation. The qualification was to be found, as William Booth saw it, at the penitent-form. Those who could not wear his uniform, march in his ranks, and accept his orders, had to look from the outside in. This did not matter so much while the Army was almost wholly a preaching, singing, evangelical form of church.

Yet, as conquest followed conquest, and often in lands where the British capacity for minding one's own business did not exist, this Salvationist insularity broke down. As preachers and seekers of souls in streets, brothels and slums, Booth's priesthood and sisterhood sufficed; as social workers in a complex society go-it-alone tactics had to be abandoned. Diversification became necessary.

In America today, and, to a lesser degree, in other lands, participation by non-Salvationists in Army endeavour is widespread. Without the nation-wide chain of Advisory Boards on the American continent and Canada there could not have been the dramatic advances and large financial resources now existing. Yet Advisory Boards are not merely 'talking shops'; neither are their members merely allowed the privilege of writing out cheques. They are active aids to Salvation Army service, exerting considerable influence upon the Salvation Army where the Army is faced with tremendously complex legal, social, administrative, property, labour and other problems.

Some Salvationists fear this liaison with non-Salvationists, because of the threat in it to independence. They recall that William Booth's freedom of action was compromised on occasions by those who gave him assistance in money and effort. Recent large-scale experience in the United States and Canada shows that such fears are unfounded.

The city of New York is apt illustration. The informant is Arthur B. Langlie, an Advisory Board member, who is also Chairman of the McCall Publishing Corporation and was for twelve years Republican Governor of the State of Washington. Previously, he had served three times as Mayor of Seattle. He says:

'Close liaison with the Salvation Army does something worthwhile for a business or professional man. It is good for a man because it give him a challenging and worthwhile cause outside himself. As we help the Army, we help ourselves. As a churchman, I find that my work on the Advisory Board of New York helps me in a manner my church does not. Sometimes I say, jocularly, "My religion is Salvation Army." But there is more than a little truth in this. There is a little tension, occasionally, between the Army officers and the members of the Advisory Board. The Salvationists tend to look at things in a ministerial way: we look at it as business men. But we have great respect for the Salvation Army officer, and because that respect is mutual, we can work together.

'Interaction of tension makes for efficiency: differences of opinion being an anvil on which hard conclusions are reached. Sometimes we give ground: sometimes the Army does. We could not accept any attempt to make mere ciphers of us, and we certainly do not expect the Army officer to accept such a role . . .'

Governor Langlie, as he is still termed by Salvationists in New York, tells of a business friend who was suffering from strain, and who did not take kindly to the invitation to become a member of the Advisory Board.

'Do it', said the Governor, 'it will grow on you and do you good.' He did, attending the meetings regularly and developing keen interest in its many projects, one of which is to raise about 4,000,000 dollars, annually, to finance the Army's New York deficit. In time, this man took it as a personal affront if anyone gave a donation to another movement while forgetting the Army! His tension eased off; he became happier, relaxed. In thinking of others more frequently, he thought of himself less. He was much better.

At a private lunch in the Union League Club off Central Park, New York, the room crammed with business men, pressmen and politicians, one caught a glimpse, in Arthur Langlie, of the essential quality needed in the good Advisory Board member.

As the meal ended, the Army's Public Relations Officer, Major Andrew Miller, said, 'Will you pray, Governor?'

The shyer Englishman who made up the trio looked about him, startled and embarrassed. The act, if the Governor achieved it, would have to be accomplished in full view of hundreds of men. But the Governor batted not an eyelid. In the manner of one not unaccustomed to prayer, he lifted his voice—no conspiritorial whispering—and petitioned God concerning the Army and the needy whom it served.

The Salvation Army in the United States could not function adequately without the aid of such men. With the Governor on the New York Board are a cross section of business and professional life which gives incalculable aid.

New York also provides a glimpse of what the Advisory Board does in practical ways, apart from assistance with money-raising. The mass media are, normally, outside the scope of the average

Salvationist so, although New York's Publicity Officer is exceptionally good in liaison with press, radio and TV, he appreciates the Board's aid in enlisting journalists, copy-writers, commentators, and advertising agents and artists. Such people, by and large, donate professional services to the Army in America, which would be quite beyond its financial resources if they had to be paid for.

Influential Board members encourage newspapers, magazines, radio and TV stations to help the Army. *Time, Life, The New York Post* and other journals regularly give space, plus writers and photographers for the good cause. *The New York Times* annually produces a full-colour supplement devoted to the Army's work. The first print is 1,000,000 copies. Though the cost is about 10,000 dollars, and most of the issue is give-away, it does, apart from its immense value as publicity, make a direct financial profit for the Army. Obviously, this can only be achieved because expensive professional services are donated to the Army.

Other assistance, in a country where there is no National Health Service, includes the provision of medical and psychiatric service for the poor. A veritable army of doctors and sociologists give time and service.

Millionaires lend not only their names to appeals, but their homes for functions on the Army's behalf. Entertainers, film, radio and TV stars give their talents. Novelist Fanny Hurst will not only write a story about the Army—which she knows well at first hand—but also give advice or editorial assistance for the preparation of publicity material. Joan Crawford will donate not only some of her husband's coca-cola profits, but her own 'personal appearances' and high skill as a public speaker, for the Salvation Army she so much admires.

There are many, many others—an army in mufti which marches side by side with William Booth's legions.

Even more secret—because of the nature of the good cause—is the Advisory Board of Oakland Salvation Army hospital for unmarried mothers, just across the bay from San Francisco. Here again, if the services rendered were just money-raising or good advice, conditions would be much less favourable. As in New York, the Oakland Board supply know-how and positive action. When they gather for their regular lunch and meeting, there is opportunity to study them.

The Chairman of the Board is Superintendent of Parks for thirteen cities around the Bay. Typically, in Board members, he is deeply religious and possessed by warm admiration for the work of the Army. Fellow board members include a bank manager, a superintendent of schools, a constructional engineer, a member of the Women's Auxiliary of the hospital, a public relations expert, a lawyer, an accountant, and various Salvation Army officers.

It can be seen that in the regular meetings at which these people discuss the hospital's problems they are professionally competent to give advice and assistance which would, in terms of fees, need large sums to buy. Though the Army in the United States is relatively wealthy, as compared with the Army in other lands, the cost of hospital administration is so high that the Army could not then do its task. The Advisory Board system makes the present large-scale work possible.

West Coast citizens are perhaps even more vocal and zealous than Easterners in doing all possible to avert that particular bogey of the average American: State or Federal 'interference'. If the community did not of its own choice assist voluntary societies to function efficiently as welfare agencies, then that dreaded spectre would emerge—to be feared more than the return of the Indians!—the Welfare State.

In other parts of the world where the Advisory Board has been considered, objections include one which William Booth might have made, and which he knew from experience to be sound—in such company the Salvation Army officers will be out-talked, out-gunned, unable to resist the expertise with which they are faced. But to an observer from Britain it seemed that the woman officer in charge at Oakland managed the Advisory Board as well as Queen Victoria controlled her Privy Council.

A reason for this, and members of the Advisory Board at Oakland admitted it, is that the competent Salvation Army officer is a considerable person in his or her own right, possessing the habit of authority, plus experience, dedication, and sense of vocation that make such authority effective. Indeed, nowhere in the United States or Canada, where hundreds of Advisory

Boards exist, staffed by wealthy and influential people from all walks of life, could one find evidence that the Salvation Army was a sleeping partner when projects were hammered out.

Sometimes, round the table where executive types gather, it is quite probable that the best equipped mind, the surest touch, will be found in that quiet-voiced, almost diffident lassie officer. She knows these unloved, feckless girls; she has the greatest understanding of their squalid homes, their sordid backgrounds; she it is who wins the respect and even affection of these sexually promiscuous teenagers, betrayed and hardened as they have been throughout their benighted lives.

Without suggesting that she has a monopoly of Heavenly grace, she it is who is most involved with the angels in that divine task of effecting profound and lasting change for the better among the modern magdalenes, who are guests at Oakland. When the Advisory Board members are in their offices, or happy at home or golf club, the Army Major will be kneeling at the altar, praying, weeping, whispering 'amen', when the sobbing girl murmurs hesitantly: 'God, I am sorry! Please forgive me, and help me to be good . . .' The knowledge that spiritual reclamation is her constant task, ensures that she is not regarded lightly by any Advisory Board member, whether she speaks or is silent. And now, brief and simple lunch over, the business of the Oakland Advisory Board meeting begins with a short prayer.

Item: The ninety thousand dollar extension. Neighbours have objections. They didn't want the original Oakland, a home for 'no-good girls', in their exclusive neighbourhod. They certainly are cool about extensions to it. Now, to the great joy of all the Chairman announces that the community's objections have been withdrawn. (He does not mention what all the board knows, that he personally canvassed from house to house, to win over the objectors.)

Item: What shall be done with the money from the '100 Club'? There have been some doubts about accepting this because it comes from a night-club. The public relations expert advises that it should be spent on publicity for the coming drive for funds. Agreed—William Booth believed that one could take money from the devil himself and sanctify it by Salvationist usage. For the benefit of the Salvationists who would not know, the public relations man says that the '100 Club' is quite respectable even though it is a night club.

Item: Need for new elevator. Considerable discussion on costs. The engineer Advisory Board member gives opinion. Decision—to make allocation from reserves.

Item: Cost of painting outside of Oakland. Agreed to spend 8,640 dollars. Representative of Women's Auxilliary asked to confer with her committee of local housewives on colours.

Item: Should we invite representative of labour unions to join board? Said union generous donor financially. Agreed to look into the matter.

Item: We have doctors here at the hospital but not one on the board. Is there a suitable man who will serve? A name is given and it is agreed that he should be asked.

At the Grace Hospital, Winnipeg, one gets a glimpse of how the Canadians operate Advisory Boards. The board members come from banking, accountancy, law, the city hall and other business and professional walks of life. There are two Salvation Army officer members—others attend by invitation. The board operates on behalf of all Salvation Army work in the city. After prayer:

Item: Allocating last year's income of 187,872 dollars. Written statement agreed.

Item: Agreed budget for next year at 197,000 dollars.

Item: Sunset Lodge rebuilding scheme. Mr. George Jackson's statement: need of elderly people acute. The present building is too small and the site is required for a new road. Option on land for rebuilding acquired as directed by the board. Cost of new building will be 500,000 dollars. Board can rely on gift of 200,000 from the Province of Manitoba, and 100,000 from women's charities. Site is four-and-a-half acres, ideally located. Motion that 50,000 be advanced for purchase of land. Agreed.

Item: Salvation Army Home for unmarried mothers: new roof garden. These girls need fresh air and privacy. It is not convenient for them to take their walks in the parks. Board sympathetic. Matron asked to obtain estimates of cost.

Item: New Men's Social Services project. Present building more or less a fire trap. Some of men smoke in bed secretly. Cost 600,000. Provincial Government will help. The number of itinerant men coming into the great prairie city is tremendous, and grows every year. It is associated with the seasonal needs of farming, but many of the men get into trouble because of unsuitable acommodation. Agreed to proceed.

Item: Fresh air camps for the young and poor mothers with babies. Extension well under way. The Kiwani Clubs are giving 6,000 dollars a year for six years. Other aid is coming from the Winnipeg Charity Foundation. Agreed to push ahead.

Item: New hall for City's Weston Corps. This is growing; need for better accommodation acute. Two Sunday Schools in operation. Good work being done for teenagers; attendances so high that repeat meetings held on Sunday at 3 p.m. to accommodate all who wish to attend.

Item: The New Grace Hospital project. Great pleasure at announcement that the City fathers asked for present hospital to be kept in service—so Winnipeg is to have two Grace Hospitals: a unique situation. There is some frustration at the hold-ups to this multi-million dollar scheme, but it is really moving now, and promising to be the largest Salvation Army Hospital anywhere—possible exception, Flushing, New York. There have been four meetings with Hospital Commissioners. Air conditioning must be installed. This will add greatly to the cost. City wishes street by new hospital to be named Booth Avenue, after the Territorial Commander for Canada, Commissioner Wycliffe Booth, and his grandfather, the Founder, William Booth. Modern standards in this hospital will require that large sums be spent on new type equipment, staff accommodation, heating, and electrical requirements. The Provincial and Ottawa Governments have agreed to help.

Item: The New Harbour Light. Present building for shelter and treatment of down-and-out men, mostly alcoholic, is quite inadequate, and must be replaced. A new one will cost half-a-million dollars. Architect's plan herewith. It is thought that sale of old building should finance purchase of new site. 13,000 free meals were given at the Harbour Light last year. There are normally about 200 men in residence. Twelve of them reconciled to their wives and families as a result of the Captain's efforts. The Army has, or is promised, aid as follows:

2,000 dollars from City appeal.

20,000 dollars from Provincial Government.

10,000 dollars from City authority.

15,000 dollars from last year's allocation.

Must act quickly. Cost of new citadel site was 800-1,000 dollars a foot, and land values are still rising.

Item: After this glut of business, thanks from a Salvation Army officer is appreciated. The men are in haste to get back to their paying work. Meeting lasted two-and-a-half hours, including lunch.

At moderate estimate, the value of the professional and business ability donated to the Army by this board would work out at about 10,000 dollars per annum. Some of the members have been giving it with pride, year after year. In their hearts—they would be reluctant to admit it publicly—they know they are doing it for God.

42. THEY DARE NOT DIE

Though the 25,000 officers and countless men and women in the Salvation Army are ordinary human beings who laugh and love, raise families, work hard, grow old and are generally subject to the ills that flesh is heir to, one thing about them is odd—they dare not die. It is forbidden by the regulations.

To William Booth death was undignified and un-Biblical; he forbade it. A salvation soldier can be 'promoted to Glory' but not deceased. After the old man took to his bed and breathed his last the massed bands of the Army played 'Sweeping through the gates of the New Jerusalem', singing Salvationists marching past the Mansion House in London with colour and panoply, an air of triumph suggesting that it was the Lord Mayor's Show, not the final obsequies. No true Salvationist wore mourning garb.

Perhaps because of the conviction that General William Booth is still alive, and watching them from wherever Heaven is, he still looms large in the lives of the people in the Army.

Though officers, as ministers of Christ, are not rich and bear many burdens, usually not their own, they are happy people. They have their compensations. One is that they are not prone to cirrhosis of the liver: they are total abstainers, with no option —William Booth again. And if smoking is causally related to diseases of the heart and lungs, then they are safe on that account, too. The Army's Founder regarded tobacco smoking as wickedly anti-social, strictly prohibited to the officer. 'If God meant people to smoke,' he growled, 'He would have given them chimneys at the top of their heads.' His eloquent contemporary, Charles Hadden Spurgeon, the fumes of whose tobacco contributed to the Victorian smog about the Elephant and Castle, took a poor view of this *bon mot*.

However, though they are not 'by regulation' allowed to die, officers, with those whom the gods love, often go early to the eternal home God has appointed. The burial places in India,

Africa, China and other lands mark their promotion to Glory after typhoid, cholera, overwork, privation in internment camp, murder by savages and the many other vicissitudes belonging to those who accept Christ's cross. They rest in the Lord.

Present-day officers, and the soldiers they lead in many lands know that their war is not over. There never can be an armistice: peace will not be signed. The frontiers are new, the garb worn by the enemy is different in these modern times, but he is still the devil and while his legions are arrayed for the hurt of mankind the Army must fight on.

With faith as to the outcome it sings as it fights:

> *We meet the foes of all mankind,*
> *And fight to win;*
> *That all the wretched joy may find,*
> *We fight to win.*
> *Though they the slaves of sin may be,*
> *And have no hope to be set free,*
> *That they may God's salvation see,*
> *We fight to win.*

BIBLIOGRAPHY

BIBLIOGRAPHY

In addition to books already quoted the following have also been consulted in the preparation of this work:

The History of The Salvation Army; (4 vols.) (vols. 1-3 by Robert Sandall; vol. 4 by Arch R Wiggins), Nelson.

The Year Book of The Salvation Army; published annually by Salvationist Publishing & Supplies Ltd., Judd Street, King's Cross, London, WC1.

The House of my Pilgrimage; by Albert Orsborn, Salvationist Publishing & Supplies Ltd.

Bramwell Booth; by Catherine Bramwell-Booth, Rich & Cowan.

Echoes and Memories; by Bramwell Booth, Hodder and Stoughton.

These Fifty Years; by Bramwell Booth, Cassell.

The Founder Speaks; by William Burrows, Salvationist Publishing & Supplies Ltd.

Soldiers without Swords; by Herbert A. Wisbey, Junr., MacMillan (USA).

God in the Slums and *God in the Shadows;* by Hugh Redwood, Hodder and Stoughton.

Hallelujah Army; by Harry Edward Neal, Chilton (USA).

The Young William Booth; by Bernard Watson, Max Parrish.

Muktifauj—Forty Years with The Salvation Army in India and Ceylon; by F. St. G. de L. Booth-Tucker, Salvationist Publishing & Supplies Ltd.

Father of Salvation Army Music—Richard Slater; by Arch R. Wiggins, Salvationist Publishing & Supplies Ltd.

The First Salvationist; by Frederick Coutts, Salvationist Publishing & Supplies Ltd.

Queen of Protests—Catherine Booth; by S. Carvosso Gauntlett, Salvationist Publishing & Supplies Ltd.

William Booth; by Minnie Lindsay Carpenter, The Epworth Press.

The best full biography of William Booth in English is undoubtedly *God's Soldier*, by St. John Ervine, (2 vols.). Wm. Heinemann. It is out of print but obtainable in many public libraries.

Harold Begbie's *William Booth, Founder of The Salvation Army;* (2 vols.), Macmillan, is an official life. Lacking Ervine's independent and critical approach it is somewhat adulatory in tone but none the less a mine of information.

English Social History; by G. M. Trevelyan, Longmans.

The Churches and the Working Class in Victorian England; by K. S. Inglis, Routledge and Kegan Paul.

The Maiden Tribute; by Charles Terrot, Frederick Muller.

Maiden Tribute; by Madge Unsworth, Salvationist Publishing & Supplies Ltd.

Missions in Crisis; by Eric Fife and Arthur Glasser, I.V.F.

Rhodes; by J. G. Lockhart and C. M. Woodhouse, Hodder and Stoughton.

Northcliffe; by Reginald Pound and Geoffrey Harmsworth, Cassell.